SECOND EDITION

BOWLING FUNDAMENTALS

Michelle Mullen

Human Kinetics

Library of Congress Cataloging-in-Publication Data

Mullen, Michelle, B.S.
 Bowling fundamentals / Michelle Mullen. -- Second edition.
    pages cm.
1. Bowling. I. Title.
 GV903.M85 2014
 794.6--dc23

                              2013042015

 ISBN-10: 1-4504-6580-3 (print)
 ISBN-13: 978-1-4504-6580-9 (print)

The web addresses cited in this text were current as of March 2014, unless otherwise noted.

Acquisitions Editor: Justin Klug; **Developmental Editor:** Cynthia McEntire; **Managing Editor:** Elizabeth Evans; **Copyeditor:** Patsy Fortney; **Graphic Designer:** Joe Buck; **Graphic Artist:** Tara Welsch; **Cover Designer:** Keith Blomberg; **Photograph (cover):** © Anton Balazh/Panther Media; **Photographs (interior):** Neil Bernstein; **Visual Production Assistant:** Joyce Brumfield; **Photo Production Manager:** Jason Allen; **Art Manager:** Kelly Hendren; **Associate Art Manager:** Alan L. Wilborn; **Illustrations:** © Human Kinetics, unless otherwise noted; **Printer:** United Graphics

We thank Country Lanes in Farmington Hills, MI, for assistance in providing the location for the photo shoot for this book.

Human Kinetics books are available at special discounts for bulk purchase. Special editions or book excerpts can also be created to specification. For details, contact the Special Sales Manager at Human Kinetics.

Printed in the United States of America   10 9 8 7 6 5 4 3 2 1

The paper in this book is certified under a sustainable forestry program.

Human Kinetics
Website: www.HumanKinetics.com

United States: Human Kinetics
P.O. Box 5076
Champaign, IL 61825-5076
800-747-4457
e-mail: humank@hkusa.com

Canada: Human Kinetics
475 Devonshire Road Unit 100
Windsor, ON N8Y 2L5
800-465-7301 (in Canada only)
e-mail: info@hkcanada.com

Europe: Human Kinetics
107 Bradford Road
Stanningley
Leeds LS28 6AT, United Kingdom
+44 (0) 113 255 5665
e-mail: hk@hkeurope.com

Australia: Human Kinetics
57A Price Avenue
Lower Mitcham, South Australia 5062
08 8372 0999
e-mail: info@hkaustralia.com

New Zealand: Human Kinetics
P.O. Box 80
Torrens Park, South Australia 5062
0800 222 062
e-mail: info@hknewzealand.com

E6064

To all my students who entrust me with the privilege to coach you

Contents

Acknowledgments

A very special thank you to my family, friends, teammates, coaches, peers, and tour roommates over the years, who have supported and inspired me to greater heights and joys; Dave Seidler and Coach Griffy for starting our high-school championship bowling team, the Edwards family for all your support and rides home from practice; Sheila Clegg for taking me under your wing all those years ago; Steve Lawson for coaching our college team at Illinois; Professor Dan Gould for believing in me and shaping my sports psychology studies at Illinois; Tom Kouros for coaching and inspiring the coach in me and Heather (Hohm) Sauder for introducing us; John Sommer and John Falzone (PWBA) for the opportunity to compete and a special thanks to all who gave me complimentary practice so I could compete; Paul Marcinek, Donna Adamek, Don Moyer, Todd Kurowski, Aleta Sill, and all ball representatives, especially Doene Moos, for drilling my equipment on tour; Bill Supper for the Pro Staff opportunity; Don Moyer for the friendship and PBI; Bill Vint for my first column in *Bowling Magazine;* Fred Borden for coaching and mentoring; Eva Burridge for your wisdom and support; Mark and Diane Voight and Aleta Sill for the vision of Your Bowling Coach; Jim Hamlin and staff at Country Lanes for your patience and accommodations; Aleta Sill for Aleta Sill's Bowling World, and for your insight throughout this project; Neil Bernstein for your amazing photography and insights; Cynthia McEntire, Liz Evans, and Sue Outlaw for your editing, patience, and guidance, and all other editors and graphic artists involved in this project, especially the illustrators (sleuths!) for translating my sketches; Justin Klug and Human Kinetics for believing in me; my amazing models Jordan Bryant, Ryan Hinman, Mike LaRocca, Allison Morris, and Aleta Sill; Jeff Bleiler; Tom DiDonato, Barb Gamber, Mike Meager, Jim Taylor, and Linda Witbeck for proofing; Todd Kurowski for your expertise and help with illustrations; Mark Robey for "Swing is King!"; Kent Shafer for the author photo; Sook and Walter, just because; Bobby Michael, Emma, and Rigby for your company and patience; and my mom and Aleta, as I turned inward to write this book, thank you for your patience and support.

To my students, you each have given me the greatest honor, which is the privilege to coach you. My passion is to help bowlers bowl better, and not only have you given me this, but you have prepared me to share these insights. I relish this opportunity to help even more bowlers bowl better. This book is for all of you.

Finally, to you, the reader, thank you for giving me this amazing opportunity. If you want to become a better bowler, I cannot wait to help you!

Introduction

My love affair with bowling spans more than 30 years. Though I have competed and won at high levels, I love to coach more than I love to bowl. Every day I am reminded how much bowlers love the sport, and my true passion is to help them improve. It is a privilege to witness the joy they experience as they see themselves getting better. I am so excited to bring together my competitive bowling and coaching experiences into this book, to inspire your love of bowling and help you fall in love with the process of learning to bowl better.

Over the last 10 years since the first edition, I have chronicled the tips and insights that really helped bowlers. This new edition includes these insights as well as updated strategies and anecdotes from my professional career, including thorough and specific information for both right-handed and left-handed bowlers.

In the last decade, I developed a deeper understanding of the mental challenges that accompany making physical changes to technique. In this book, you will learn about the psychology involved in making changes, and I will prepare you for how you can expect to feel, both emotionally and physically, as you make these changes. This will ease the process of becoming a better bowler.

Whether you are a recreational or competitive bowler, bowling fundamentals apply to you. You may be learning them for the first time or reinforcing them; either way, they will certainly help your game. To this day, I teach and instill fundamentals to help bowlers of all skill levels improve their game. Although technology has changed, the need to apply fundamentals remains intact.

In this book, the movements that make up the bowling approach are broken down so that you can develop your physical game, step by step. I reinforce the basic principles of the physical game, including timing, footwork, arm swing, delivery, and release, and will help you understand their relationship to each other so you can bowl better than ever before. In addition, I address the release, lane play, equipment, spare shooting, and the mental game in greater detail than the first edition of *Bowling Fundamentals*.

Advances in technology have brought changes to the equipment we use and lane conditions. I will help you learn how to play the lanes, whether you are bowling on typical lane conditions or more challenging sport patterns. I also provide in-depth information on equipment, breaking down the variables involved to create proper ball reaction on the lanes. Chapters 8 and 9 are dedicated to these topics.

Additionally, spare shooting strategies have evolved since the first edition of this book was published. I will teach you a traditional spare shooting system (complete with adjustments that consider lane conditions), as well as an advanced spare shooting system that eliminates the need to consider lane conditions altogether.

Beyond the physical game, lane play, and spare shooting lie the many mental aspects of the game, which become increasingly more important as you learn to bowl better physically. I have included a new chapter on the mental game, which addresses what it takes mentally to become a successful bowler.

Finally, I am really excited to address the psychology involved when making changes to your game. I shed light on the powerful interactions between your mind and your body to help you be more effective throughout the process and to expedite your progress.

Inspired by every student I have coached, I have realized that the better you understand what you are going through and how you will feel, the less frustrated and more successful you will be at making changes. You have to feel different to reach the next level. I hope this insight will *spare* you frustration and encourage you to stay the course for a more productive transition as you take your game to the next level.

GUIDING PRINCIPLES

In 27 years in bowling, I have learned to appreciate the mental challenges that come with making physical changes. Making changes and feeling different in the process is necessary but not easy. In fact, I have always believed that the many things I've had to work on in my own game have made me a better coach. I know what it is like to have to work hard to bowl better, and what it feels like to make changes.

Often, a lot of effort is required to accomplish a small change. It's hard to feel different. Often what we think we are doing is not what we are doing at all, especially when we attempt to change. It helps to know what to work on and how you can expect to feel as you do to remain on track. Another challenge is overcoming muscle memory.

To improve as a bowler, you need to be willing to get out of, and expand, your comfort zones. Whether you are learning to play a different arrow on the lane or adjusting to a different feel with your timing, you need to get out of your current comfort zone to become a better bowler.

To make changes and improve your game, keep in mind a few guiding principles. The challenges you meet will center on how you *think* and how you *feel*. Once you have decided that you are willing to get out of your current comfort zones, you are ready to consider the following four concepts when facing the challenges of making changes.

Change Occurs in Two Parts and Involves Compensations

When you improve your performance of a skill, that skill will feel different and so will the rest of your motion. Your body then has to learn to stop making the compensations that it used to make as a result of poor technique.

You have to be patient and understand that while you are improving a technique, you may not see the results right away. This is because your body is still getting used to the difference that the change makes on the rest of your approach. Furthermore, your body no longer has to make the compensations it used to, and it has to learn to adapt to the change in technique, essentially to "forget" the need to continue to compensate.

Consider the common issue of pushing the ball late in the start. When you have a late start, you have to pull the ball to get it to catch up. So, when you are learning to push the ball out sooner, which requires a lot of focus and repetition, you may be fixing your timing, but you will likely still pull the ball at the finish out of habit.

It requires patience and understanding to realize that you really are making the fix, but your body simply hasn't acclimated to it yet. The best way to get your body used to the change is to repeat it many times and give your body a consistent movement to get used to so it can adjust. As you repeat the new technique over and over, your body will begin to sense the new timing and will likely adapt to it. You will eventually stop pulling the ball down to compensate for the previously poor timing.

If after lots of repetitions of the new movement you are still pulling, you just have to give a little extra focus to learning to relax the swing into delivery, because the need to pull has been fixed. Sometimes it is just a matter of undoing the old muscle memory that you had developed prior to improving your technique. This is especially true if you have bowled a certain way for a long time and are working on changing your technique. Just stay the course and you will begin to see the changes.

I have so much respect for my students who want to make changes and who entrust me to help them. I have learned over the years to explain how things are playing out as students make changes, especially when I sense their frustration while I am seeing improvement. It can be frustrating when you try so hard but do not see the results you want, at least not right away.

That is why I want you to understand that *the process of making changes occurs in two parts*, to offer reassurance that you are making progress; you just need to stay the course until your body gets used to the feel of the new technique and its effect on the rest of your approach. Stay calm and be patient while you work through it, and soon the results will begin to show.

Overexaggeration Can Help Overcome Old Muscle Memory

When you have been doing something a certain way for a while, exaggerating the correction can help your body make the change more quickly. Our tendencies are strong and difficult to overcome. For this reason, I am a big fan of overexaggerating any change; experience has shown that doing so speeds the process of change. This means creating an opposite motion (in your mind) to counter your current muscle memory. When you do this, it will feel even more different at first, but it will help you overcome the old muscle memory more quickly.

Let's say that you have a late push-away, which is a very common timing problem. Reading about how to fix it might make it seem easy, but I assure you it is not. In lessons, when I point this problem out to students, fixing it sounds easy, but video after video reveals that although they believe they are pushing it out with the first step, they still are not.

In most lessons, when students try to push and step at the same time to fix a late push-away, they still push late. (This is extremely common, and it is hard to detect without a camera.) For this reason, overcoming late timing requires an overexaggeration in technique. This is because your body has created its own idea of timing, and overcoming it requires work.

Almost every time, the attempt to push and step together does not work. So, rather than continue trying to push and step at the same time, you should overexaggerate and try to push the ball even sooner, *slightly before* you step; this often results in both the push and the step happening together. This is not easy to do, or to feel, because you are so used to pushing the ball too late and the rhythm created. Your body is so used to taking the step first that trying to move the ball first may seem almost impossible. The point here is that your tendency to push late is so strong that you have to try to push early, just to get the push and the step closer together. This is the concept of overexaggeration.

Often, what you think you are doing and what you are actually doing are not the same. Most likely you are still late, because muscle memory is hard to overcome, especially when it comes to timing in the start. I could count on one hand the bowlers I have met who naturally have a good start (professionals included), and not use all my fingers to do so.

Suppose you are pushing the ball downward too soon in the start, getting your ball into the swing too early. Although your goal might be to push it out more (rather than down), you will likely have to overexaggerate pushing it up (to combat the tendency to push downward) to actually just push it straight out.

Chapter 4, Footwork, addresses using overexaggeration to conquer a drift to your walk. Again, muscle memory can be a strong force, just as wanting to stay in our own comfort zones can be. You will learn to make changes more quickly and move out of your comfort zone faster if you overexaggerate your changes until the desired movement becomes more natural.

What You Think You Are Doing and What You Are Actually Doing Are Often Two Different Things

The discrepancy between what you think you are doing and what you are actually doing is especially pronounced when you are working on your game. It may help to watch yourself bowl to bridge this gap. It's best to work with a qualified coach when analyzing video to troubleshoot problems, but even on your own you can use photos or video to provide visual feedback on a skill you are developing.

I am continually amazed at how deceived bowlers can be about what they are doing. I remember going through this, too, when I practiced for tour. When

I worked on lowering my backswing, I felt like I barely had a swing at all even though it was still shoulder high. In lessons, I have the benefit of being able to show bowlers on video what they are actually doing. Telling them is one thing; showing them, however, is invaluable.

Being able to see yourself bowl expedites the process of change because you can clearly see what you are doing. This will help you make the change you desire. In lessons, I use a state-of-the-art video analysis system to provide instant feedback. With advances in technology, you can now use smartphones and tablets equipped with cameras to take videos of yourself bowling.

This book pays special attention to specific changes, including how to go about making them and what you can expect to feel when you do. Remember, as a result of working on a specific technique, you will experience a different feeling not only when performing that skill, but also throughout the approach. I will help you make sense of what you are feeling and provide a better understanding of what to expect when you make changes to your game.

Timing Changes Everything

Often, you have to change the way you think about the bowling motion—that is, better understand how it is supposed to feel—to be able to do it differently. This is true especially regarding timing and leverage at the foul line. Once you have an idea of what you can expect to feel, you can begin to make a change.

Over the years, I have realized that what a bowler thinks should be done affects the motion she creates. I have learned that I often have to change her "helmet"—that is, how she thinks about the motion. The great champion Aleta Sill always says, "You have to think differently to do it differently." That is, your perception of how a technique should be done has to change to be able to change the way you perform it.

There is a mentality to establishing the proper timing at delivery. I often see that my students' mentality needs to change to produce the desired results. So, I often pose the following question:

At delivery . . .

a. Should the ball be there before you?

b. Should you be there before the ball?

c. Should everything be there together?

You might think the answer is C, but the answer is B. However slightly, you should be there before the ball for power and leverage. It's a question of milliseconds, but you want your legs to be solid and balanced at delivery so they can impart power and leverage to the release. As in most sports, you use your body to create power to deliver or hit an object. Take a baseball pitcher who winds up and *then* throws, or the batter who steps and *then* swings. Understanding this sequence to movement influences how you develop your motion to the line. You tend to bowl the way you think you should.

HOW TO PRACTICE

How you practice is as important as what you practice. Here are a few tips to help you get more out of your practice sessions.

Do Not Keep Score

Do not worry about keeping score when you are working on technique (which is what practice is for). If the score is running because it is the only way the bowling center knows how much to charge you, then don't pay any attention to it. We never kept score while we practiced in the off-season to get ready for tour. Score was just irrelevant, a distraction at best. Furthermore, do not let the pins distract you when you are working on technique. When you are working on developing a specific skill, focus solely on it, not on where the ball goes. This can be challenging when you just want to knock down pins!

Use the Drills

Do your drills frequently to recognize the feel of a skill you are trying to improve. Drills are stepping-stones between what you have learned and your ability to create that motion, or feel, when you actually bowl. Drills help you become familiar with how the technique feels as well as help you become proficient at it. They help you apply what you have learned and incorporate it into your bowling game. Drills also reinforce proper technique and train your body to create new muscle memory. This training effect often includes strengthening your body to endure the repetition of the motion, as you have to when you actually bowl.

Take One Thing at a Time

Limit your thinking to one, maximum two, things at a time. Having 100 correct thoughts does not mean you will be able to execute the proper motion. Trust me on this. You will fare much better by staying focused on a specific part of your technique; then, once you start to "own it," you can move on to practice something else.

Give yourself a game, or time yourself for 15 or 20 minutes, to focus on that one thing. Get used to how it feels. It will take a lot of effort to get it down, so do not allow any distractions, including trying to work on something else at the same time! Avoiding this urge can be difficult.

Once you have worked on that one thing and believe you have made adequate progress, move on. It may take more than a game or 15 to 20 minutes. Be flexible. It's better to have developed a single skill than to have tried to do too much and accomplished nothing.

Sometimes it helps to create a visual in your mind. Create an image and try to execute it. Or model yourself after a bowler who exemplifies the desired technique. A single image can combine what would otherwise be many thoughts and make it much easier to develop a skill.

Reserve Judgment

Do not judge another part of your execution when you are working on something else. Judge only how you did on the one thing you are working on. Resist the temptation to beat yourself up about the other part of your approach that you were not so good at. It's hard enough to make one change, let alone to do multiple things at once. Change requires a lot of focus and dedicated effort without distraction.

When you develop some key aspects of your approach, some of the other parts may start to come naturally. So it pays to stay the course on those key things, such as timing and swing. The rest will come. If the other parts still need a little polishing, doing so is typically easier once you have improved your start and created a looser arm swing.

Stay on Task

Often, the release improves as a result of improving timing and leverage. But, it is easy to chase symptoms rather than stay focused on the issue at hand. If you are working on your timing, but you don't release the ball right, don't jump ship and start working on your release. Stay the course on your timing until you have it down. Then, once you start repeating your shots more, see how your release has evolved from the timing change. If after many repetitions of your new timing you still have an issue, then you may have to work on the release itself. But abandoning ship on your timing just because your release is poor or inconsistent on some shots can result in missing the boat on the cause of your poor or inconsistent release.

Remember, change often comes in two parts. Once you have made a change, your body has to get acclimated to it. In many cases, you just need to show your release what kind of timing to expect, so it can settle into it. Continue to create more consistency in your timing, for the sake of your release, and likely *both* will improve.

Coach Yourself in Dos Rather Than Don'ts

Your focus needs to be on the things you can do, rather than on what you do not want to do. In other words, coach yourself in dos rather than don'ts.

For example, rather than tell yourself not to pull the next shot, tell yourself to relax and just let your arm swing. Your mind will tend to hear and remember the verb in the thought. In this example, the verb in the negative thought is *pull*. In the second thought, the verbs are *relax* and *let your arm swing*. You are more likely to end up pulling the ball following the first thought than following the second one.

I am very sensitive to this principle when I coach. I ask bowlers to do what I want them to do, rather than tell them what *not* to do. Doing something is simple; trying to avoid doing something is more difficult and often counterproductive.

It all comes down to fundamentals. I strive here to break down bowling in such a way that you can understand and apply the concepts, just as I do when I coach. Welcome to *Bowling Fundamentals, Second Edition.*

Bowling Ball and Grip

Bowling requires a balance between power and consistency. That is, it is a sport of repetition and power. Although the approach is made up of a sequence of movements meant to develop this power, the key to developing consistency and accuracy lies in the swing. As we say, "Swing is king!" The key to developing a healthy, natural arm swing is to relax. A natural swing is easiest to repeat. To keep tension out of the swing and be able to relax, you must have the proper grip.

Both a good ball fit and the application of proper grip pressure have a major impact on the swing. In other words, to develop a consistent swing, you need a ball that fits properly and you need to apply minimal grip pressure throughout the swing. You should be able to do this if the ball fits right. This will allow you to relax and repeat shots to become more consistent and accurate.

In addition, a proper ball fit helps you avoid injury when you bowl. Bowlers with poor ball fit often complain of sore tendons or fingers or have abrasions on their skin. Worse, some bowlers experience soreness in the arm, shoulder, or back when the grip is poor, as a result of all the tension caused by trying to hold on and all the compensations the body makes during the approach—all so that the ball does not slip from the hand! Finding a skilled ball fitter is invaluable when you take up bowling. We have had people come from far away to get help, and I always say that just getting the proper fit is worth the trip.

Some accessories can enhance ball fit. Using bowler's tape to adjust the size of the thumbhole to keep up with the swelling and shrinking of your thumb when you bowl is critical.

It also is important to use a ball that is the correct weight. If the ball is too light, your arm can overpower it, inhibiting the pendulum effect you are trying to achieve in the swing. However, if the ball is too heavy, it is difficult to develop a full and loose arm swing. With the importance of ball fit and ball weight in mind, you need to decide whether to purchase a ball. Owning a ball is clearly advised. When you purchase your own ball, you can get the proper fit in the correct weight, as well as the proper type of ball for your game.

The quality of the ball, particularly the ball's cover, can help you achieve optimal performance. Advancements in research and technology have improved the performance of today's bowling balls. They have differing amounts of hook potential, depending on their covers and the weight blocks inside them. Matching the type of ball to your game is the responsibility of your pro shop professional.

Taking care of your new bowling ball is also very important. This chapter provides some maintenance guidelines for keeping your ball performing better, longer.

BALL FIT

There are three aspects to ball fit: hole size, span, and pitch. Hole size speaks for itself. The span is the distance from the finger holes to the thumbhole. This is carefully measured to ensure that both the fingers and the thumb insert securely at the joints. Finally, the pitches are the angles at which the holes are drilled into the ball. Proper pitches are very important and are based on flexibility and hand span.

Hole Size

Having proper size holes (figure 1.1) is important. You should be able to get your fingers and thumb in all the way, without the holes being so large that you need to squeeze the ball to keep it on your hand. The holes should provide a snug fit, but they shouldn't be so tight that you cannot get your fingers or thumb in all the way. Hole shape also is a consideration for a good fit. The thumbhole can be drilled to accommodate the shape of your thumb, whether it's thicker on the sides, has an oval shape, or any other quality. This allows you to keep the thumbhole snug while preventing any unnecessary friction on release.

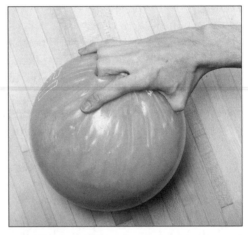

Figure 1.1   Correct hole size. Fingers and thumb fit snugly.

Span

The span is the distance between the finger holes and the thumbhole. Your hand has to be carefully and skillfully measured for span. With a proper span, you can get both your fingers and your thumb in all the way with ease. If you have to stretch your hand to get your fingers and thumb in all the way, or if you have to choose between one or the other, the span is likely too long. At the same time, you do not want the holes so close that there is a lot of space between the ball and your palm. A span that is too long or too short will cause you to squeeze the ball.

Although the proper way to put your hand in the ball is to put your fingers in before the thumb, try this raw test to check your span. Put your thumb all the way in and lay your fingers out on top of the ball over the finger holes (figure 1.2). The joints should be about three-fourths the way over the holes, rather than barely making it to the front edge of the holes (closest to the thumb). Considering how your fingers line up with the holes in a straight line allows you to properly gauge if you will be able to properly reach the span once your fingers are inserted.

Figure 1.2 Raw test for proper span: *(a)* conventional grip; *(b)* fingertip grip.

Pitch

Pitch (figure 1.3) is the angle at which a hole is drilled into the ball. When the hole is drilled directly toward the center of the ball, the hole is considered to have no angle, or zero pitch. A hole drilled at an angle in either direction away from the center of the ball has pitch, either forward or reverse. Forward pitch is a hole drilled on an angle toward the palm of the hand. Reverse pitch is a hole drilled away from the palm. A gauge is used to measure pitches.

Forward pitch provides a more secure fit to help you hold on to the ball. Reverse pitch

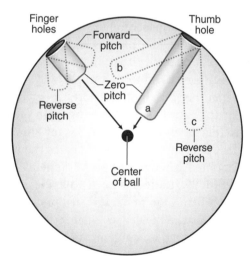

Figure 1.3 Various pitches of the thumbhole and finger holes: *(a)* zero pitch; *(b)* forward pitch; *(c)* reverse pitch.

helps you release it sooner. The proper pitches for you depend on your span and flexibility. Again, your hand has to be carefully and skillfully measured to determine the amount of pitch you need in each hole.

Generally, the shorter the span is, the more help you need holding on to the ball, so forward pitch is necessary. That is why forward pitches on both the finger holes and the thumbhole are necessary with a conventional span for proper grip pressure. The amount will further depend on your flexibility. Both conventional and fingertip grips are addressed later in the chapter.

In a fingertip grip, however, thumb pitch is based on your span, whereas finger pitches depend on your flexibility. If you have a longer span, you should have some reverse

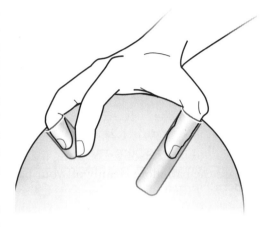

Figure 1.4 Fingertip flexibility and pitch.

pitch in the thumb to help you release the ball soon enough off your hand. The flexibility in each of your fingertip joints determines the angle at which to drill the hole (figure 1.4). The goal is to have the pads of your fingers flush against the front of the holes without your nails pushing out toward the back of the holes (which would indicate that you would need to change the pitch).

Thumb Pitch and Backswing

Although some reverse pitch may be necessary (depending on your skill level and span) for a clean thumb release, excessive reverse pitch leads to excess gripping in the backswing, leading to swing and release issues. The top of the backswing is the first time your hand is actually on top of the ball during the swing. If the pitch is excessive, you will have to squeeze it at that point so the ball does not come off your hand too soon.

When the thumb pitch is off, the grip pressure forces you to tighten up the swing and can cause you to hang up in the thumb at release. But then, when you try to relax your grip pressure (as my students often do during lessons), you end up dropping the ball. This indicates the need for a different pitch.

Caution: Although reverse pitch helps the bowler clear the thumbhole a little more quickly, there has been an epidemic of putting too much reverse pitch in the thumb and too much forward pitch in the fingers. Excessive reverse thumb pitch forces the bowler to squeeze the ball to keep it on the hand long enough. This has created an epidemic of bowlers who end up grabbing and pulling the ball in the downswing. I was a victim to this for years! There is a difference between having enough reverse pitch in the thumb so you can get it out of the ball clean and having so much pitch that you have to squeeze so that your thumb doesn't come out too soon. Fortunately, through a better understanding of progressive fitting techniques, we've been able to help many bowlers get rid of or even avoid this problem.

Fingertip Pitches and Flexibility

With some exceptions, most players who use a fingertip grip need some reverse pitch to accommodate the lack of flexibility in their fingertip joints. In a fingertip grip, the hand is spread across a longer span, which requires more joint flexibility to bend the fingers forward and have the finger pads flush against the front of the finger holes. Reverse pitch helps the bowler achieve this feel. It used to be common to drill the finger holes forward to try to create lift on the ball. But that was when the balls were much weaker and needed more action. Now, with much stronger bowling balls that naturally hook more, you want to release the ball more cleanly off your hand and roll it into the lane for the best reaction. Although many bowlers still refer to the concept of lifting the ball, I haven't taught it since I have been coaching!

Age and Ball Fit Changes

As we age, we become less flexible in the joints. Sometimes arthritis settles in. Ball fit should be adjusted to keep you comfortable when you bowl. Your grip should be changed to match the changing flexibility and strength of your hand.

If you use a fingertip grip, you especially need to have the finger pitches adjusted to match the current range of motion in those joints. Eventually, you will likely need to add more reverse to the pitches so that the pads of your fingers can remain flush against the front of the finger holes. And, depending on the strength of your hand, you may even

Figure 1.5   Bowling ball with a pinkie hole.

decide to add a fourth hole, or pinkie hole (figure 1.5), for more support. Like some of bowlers, I love using a pinkie hole. The ring finger and pinkie typically share a tendon, so when one bends, so does the other. I used to tuck my pinkie finger on the ball to get a better feel on my ring finger. I no longer do this because of arthritis, and the pinkie hole made the grip more comfortable.

The bottom line is that your hand should not hurt when you bowl. As your hand changes, so must your grip so you can stay comfortable and avoid injury. This is especially important if you become less flexible or develop arthritis.

BALL WEIGHT

Bowling balls range from 6 to 16 pounds in weight. For youths, a general rule of thumb is to use a ball that is about 10 percent of their body weight, give or take a pound or two. That can be a bit vague. When instructors help bowlers decide what weight to use, they watch them bowl, with a house ball if necessary, to determine when their swings look best.

If you are trying to choose a house ball, you have to consider that they are predrilled, not custom fit to your hand. Therefore, you may not find a ball that is the desired weight. When instructors watch bowlers use a house ball to determine the proper weight for a new ball purchase, they have to take into consideration that the new ball will fit so much better and, therefore, that the bowler may be able to go a pound heavier than the house ball. Balls that fit well feel lighter.

If your ball is too light, you will be able to overpower it and it will be hard to have a consistent swing that also stays in alignment. You need a bit of an anchor at the end of your arm to develop the pendulum effect in the swing. However, you do not want a ball that is too heavy. Bowling well does not require choosing the heaviest weight. It takes strength to let a heavy ball swing through a full arc. If you labor at all to let the ball easily swing through a full arc, or if you struggle to do this easily over the course of the number of games you typically bowl, then a lighter ball would be better. Go only as heavy as you can while still being able to stay in form for the duration of time that you bowl.

I liken this concept to that of being at the gym and wanting to lift heavy weights but not being able to do so with proper form or to complete any substantial number of reps with them. It takes strength training to develop the ability to stay in form with more weight.

More weight is not necessarily better! At one time, the cores of bowling balls were a lot weaker, and the hitting power of the balls did depend more on ball weight. Nowadays, cores have gotten so strong that in some cases they account for approximately half the weight of the ball! Bowling balls today hit harder, even in lighter weights. For this reason, many of the male professional bowlers do not throw 16 pounds. If you have to labor to push the ball out into the swing or cannot let the ball swing fully into the backswing, or if your ball speed is too slow, consider using a lighter ball.

Just because you throw the ball hard does not necessarily mean that you need a heavier ball. Consider that the top professional bowlers have good speed and strong ball roll. Sometimes, the illusion of throwing it too hard is really a matter of having ball roll that is too weak for your speed. If this is the case because your wrist is in a weak position, more ball weight is not the answer. Rather, a firmer and stronger wrist position is necessary to create a stronger ball roll. This would be harder to achieve with a heavier ball.

In some cases, a wrist guard is warranted to strengthen the wrist position and create stronger roll. Candidates for wrist guards are those with weaker wrists or who firm up the wrist by creating more grip pressure or tightening the muscles during the swing. This is very common. Different muscles are used to strengthen the wrist position than are used to hold or swing the ball. Wrist strength aside, bowlers need to firm up wrist position without increasing grip pressure or tightening the swing. Those who can't should consider a wrist guard.

BALL TYPE: PLASTIC AND REACTIVE RESIN

Three types of bowling balls commonly used in today's game are plastic, urethane, and reactive resin. Reactive resin balls are urethane-based with the additive reactive resin, which gives these balls their hooking motion down lane. The additive creates more reaction, which is why these balls are the preferred performance balls and have essentially replaced regular urethane balls. However, a few urethane balls have been reintroduced into the market for high-level players who need more control with certain lane conditions. For our purposes, however, let's stick to the two most popular types, plastic and reactive resin.

Plastic Balls

Plastic balls are just that, balls made of plastic. Plastic is very smooth and does not create much friction with the lane. Liken it to a bald tire on a car, which has little traction on the road.

In addition to the cover, the inside of most plastic balls is composed of a very small weight block surrounded by filler material. This creates a less dynamic ball reaction for bowlers who impart rotation to the ball. Like the cover, the weight block is very weak and does little to help the ball hook. A plastic ball virtually goes straight on the lane.

Typically, plastic balls are good for novice youth bowlers who throw a straight ball and who will need to purchase heavier balls and be refit for larger hands as they have growth spurts. Plastic balls are good for adults who throw the ball straight and want their own ball with the proper fit to enhance proper form. Plastic balls also are effective for senior bowlers who roll the ball very slowly. If a reactive resin ball hooks too much for a bowler's ball speed, a plastic ball can be used (although it won't hit as hard) and still hook, because of the very slow ball speed, as long as the bowler imparts rotation at release. The predrilled house balls at your local bowling center are plastic.

Plastic balls may also be used for shooting spares. If you throw a hook ball, especially if you use an aggressive ball that hooks a lot, shooting the corner pin with a plastic ball can help you avoid having the ball hook away from the pin. This is discussed at more length in chapter 10, Spare Shooting. In addition, chapter 11 describes an advanced spare shooting system that uses a plastic ball for all spares to take ball reaction out of the equation.

Reactive Resin Balls

Reactive resin balls hook more, provided the bowler imparts rotation at release. They hook more as a result of the cover material and the size and shape of the weight block inside, which is referred to as the core. With the exception of the lightest-weight balls, reactive resin balls have bigger and specially shaped cores that create a more dynamic reaction on the lane.

Reactive resin balls are referred to as performance balls. Their composition creates more friction with the lane, enabling them to hook more and hit harder. Referring to the tire analogy, they have more tread with which to grab the oil conditioner on the lane. They are much stronger and have a more angular shape as they hook on the lane. And like the various tires on various vehicles, they can have the gripping power of a sedan tire, a tractor tire, or even a tire with chains!

Reactive resin balls can be broken down into three basic categories with regard to their covers: solid, pearl, and hybrid reactive resin. Solid balls tend to have a plain, matte finish. Pearlized balls have more swirls and tend to be shinier. The hybrid is the cross between a solid and pearl bowling ball, a combination of the two types.

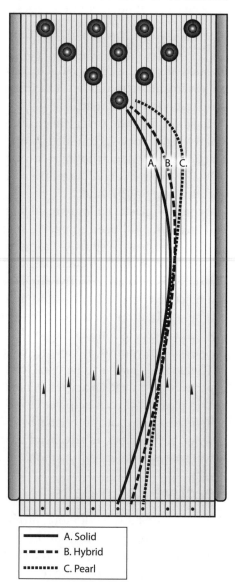

Solid Reactive Resin Balls

Solid balls have strong, aggressive covers that tend to create a lot of friction early on the lane—that is, soon after release. Because they hook sooner and use up a lot of energy more quickly, they tend to have a smoother arc (figure 1.6a) on the back end of the lane as they hook into the pins.

Hybrid Reactive Resin Balls

The hybrid ball combines the characteristics of the solid and the pearl balls. A hybrid ball does not hook quite as early as the solid and does not hook as much on the back end of the lane as the pearl. It is between the two in its reaction (figure 1.6b).

Pearl Reactive Resin Balls

Pearl reactive resin balls have a pearl additive that causes the ball to skid further and hook later on the lane. Because they skid longer, they store more energy for later on the lane. These balls react more on the back end of the lane, with a bigger arc into the pins (figure 1.6c).

You may be inclined to pick one of these ball types based on its description. However, keep in mind that they all are effective, depending on conditions. Back to the tire analogy, you

——— A. Solid
- - - - B. Hybrid
••••••••• C. Pearl

Figure 1.6 Types of reactive arcs: solid, hybrid, and pearl.

would not use tractor tires with chains on a dry pavement, nor would you want bald tires in a snowstorm. Properly matching up the ball's friction with the lane condition is key. This is addressed further in chapters 8 and 9 on lane play.

Beware of the fact that often what you think you need is not actually what you need! The right ball for you depends on many variables, including your release, ball speed, lane conditions, and how you like to play the lane. That is why you should consult with a qualified professional ball driller or coach to determine what type of ball is right for you.

GET A GRIP

The two types of grips are the conventional grip and the fingertip grip. Most bowlers begin with the conventional grip and eventually graduate to a fingertip grip.

Each finger has two joints. For ease of reference, think of the joint nearest the fingertip as the first joint and the joint in the middle of the finger as the second joint. In a conventional grip (figure 1.7), the fingers go into the holes up to the second joint in the middle of the finger. On a ball that is drilled for a conventional grip, the finger holes are closer to the thumb and are larger to accommodate the size of the fingers up to the second joint. Once the fingers are in, the thumb should go into the hole *all the way* to the base of the thumb. Most bowlers start out with a conventional grip because it makes them feel more secure when swinging the ball.

In the fingertip grip (figure 1.8), the fingers go into the holes up to the first finger joint. On a ball that is drilled for a fingertip grip, the finger holes are drilled farther from the thumb, compared to a ball drilled for a conventional grip, and the holes are smaller to accommodate the smaller size of just the fingertips, from the first joint to the tip. Once the fingers are in, the thumb should go into the hole all the way to the base of the thumb.

Figure 1.7   Conventional grip.

Figure 1.8   Fingertip grip.

A fingertip grip eventually is the preferred grip because it allows you to create more revolutions at release. In the fingertip grip, the thumb comes out much sooner than the fingers, as compared to the conventional grip, in which the thumb and fingers come out closer together. Because the ball has more time over the fingers, it has more roll. *Note:* It is a myth that it is more difficult to hold on to a ball using the fingertip grip because only the very tips of the fingers are in it. The ball is actually still fit securely at a joint (which is why a semi-fingertip grip is not suggested—you should be fit to the joints). If the ball is fit properly for your hand, you can easily hold on to it using the fingertip grip without increasing grip pressure.

With both grips, the thumb exits before the fingers during release (see chapter 7). The length of time from thumb release to finger release varies between the two grips because of the amount of hand spanning over the ball.

To maintain a loose, natural arm swing, use a minimal amount of grip pressure to hold on to the ball. With a proper fit, both fingers should be able to go into the ball all the way to the proper joints, depending on grip type, and the thumb should go into the thumbhole all the way (see figure 1.9). If the thumb does not go all the way in, the grip will feel insecure and you will tend to squeeze the ball. If the thumb cannot go all the way in, either the thumbhole is too tight or the distance from the finger holes to the thumbhole, called the span, is too wide.

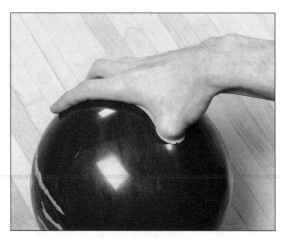

Figure 1.9 The thumb goes in all the way.

Most bowlers start out with a conventional grip because it initially feels like a more secure grip. Once you develop an established level of consistency—typically when you average around 150 or so—a fingertip grip becomes the preferred grip. At this level, you are hitting the pocket and picking up spares more consistently and need to begin developing more pin action when the ball hits the pocket. A fingertip grip will help you strike more as well as create better pin count on the first shot to leave easier spares (with fewer pins) to pick up on the second shot.

In a good release, the thumb exits the ball before the fingers. Because the fingers and thumb release closer together using a conventional grip, whereas the thumb clears much sooner than the fingers using a fingertip grip, a fingertip grip creates more revolutions on the ball. Releasing from a fingertip grip creates a quicker transfer of ball weight from the thumb to the fingers to impart more roll off the fingers at release. Bowlers with higher averages and professional bowlers use a fingertip grip for its superior effect on the roll of the ball. It creates better pin action when the ball strikes the pocket.

FINGERTIP GRIP ACCESSORIES FOR BETTER FEEL

If you use a fingertip grip, you may opt to have finger inserts, also called finger grips, glued into the finger holes (figure 1.10a). These accessories are made of rubber and offer a different feel to the fingers. The majority of bowlers who use a fingertip grip use finger inserts. The holes are drilled bigger to accommodate the circumference of the grip, and then the finger inserts are glued into the holes. Most bowlers decide whether they want them when they purchase the ball; however, the finger holes can always be redrilled later to add them.

Many bowlers like the smooth feel of a thumb slug (figure 1.10a) to facilitate a clean thumb release. The thumb slug is glued into the ball and then the hole is drilled right into it. If you have more than one ball, a thumb slug will give you the same feel from ball to ball. You do not have to decide whether you want a thumb slug when you purchase your ball; the thumbhole can always be redrilled later to add one.

If you have multiple bowling balls and are more sensitive to the feel of the thumbholes as you switch from ball to ball, consider using an interchangeable thumb slug (figure 1.10b). Basically, a slug is made with a locking mechanism that you can move from ball to ball. You can have different sizes made to accommodate the fluctuations in your thumb, especially if your thumb size changes drastically while you bowl. These slugs click into place in a receptacle installed into each bowling ball you own. However, this does not alleviate the need for bowler's tape within these slugs because your thumb will still have slight fluctuations that require tape to size the hole just right.

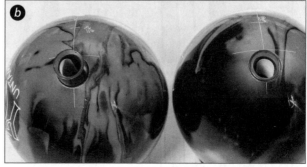

Figure 1.10 Fingertip grip accessories: *(a)* finger inserts or finger grips and thumb slug; *(b)* interchangeable thumb slug.

Making Changes: Grip Pressure

You may believe that your thumbhole is too tight because you hang up in it and can't easily let it go; however, the problem may not be what it appears to be because of the variable of grip pressure. What you might think is too tight a hole is often too loose! One of the most common requests in our pro shop is to open up a thumbhole because the bowler cannot let go of the ball without getting stuck in it. About 75 percent of the time, the issue is actually that the hole is already too big, which causes the bowler to squeeze the ball to hold on to it. Instead of opening up the hole on the ball, the bowler needs to learn to relax and, often, to make the hole smaller with bowler's tape. Relaxing and gripping the ball properly often solves the problem and leads to a better arm swing, too!

The same can be true of thumb pitch. Although reverse pitch in the thumbhole helps you release the ball sooner, hanging up in the thumbhole at release does not necessarily mean that you need more reverse pitch. You may need less! Reverse pitch that is excessive for your hand will cause you to squeeze to keep from letting go too soon. As a result, the thumb hangs up and you end up releasing the ball too late.

Bowling with a ball that does not fit properly, whether a generic house ball or your own ball that was badly fit, will lead you to develop excessive grip pressure. You may then want to increase the size of the thumbhole because you are afraid of hanging up in the ball and launching it onto the lane or, worse, not being able to let go of it at all.

This issue is common. However, the solution is counterintuitive. Although you may be inclined to have the thumbhole opened and enlarged, actually you need to lighten up your grip pressure to bowl with the hole a little tighter than normal. It's the only way you will ever learn to relax.

If you open up the hole out of fear of not being able to let go of it, you will end up just squeezing it more and exacerbate the problem. The tension will affect your swing and your performance. Learn to relax and let the ball come off your hand. I am not saying that you *never* need to open up the hole; I am just sharing the tendency of many bowlers to want to enlarge holes without realizing the actual problem. The key is to maintain proper grip pressure.

A couple of tosses on the carpet to your pro shop person (standing still, of course!) will help you acclimate your grip pressure and ease the anxiety of not being able to get it off your hand when you bowl. We do this all the time in our shop when people ask for their thumbholes to be bigger than we believe they should be. We teach proper grip pressure. When you roll the ball across the floor while standing still, be sure to use a full swing. Without that momentum, or centrifugal force, you need to grasp the ball to keep it on your hand. Although you are tempted to half swing it, you must have a full swing to be able to relax your grip and let the ball go.

When you have trouble letting go of the ball, a good trick for learning to stop squeezing and clear the thumb better at release is to think about pressing your thumbnail against the back of the hole, essentially "unsqueezing" the ball at release. This helps when you first learn to get the thumb out easier. It is doing the opposite, straightening the thumb, to overcome squeezing. This trick works really well for bowlers who have been using house balls or for those who have come out of a poorly fit ball to finally have their own ball that fits properly. You only have to think about doing this until you learn the proper grip pressure when you bowl.

BOWLER'S TAPE

Use bowler's tape in the thumbhole to fine-tune the ball fit. Tape is meant to be used during play to maintain the proper hole size to keep up with the natural fluctuations in your thumb size. Put it in and take it out as necessary for any given shot. Never give up a shot if the size of the hole is not right.

Bowler's tape comes in two colors and two sizes. Black tape has a smooth finish, and white tape has a little bit of texture. They both come in either 3/4-inch or 1-inch widths, for smaller or larger thumbs. Using black tape on the back side of the hole (figure 1.11) is common. Notice that your thumb goes into the ball at an angle. Put the tape in rounded side up on either the pad side or nail side of your thumbhole. Use a tool to help you.

If you do use the white tape in the front, use only a piece, because this adjustment can affect your span. Insert it directly across from the black tape, where the pad of the thumb lies. You need only one piece because you are using it for the feel it provides. Then make the rest of your adjustments in the back with the black tape. Replace the white tape only when it starts to absorb oil and changes color or when it loses the feel it had. Keep the exits clear to facilitate a smooth, clean release. This adjustment will not affect your span. Some bowlers like a piece of white tape in the front (pad side) because the texture helps them feel more secure. Experiment to find the feel you like.

You may notice a trend in how your thumb fluctuates in size, either shrinking or swelling when you bowl. In either case, use tape to make sure the ball fits your hand properly for the next shot. Your goal is to maintain a constant grip pressure from shot to shot. This means adjusting the ball to your hand rather than your hand to the ball.

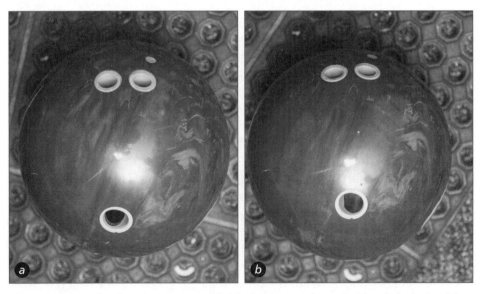

Figure 1.11 Using bowler's tape, with black tape on the nail side of the hole: *(a)* right-handed bowler; *(b)* left-handed bowler.

GRIPPING TAPE

Gripping tape put on the back of the thumb (figure 1.12) is not to be confused with bowler's tape that is put into the thumbhole. Gripping tape comes in various textures and is used to achieve the desired feel at release. Experiment to see what you like, if any. If you use it, though, it will technically take up a little more space in the thumbhole; you will still need to use bowler's tape to keep up with the changes in your thumb size as you bowl.

Learning to use bowler's tape and gripping tape properly is a sign of maturity. First, it indicates that you recognize when you need it. Second, the fact that you can handle the tighter hole means that you are learning proper grip pressure!

As your grip pressure improves, your ball fit will evolve. When you learn to relax more, you will be able to handle less reverse pitch in the thumb and still get out of the ball cleanly. Being able to get out of the ball just as cleanly with less reverse pitch (or more forward pitch) indicates that you are more relaxed.

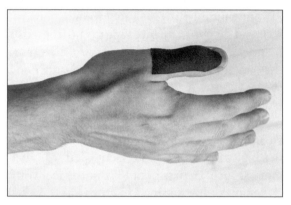

Figure 1.12 Gripping tape applied to the back of the thumb.

BALL MAINTENANCE

It is good to clean your reactive resin ball every time you finish bowling, before you put it back in the bag. These balls absorb the oil on the lane, and it should be cleaned off to restore the ball's tackiness and maintain its ability to hook. You do not have do maintenance on a plastic ball.

It is good practice is to use a tested and approved bowling ball cleaner. Use a dedicated rag that you keep in your bag. Just spray and wipe. This is the most user-friendly way to clean it. Again, clean your ball with an effective cleaner every time you are finished bowling. Do not waste your quarters using the ball-cleaning machines. They only wax the ball; they do not clean it.

From time to time, it is a good idea to soak the ball in hot tap water with detergent. Do not worry about water getting into the holes. Let it soak for about 20 minutes or until the oil stops coming to the top of the water. This is an effective way to degrease the ball. This is especially true for balls that have more of a matte finish because they soak up the lane oil quickest.

Never use only a towel when cleaning your ball, do not use rubbing alcohol on your ball, and do not put your ball away without cleaning it. Rubbing the ball with a towel does not clean out the oil, and rubbing alcohol does not penetrate the amount of oil currently applied to lanes. Avoid exposing it to extreme temperatures, such as leaving it in the car on extremely cold or hot days or putting it in the dishwasher. This can damage the ball and may extract some of the material that makes it hook.

Have your ball's surface refreshed every 10 games or so, as needed. To maintain consistent performance in a dull ball, refresh the surface to maintain its dull finish. Repolish a ball that works best when shiny. The surface of the ball will change as you bowl with it. You will begin to recognize when a ball works best for you; have the pro shop restore the cover to that finish from time to time.

Even with the topical cleanings after each use, you will not be able to get all of the oil out of the ball. For this reason, you need to purge the oil that goes deeper into the ball from time to time. Pro shops offer this service. Depending on the conditions you bowl on, purge oil from your ball every 75 to 100 games or so.

Because your ball makes direct contact rolling on the lane and hitting pins, the cover of the ball will get wear spots and nicks in it. Of particular concern to performance is track wear. This is the actual area that makes continual contact as the ball rolls down the lane, depending on your type of release. Once that begins to show enough wear and the ball gets sluggish, it is a good idea to have it resurfaced to restore performance. This service is provided by a pro shop and should be done every 60 games or so, as needed.

To properly maintain your mid- to high-performance bowling ball, follow the maintenance procedures here. Remember, these are guidelines. Depend on your pro shop professional to help you determine the maintenance you need to restore performance.

- Clean your ball every time you finish bowling.
- Have the ball's surface refreshed every 10 games or so, as needed.
- Have a thorough ball resurfacing performed with pads every 60 games.
- Have the oil purged from your ball every 100 games.

Note: Resurfacing the cover refers to bowling ball maintenance and is not to be confused with making adjustments to the surface for the immediate purpose of managing the ball's friction on lane conditions in league or other competition. Because ball surface adjustments are a significant part of fine-tuning a ball's reaction for lane conditions, they are addressed in chapters 8 and 9 on lane play.

SUMMARY

If you plan to bowl regularly and want to improve your skills, buy your own ball. Having the proper type of ball that is the correct weight with a good fit will lead you to develop good habits that help you bowl better. You will learn to have the proper grip pressure to create a more relaxed and consistent arm swing.

The quality of the ball fit is extremely important for comfort and performance. A good ball fit enhances performance and avoids injury. Furthermore, a poor fit hinders performance and can cause injury. An excellent ball fit is invaluable.

If you notice marks or develop blisters or callouses on your skin, take your ball to a reputable pro shop to have the grip checked and adjusted.

When I first gave lessons, I eventually got around to checking the ball fit toward the end of a lesson. Now, it is the first thing I consider when I watch a bowler warm up and I see a swing issue. In fact, on occasion I have had to reschedule a lesson because the ball fit was too inadequate for the bowler to be able to relax and do the things required. It is amazing to see what happens to a player's swing when a poor fit is fixed.

You want to be able to maintain a gentle grip pressure at all times when you bowl. Use bowler's tape properly to keep the thumbhole snug, and adjust the fit to accommodate the fluctuations in your thumb size. You have to relax your grip pressure to even know you need to use tape; however, you need to use enough tape to be able to lighten up your grip pressure. Sometimes, it takes just a piece or two to get your swing loosened up again because you no longer have to squeeze the ball. Using tape properly makes a huge difference!

Finally, make sure you do the maintenance on your bowling ball to maintain its performance.

Chapter 2

Stance

When you get on the approach, you have to determine where to stand and how to set up. The starting position, or stance, sets the tone for the motion that follows. Knowing how to position your body and where to stand is important for a good delivery. Starting in a sound, leveraged position with a relaxed body will help you develop a good approach. This chapter provides basic guidelines on where to stand and where to target based on your release. Keep in mind that where you stand and target will evolve as you develop your game, especially your release, because lane conditions have to be taken into consideration when you throw a hook.

Two factors must be considered when determining where to stand: how far from the foul line to start and which board of the approach to stand on. To create a smooth motion with good rhythm to the foul line, walk naturally during the approach. Many bowlers end up short of the foul line or attempt to overstride and rush to the line because they start too far back on the approach. The distance to stand from the foul line on your approach depends on the length of your natural stride and the number of steps you take.

Your method of release and perhaps lane conditions (if you throw a hook) determine which board to start on. Your release causes the ball to rotate in one of three directions: clockwise, straight forward, or counterclockwise. The type of rotation determines which pocket to use and whether to target on the right or left side of the lane. From there, you can determine where to stand on the approach. To maximize pin action and minimize ball deflection on impact, your ball should hit the correct pocket upon making contact with the pins for the way you roll the ball. The area between the 1 pin and the 3 pin is the right-side pocket; the area between the 1 pin and the 2 pin is the left-side pocket. The 1 pin is also referred to as the headpin.

Whereas the pin numbers are standard and do need to be memorized, the way boards are counted differs for right- and left-handed bowlers. Right-handed bowlers count the boards and targets from the right; left-handed bowlers count them from the left (figure 2.1).

There are always 39 boards and seven arrows (targets) on a lane. There are always seven dots at the foul line to line up with the seven arrows. What varies is the number of dots at the beginning of the approach. There either will be seven dots, which line up exactly with the seven dots at the foul line and arrows on the lane, or there will be only five dots, which line up with the inner five dots and arrows on the lane. Therefore, you would be missing dots on board 5 and on board 35. When you have only five dots in the start, the first dot lines up with the second arrow, or board number 10.

ESTABLISHING YOUR STANCE

Stand with your feet close together and knees slightly bent so that you feel ready to move. Flexed joints move more easily than locked joints. Your body should be relaxed and ready to move. Your spine should have a slight tilt to it, about 15 degrees, to main-

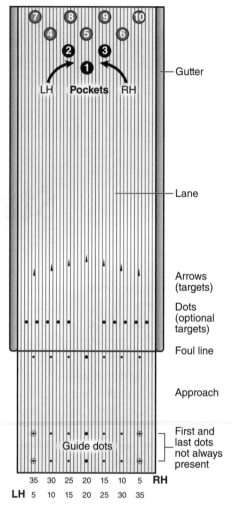

Figure 2.1   The bowling lane.

tain a leveraged position of your upper body. Maintain good balance by keeping your center of gravity over your base of support. Centering your core over your legs will put you in control of your first step, rather than having to react to an imbalance in your body position.

A right-handed bowler starts with the right foot slightly behind the left to preset the hips and shoulders as they will be at the delivery (figure 2.2a). A left-handed bowler puts the left foot slightly behind the right to preset the hips and shoulders (figure 2.2b). At delivery the right-handed bowler ends up on the left foot with the right leg behind, setting the hips in an open position. A left-handed bowler ends up on the right foot, setting the hips in an open position. The shoulders, hips, and feet should all be in alignment and facing toward the target. It is important to relax your spine rather than have it twisted to be able to maintain this preset position throughout your approach.

You should have slightly more weight on the nonstarting foot. So, if you start with your right foot, you will put more weight on your left to free up the right

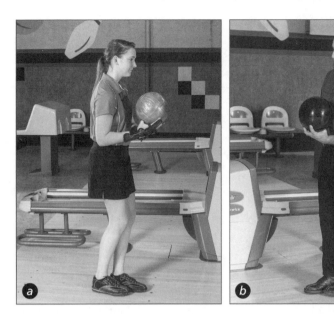

Figure 2.2 Feet staggered to preset feet, hips, and shoulders: *(a)* right-handed bowler; *(b)* left-handed bowler.

foot to move. You will learn more about which foot to start with in chapter 3 in the section on timing.

Overall, your body should feel balanced, ready to move both the starting foot and the ball on the correct key step.

Your upper body should be relaxed. Support the weight of the ball using the leverage of both hands, with the weight primarily in the hand without the ball, or the nondominant hand, to allow the swing arm to relax as you push the ball away.

The elbow of the swing arm should be by your side, next to your ribs. Identifying a place for your elbow enables you to start with the ball in the same position every time. Hold the ball in line with the inside of your shoulder (figure 2.3). Keeping the elbow by your side and holding the ball in line with the shoulder joint facilitates a consistent and straight arm swing.

Hold the ball close to your body in the stance. This helps you relax because the closer it is to you, the lighter it feels. The farther it is from you, the heavier it feels. This is why you would carry a heavy box close to your body, rather than with your arms extended. The closer it is to your center of gravity, the more leverage you have and the lighter it feels. The key to a good arm swing is to relax!

Generally, putting your arm by your side and your forearm parallel to the floor is a good position from which to push the ball out in the start. Depending on your timing tendencies, you might position the ball higher or lower in the stance. Holding the ball higher or lower changes the shape of the push-away in the start. This can be strategically engineered to improve your timing, which is discussed in chapter 3.

The next goal in the stance is to align the ball with your shoulder and then stand in a place to get your swing shoulder lined up with the appropriate target

Figure 2.3 Ball in line with the inside of the shoulder: *(a)* right-handed bowler; *(b)* left-handed bowler.

to hit the pocket. Start by identifying what type of bowler you are, based on your release. From there, you can fine-tune your angle to the pocket.

DETERMINING STANCE DISTANCE

To determine how far back to stand on the approach, walk up to the foul line and put your heels on the dots with your back to the pins. From the foul line, take four comfortable but brisk steps toward the back of the approach (figure 2.4). (Add a step, if you use a five-step approach.) After the fourth (or fifth) step,

Figure 2.4 Take comfortable, brisk steps toward the back of the approach.

add approximately another half step to allow for the slide (figure 2.5). This will determine your approximate starting point for the approach. Again, walk naturally but briskly, because taking normal-sized steps, with momentum, is the key to a comfortable approach and the ability to repeat shots.

DETERMINING STANCE POSITION

To figure out which board to stand on, you need to identify the type of release you have, which influences the pocket you should use. Your positioning on the lane depends on your swing arm and the type of release. The type of release is determined by the direction of rotation imparted to the ball, which in turn determines the side from which the ball should enter the pins for maximum drive through the pocket. The ball should rotate toward the middle of the rack of pins for minimal deflection on impact. So determining which pocket to use and your position on the approach depends on the rotation of your ball.

A ball that does not curve or significantly rotate in either direction and whose path is virtually straight down the lane with a forward roll is called a straight ball. It does not hook in one direction or another. A bowler who throws a straight ball must be sure to hit around the head pin. A right-handed bowler with a straight ball uses the 1-3 pocket; a left-handed bowler uses the 1-2 pocket.

For the right-handed bowler, a ball that curves from right to left is a hook. Another way to define hook is to say

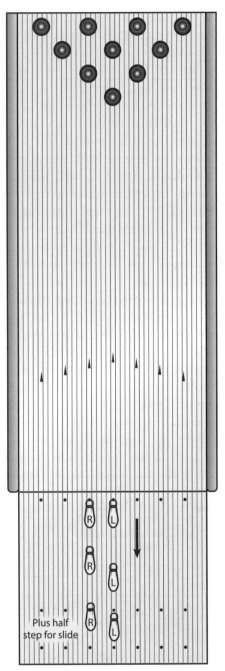

Figure 2.5 To determine how far back to stand, take four steps toward the back of the approach, adding a half step to account for the slide.

that it is a ball that spins in a counterclockwise direction. A right-handed bowler with a hook uses the 1-3 pocket to maximize drive into the pocket through the pins on impact; a left-handed bowler uses the 1-2 pocket.

The exception to a right-hander using the 1-3 pocket and counting the arrows from the right is the bowler who throws a reverse hook, or back-up ball. A reverse hook curves from left to right because it rotates in the opposite direction of the traditional hook. The reverse hook of a right-handed bowler rotates in a clockwise direction. To minimize ball deflection, a right-handed bowler who throws a reverse hook should use the 1-2 pocket to maximize the drive of the ball into the pins. Because the spin is like that of a left-handed hook, for simplicity I suggest that this bowler count the arrows from left to right, like a left-handed bowler, because he is using the left-side pocket.

Basically, right-handed bowlers use the right-side 1-3 pocket and count the boards and arrows starting from the right side of the lane. Left-handers use the left-side 1-2 pocket and count the boards and arrows starting from the left side. The exception is the bowler who throws a reverse hook, or back-up ball (see tables 2.1 and 2.2). These bowlers use the opposite pocket, counting the arrows and target from the opposite side of the lane because of the reverse rotation on the ball.

Note: bowlers should use the foot they end on at the finish to line up on the proper board in the stance. For right-handed bowlers, this is the left foot; for left-handers, this is the right foot. I suggest that you use the inside of your foot to line up. There is more information on this in chapter 4, Footwork.

A right-handed bowler who throws a straight ball and whose goal is to put the ball in the 1-3 pocket should stand just left of the middle dot on the approach (figure 2.6a). The middle dot is on board 20, and it is larger than the other dots. The left foot is approximately on board 23. The arm swing is lined up with the third arrow, and the third arrow is the target.

A left-handed bowler who throws a straight ball and whose goal is to put the ball in the 1-2 pocket should stand just right of the middle dot on the approach

Table 2.1 Right-Hand Releases

	Straight	Hook	Reverse hook
Direction ball curves	Doesn't curve	Right to left	Left to right
Direction ball rotates	Doesn't rotate	Counterclockwise	Clockwise
Pocket to use	1-3	1-3	1-2
Target	Third arrow	Second arrow	Third arrow*

* Count arrows from the left side.

Table 2.2 Left-Hand Releases

	Straight	Hook	Reverse hook
Direction ball curves	Doesn't curve	Left to right	Right to left
Direction ball rotates	Doesn't rotate	Clockwise	Counterclockwise
Pocket to use	1-2	1-2	1-3
Target	Third arrow	Second arrow	Third arrow*

* Count arrows from the right side.

Figure 2.6 Straight ball: *(a)* right-handed; *(b)* left-handed.

(figure 2.6*b*). The right foot is approximately on board 23. The arm swing is lined up with the third arrow, and the third arrow is the target.

A right-handed bowler who throws a hook ball uses the 1-3 pocket and can begin by standing just right of the center dot (figure 2.7*a*). The left foot is approximately on board 18, and the target is close to the second arrow. A left-handed bowler who throws a hook ball uses the 1-2 pocket and can begin by standing just left of the center dot (figure 2.7*b*). The right foot is approximately on board 18, and the target is close to the second arrow.

A right-hander who throws a reverse hook lines up for the 1-2 pocket. Unless you throw an aggressive reverse hook, line up using the third arrow from the left, with the left foot starting on approximately board 7 from the left (figure 2.8*a*). You need to stand this far over because the arm swing is on the right side of the body, but the pocket and target are on the left side of the lane. If your ball hooks a lot, you should play closer to the second arrow and adjust for lane conditions.

A left-hander who throws a reverse hook lines up for the 1-3 pocket. (*Note:* It is rare for left-handed bowlers to throw a reverse hook.) The left-handed bowler

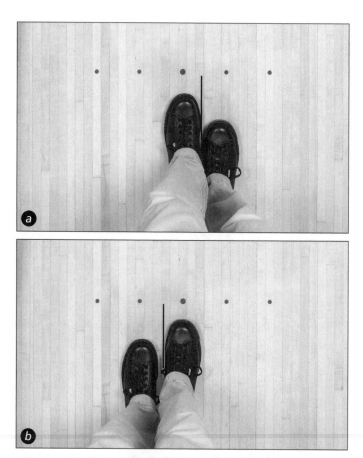

Figure 2.7   Hook ball: *(a)* right-handed; *(b)* left-handed.

lines up using the third arrow from the right, and the right foot starts approximately on board 7 from the right (figure 2.8*b*). It is necessary to stand this far over because the arm swing is on the left side of the body, but the pocket and target are on the right side of the lane. A left-handed bowler whose ball hooks a lot should play closer to the second arrow and adjust for lane conditions.

These positions are just starting points and, as such, are subject to adjustments. Depending on where the ball hits (or misses) the pocket, the quality of the ball, and the amount of rotation you impart at release, you may stand slightly to the right or left of these boards in the stance to either adjust your angle or allow for how much the ball does or does not hook. The amount of hook is influenced by the amount of friction the ball creates with the lane, which is caused by the release and the type of ball thrown.

When you throw a ball with little or no hook and you miss the pocket, move your stance in the direction of your miss. That is, if you are a right-handed bowler and the ball is hitting more of the 3 pin, move to the right, keeping the same target, to create a more direct angle to the pocket. If you are a left-handed bowler and are hitting more of the 2 pin, then move to the left, keeping the

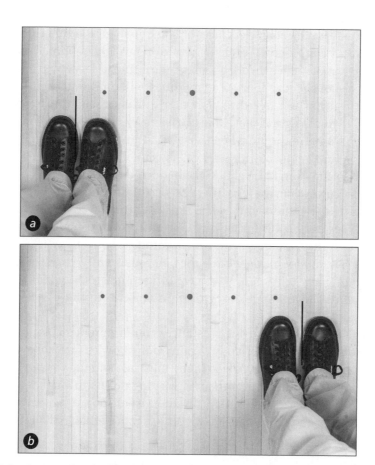

Figure 2.8   Reverse hook: *(a)* right-handed; *(b)* left-handed.

same target, to create a more direct angle to the pocket. If the ball hits more of the headpin, or even the opposite pocket, move your stance in that direction to create less of an angle toward the pocket. These adjustments are based on having thrown a good shot!

When you throw a hook, the amount of friction the cover of the ball creates also influences where you stand in relation to the target. You may need to adjust your stance according to the amount of friction the ball creates with the lane. Although you will still move your feet in the same direction that the ball missed the pocket, this adjustment involves more than just adjusting your angle; you must also adjust to the lane conditions. The key is to make adjustments to fine-tune your position on the approach. Chapter 8, Basic Lane Play, provides more information about making these adjustments.

RELAXING ON THE APPROACH

Being relaxed is one of the most important keys to creating a consistent approach and delivery. In any game of repetition, staying loose is the key to being able to repeat your performance. Bowlers face the same challenge as free-throw shooters in basketball. It comes down to being able to repeat the motion over and over. A free-throw shooter goes through a preshot routine to loosen up and get ready to repeat the shot she has done so many times. I liken the stance in bowling to the preshot routine of a free-throw shooter in basketball. Your stance is your preparation to make a good shot. Many bowlers are not aware of how tight their muscles are in a normal state when they don't think about relaxing.

It is a myth that, in the bowling stance, the shoulders must be perfectly square to the foul line and even in height. Right-handed bowlers should allow the right shoulder to be lower than the left (figure 2.9), so it can relax. Left-handed bowlers should allow the left shoulder to relax and be a little lower. To dispel a popular myth, you'll see in chapter 6 that it is OK to drop your shoulder at the finish. Here, we preset the shoulders with this in mind.

If you are having trouble delivering the ball consistently, check to see whether you are creating any tension in your grip or the muscles of your swing arm or shoulder. Many bowlers start out with tight muscles in the stance and do not even realize it.

Gripping the ball too tightly in the stance is often a problem because it creates tension throughout the upper body. Again, many bowlers are not aware of how tense they are in the stance. With so many muscles, and the various amounts of tension you could create within them at varying points throughout the swing, your approach can become infinitely different from shot to shot. *Tension makes you erratic.* Relax and let physics take over. It's more reliable than we are.

Figure 2.9 One shoulder is lower than the other. Shoulders are relaxed: *(a)* right-handed bowler; *(b)* left-handed bowler.

If inconsistency and inaccuracy are plaguing you, loosen up to allow the ball to swing naturally. With a proper lineup in the stance, natural eye–hand coordination will produce accurate shots if a natural arm swing is repeated every time. Rather than tightening up and trying to control and steer the shot, learn to relax and trust yourself!

Are You Relaxing in the Stance?

To see whether you're relaxed, put your arm in another person's hand in the same position as it is in the stance (figure 2.10). Without the ball, assume your stance position. Relax completely, allowing the other person to support the weight of your arm with his hand holding your arm up, beneath your wrist. Now have him spontaneously let go of your arm.

Does your forearm fall to your side? If not, the muscles are keeping it up. If you were relaxed, your arm would have fallen when the person withdrew his support. Repeat this from time to time. When you learn to relax your muscles, your arm will eventually fall—and that is progress!

Figure 2.10   To test your relaxation, *(a)* have someone hold your arm when you are in stance position and then *(b)* let go of your arm. If you are relaxed, your arm should fall to your side.

Progressive Muscle Relaxation

If you are not sure how to relax, do progressive muscle relaxation exercises at home. While lying in bed at night, tense and relax specific body parts, starting with your forehead and working through your face, neck, shoulders, arms, buttocks, legs, and feet. Do not progress to another part of your body until you relax the one you are working on. You may even fall asleep before finishing!

Once you achieve a relaxed state, conjure up an image in your mind that you associate with a relaxed state of being—a sunset, the beach, or whatever makes you think of relaxing. Do this every night for several weeks. Your body will involuntarily begin to associate this image with your relaxed state. It will be able to respond to your thought of this image to produce a more relaxed body while bowling.

So many people express an inability to relax. However, it can be learned! You can do research to learn more about practicing progressive muscle relaxation. It is good for you, even beyond your bowling game.

SUMMARY

A good start leads to a good finish. The stance is the position from which the entire approach occurs. You want to preset your core body position in the stance as it will be in the finish so you will have fewer moving parts throughout the approach and be able to repeat your shots.

A relaxed stance is crucial to a smooth motion and a loose arm swing. With the joints slightly flexed, the body is prepared to begin motion. It is easier to start from a relaxed position than from a tense position. Many bowlers start the stance holding the ball too tightly. Some begin tense and unaware of how tight their muscles are, whereas others are ready to try too hard during the approach. Start in a relaxed state so that you stay relaxed during the motion to follow.

Finally, when getting ready to swing the ball, too many bowlers underestimate the importance of the opposite, or nondominant, hand to the creation of a loose arm swing. Be aware of how your weight is distributed in the stance and throughout the start. Most bowlers put too much weight toward the swing hand, imposing too much stress on the muscles of the swing arm. When this happens, it becomes virtually impossible to create a loose and pure swing. Remember to support the ball with your opposite hand!

Chapter 3

Approach and Timing

In the bowling approach, you are trying to synchronize your arm swing with your footwork. This creates good leverage at delivery and enables you to repeat shots. It is easiest to develop this timing and maintain a loose arm swing by taking a four- or five-step approach. This chapter defines the proper timing zones for the swing with each step; then addresses common timing issues and how to fix them.

Timing affects all aspects of the approach. Your rhythm, finish position, release, accuracy, and ability to repeat shots all depend on timing. When you improve your timing, you will likely see these things improve as well. That is why a focus on timing is critical to a sound bowling approach and delivery.

FOUR-STEP APPROACH

In a four-step approach, a right-handed bowler starts with the right foot and ends on the left foot at the end of the approach. So, the steps taken are right, left, right, left (figure 3.1).

A left-handed bowler starts with the left foot and ends on the right foot. The left-handed bowler steps left, right, left, right (figure 3.2).

Notice that the arm moves in sequence with the feet. In the four-step approach, each step taken toward the line features a different basic ball position. These four positions can collectively be referred to as "out, down, back, and through."

• **First step: out on one.** The first step of the four-step approach begins by moving the ball forward with the first step, or the *key step*. The key step is the step that you initiate the swing with, beginning your timing sequence. The ball is pushed away from the body (often referred to as the push-away, or ball placement) and moves forward with the first step (figure 3.3*a*). This is the beginning of the approach. *Note:* your goal on the key step is to get the ball out to the place from which it will swing. (There will be more on this in chapter 5, Arm Swing.)

Figure 3.1 Four-step approach for a right-handed bowler: *(a)* right; *(b)* left; *(c)* right; *(d)* left.

Figure 3.2 Four-step approach for a left-handed bowler: *(a)* left; *(b)* right; *(c)* left; *(d)* right.

Figure 3.3 Ball positions of the four-step approach, right-handed bowler: *(a)* out on one (key step); *(b)* down on two; *(c)* back on three; *(d)* through on four.

TEXTBOOK TIMING VERSUS ADJUSTED TIMING ZONES

These traditional timing zones are a guide to developing good timing with a loose arm swing. Experienced bowlers often develop their unique approach around their release and swing mechanics. Therefore these timing positions may need to be modified into general timing zones to still be effective. The key is proper timing at the finish, which will be addressed later in the chapter. Many bowlers improve their games by heeding the fundamental principles of better swing mechanics and relaxing on the approach.

• **Second step: down on two.** On step two, the ball begins to swing into the approach (figure 3.3*b*). At the completion of this step, the ball should be down by your side.

• **Third step: back on three.** After you move the ball out on step 1 and down on step 2, the ball comes back on the third step into the backswing (figure 3.3*c*). This is in preparation to deliver the ball on the last step.

• **Fourth step: through on four.** Finally, on the last step of the four-step approach, your arm swings down to the release point and you follow through to deliver the ball (figure 3.3*d*).

FIVE-STEP APPROACH

For some bowlers, starting with the nondominant foot is just easier. A right-handed bowler who prefers to start with the left foot simply takes an extra step with the left foot, without any ball movement on the first step, and then performs the four-step approach starting with the second step (figure 3.4). A left-handed bowler takes an extra step with the right foot without any ball movement at the start. Therefore, in a five-step approach, the second step is the key step.

Whether you take a four- or five-step approach, the ball initially needs to move out with the key step. In a four-step approach, it's the first step; in a five-step approach, it's the second step. The key step for a right-handed bowler is on the right foot; the key step for a left-handed bowler is on the left foot.

Starting with the key step, the timing is the same in both the four- and five-step approach. This is why the first step of the five-step approach can be referred to as the zero step. It is simply an extra, get-started step without any movement of the ball. Therefore, the five-step approach is a modified four-step approach with an extra get-started step before beginning the four-step timing. Remember that the key step on a five-step approach is the second step.

Figure 3.4 Five-step approach, left-handed bowler: *(a)* first step with no ball movement; *(b)* second step (key step), ball goes out; *(c)* third step, ball swings down; *(d)* fourth step, ball swings back; *(e)* fifth step, ball is released and arm follows through.

EARLY AND LATE TIMING

Early and late timing refers to the position of the ball in relation to the body. Early timing is when the ball gets ahead of the body; late timing is when the body gets ahead of the ball. For simplicity while addressing timing issues, let's assume a standard four-step approach. (If you take a five-step approach, consider the first step a zero step; then refer to proper timing from the key step on, which is the equivalent of a four-step approach.)

Just about every bowler I have ever met, professionals included, has a timing issue in the start. That is, we all have a tendency to be either early or late; it seems that no one is immune to this tendency. This is why professionals often work on their starts practically every day to manage their tendency and develop a better start. As many have said, "A good start leads to a good finish!"

Early Timing in the Start

Early timing is when the ball swings ahead of the body. A good checkpoint is to identify where the ball is on the second step. If the ball is already past your body on the second step, rather than being straight down, then you have early timing (figure 3.5)—that is, the ball is *ahead* of the body. Table 3.1 lists a few common causes of early timing in the start, as well as solutions. To address early timing, you need to consider *when* you start the ball, *how* you start it, and the *shape* of your start.

Figure 3.5 Early timing. The ball is already past the body on the second step.

Table 3.1 Early Timing Causes and Solutions

Causes	Solutions
Starting to push the ball too soon	Push the ball with the key step, not before.
Pushing the ball downward too much	Hold the ball lower in the stance. Push out and slightly up.
Pulling the ball back into the swing	Keep the push-away out longer than usual; then just let the ball drop into the next step.
Taking too large a key step	Shorten the key step. Use the proper weight transfer by keeping your weight back.
Standing too far back on the approach and having to rush	Adjust stance position to start closer (see chapter 2).

Starting the Ball Too Soon

Pushing the ball out before you take the key step causes early timing, simply because you are pushing the ball early. If you are a four-step bowler, push the ball on the first step, not before. If you are five-step bowler, push the ball on the second step. If you are a five-step bowler and have a hard time waiting to push the ball on the second step, that might be a good reason to try four steps—so you can push on the first step.

Pushing the Ball Downward

If you push the ball down too much, rather than out, you likely will be early on the second step. Try to create more of an arc to the start by pushing the ball out and up before it comes down. Because you are used to pushing it downward, it will feel like you are pushing it out and slightly upward. Try holding the ball lower in the stance to help you create this upward motion. Overexaggerating and thinking upward will help you combat the tendency to push downward while fighting early timing. This will create a more circular motion, rather than a direct line toward the floor.

This arc should take two steps to complete. When you do push the ball out rather than down, wait until the second step to let it drop down and complete the arc. Pushing it out but letting it drop during the first step is another way the ball can get into the swing too early. Delaying the drop until the second step can be particularly challenging because your tendency is to be early. You need to keep your push-away out longer than usual, and then let the ball drop down to your side on the second step. Remember, out on one, down on two.

Many bowlers I coach who get early in this way have to overexaggerate and feel as though they are holding the ball out in front of them for almost two whole steps. When I take a photo and show them what is really happening, they cannot believe that they are not really holding it that long. What they think they are doing is not what they are actually doing.

Pulling the Ball Back

Using the muscles of your arm to pull the ball back into the swing is another way the arm can get ahead of the body. Rather than accelerate your arm back, learn to let your arm relax and swing like a pendulum. Your swing arm should be relaxed as you let the opposite hand do all the work to push the ball out and create the proper timing in the start. This concept of using your other hand to create a good swing in the start is of particular importance and is addressed at length in chapter 5, Arm Swing.

Taking a Long Key Step

Taking too big of a key step gives the ball too much time to drop early into the swing. You want the ball to go out with the key step and drop with the next step. The longer the key step is, the more likely the ball will be to drop during that step, because you can hold a heavy ball out in front of you for only so long! When you tend to fight the earlier side of timing, take a smaller key step as you push the ball out, so that the step is over sooner. This will make it easier to delay the drop until the next step.

It is easy to take too big a step when you shift your weight too far forward as you take that step. The imbalance of having your body lean forward creates a need for your feet to react and catch your balance. And because you are leaning your weight forward, you have to take a bigger step to get your legs back under you for balance. The result is a larger-than-natural step. Keep your weight centered as you take your step. You may even have to think about exaggerating your weight over your heels to keep from shifting the weight too far forward over your toes before you take your step.

Try this: get into a stance position as if you were practicing your start, and, just before you go, shift your weight forward over your toes and then take a step. Now, try again, but this time keep your weight centered over the heels or center of your feet and take a step. Notice that you are in much more control of your step, and its length, when your weight remains balanced.

Standing Too Far Back on the Approach

Taking a stance too far from the foul line has the psychological effect of making the approach feel like a runway you have to negotiate to make it all the way to the foul line. Your body sees a greater distance to the line than it could cover by taking natural steps. Therefore, you will throw your weight forward and tend to drop the ball early into the approach, which will make it feel as though you have to run to catch up. Because running steps are larger than walking steps, this is your body's way of making up the extra distance. I would estimate that about 80 to 85 percent of the students I see stand too far back. I am not saying that all have early timing, but standing too far back is a very common mistake. See chapter 2 for help determining how far back to start on the approach.

Late Timing in the Start

Late timing is when the ball is delayed getting into the swing. For example, the ball is not yet down by your side on the second step. In this case, the body is too far ahead of the ball (figure 3.6). Table 3.2 lists a few common causes to late timing in the start, as well as solutions. To address this issue, you need to consider *when* you start the ball, *how* you start it, and the *shape* of your start.

Figure 3.6 Late timing. The ball is not down on the second step.

Table 3.2 Late Timing Causes and Solutions

Causes	Solutions
Starting to push the ball too late	Push the ball with the key step, not after.
Pushing the ball up and outward	Hold the ball higher in the stance. Push out and down.
Tightening the arm and delaying the downward swing of the ball	Relax the swing arm after the push-away and just let the ball drop. Do not overextend or lock your swing arm.
Taking a key step that is too small	Lengthen the key step.

Starting the Ball Too Late

Pushing the ball out after you take your key step causes late timing simply because you are pushing the ball late. If you are a four-step bowler, push the ball with the first step, not after. If you are five-step bowler, push the ball on the second step. Be sure your elbows move forward, not just the ball. The ball swings from your shoulder. The only way to get the ball out far enough to swing from the shoulder is to push your elbows out. However do not lock the elbow of your swing arm as you push out the ball; this would cause the ball to pause rather than naturally drop into the swing.

If you are still late when you try to move the ball and foot at the same time, overexaggerate and try to push the ball *before* you step to get both the ball movement and the step to happen together. Many bowlers have to do this because they are still late when they try to move the ball and the foot at the same time. Sometimes you have to see it on video to believe it!

Pushing the Ball Upward

If you push the ball up too much, rather than out, you likely will be late on the second step. Try to push it out and slightly downward. Try holding the ball slightly higher in the stance to help you create this downward motion. Over-exaggerating and thinking downward will help you combat the tendency to push up. This will help you get the ball into the swing sooner by changing the direction of your push-away.

Delaying the Drop

Using your muscles to hold the ball out too long during the first step is another way the ball gets into the swing too late. Because you are used to the feeling of being late, you might tighten up and hesitate to drop the ball to your side on the next step because it feels too quick although it actually is on time. Once you push the ball out, just let it drop down on the second step.

Note: to maintain a fluid arc into the swing, do not overextend or lock your elbow. This will only keep the ball from dropping into the swing on time. Letting it just drop on the second step can be particularly challenging because your tendency is to be late. The fluid arc to get the ball into the swing properly should be completed in two steps: out on one, down on two.

Again, your swing arm should be relaxed. Learning how to use the opposite hand to get your swing arm to relax is really important to your timing and is addressed at length in chapter 5, Arm Swing.

Taking a Short Key Step

When your key step is too short, you have too little time to push the ball out with that step. The shorter the step is, the less time you have to get the ball out; the longer the step is, the more time you have to get the ball out during that step. If your timing is late, you need more time to get the ball out; a longer step will help because it takes more time to complete. This will give you more time to get the ball into the swing.

Two-Step Timing: Out on One, Down on Two

Starting with your right foot, take only two steps to combine the out-on-one motion with the down-on-two motion. When you stop on the second step, the ball should be down by your side (figure 3.7).

Figure 3.7   Two-step timing: *(a)* out on one; *(b)* down on two. The ball ends down by the side.

Making Changes: Timing Changes and Rhythm

Your rhythm will change when you adjust your timing, especially if you have been bowling for a long time. At first, it is normal to fight this feeling. Just remember that when you are feeling this difference, you are making the change!

If you were early with the swing and are learning to delay your timing, you may feel slow, as though moving through molasses. If you were late with the swing, you may feel fast when you are actually getting the swing started on time. For you, this may feel way out of control. I remind my students that it is human nature to want to be in control, and it is difficult to lose control, which you must do to correct late timing. Since late timing is caused by too much control, fixing it requires letting go of control to let the ball swing. Once you allow your swing to loosen up and get in sync with your feet, you will begin repeating your shots at a whole new level and bowl better!

Timing changes lead to changes in rhythm, or the overall cadence of your steps. For example, if you are used to pushing the ball late and you start pushing it on time, letting the ball drop into the swing sooner, your feet will actually start to move faster to keep up with the ball. Conversely, if you used to push the ball too soon and you learn to push it later, your rhythm will feel much slower as you delay pushing the ball into the swing. The change that you feel is not your imagination, nor is it bad. It is real, and it means that you are actually making the correction in your timing. If you are not feeling a difference in your rhythm, you are likely not changing your timing.

Again, what might feel like running or moving slower than molasses is not actually that extreme. Because we are sensitive to how things feel, a slight change can feel dramatic.

At first, you might fight the change in rhythm that comes with a correction in timing. However, if you understand that it is due to the correction in timing, you will be more apt to welcome the change in rhythm as a sign that you are succeeding in correcting your timing and stay the course!

Once you successfully accomplish the out-on-one motion, if the ball is already past your leg on the second step, your swing is ahead and you are early. In this case, you either need to delay the drop or just let it drop (rather than pull the ball back). Keep in mind that this will feel really slow, almost as if you are holding the ball out for almost two steps!

If your ball is not yet to your side on the second step and is still in front of you, you are late. Move the ball sooner in the push or use your nondominant hand to push the ball sooner and let it drop freely. This will likely feel fast to you until you get used to the rhythm of the new timing.

Use these suggestions until you complete the drill properly. This may take many tries! When you can do it correctly at least three times in a row, you are starting to get the feel and can attempt to take a shot. A word of advice: When you take the shot, try to walk through the first two steps as though you are still in the drill and then simply finish your steps. Although this will feel very fragmented, this is the only way you will stay technically correct and reinforce the correct timing and finish the approach. With a lot of repetition, you will become smooth and in sync. Be patient.

Note your posture as you do this two-step drill. If your swing gets a bit early in the start, you will tend to lean more forward as the ball moves into the swing (figure 3.5). This is not to say that there is no spinal tilt during the approach, but it tends to get excessive when the swing gets quick. Paying attention to posture has helped many bowlers get back to better basics when working on letting the ball swing for better timing. Chapter 6, Finish Position and Delivery, addresses getting low while maintaining good posture.

Fixing timing is a function of starting the ball at the right time (with the key step) and creating better swing mechanics to maintain good timing. More details on these mechanics are provided in chapter 5, Arm Swing.

TIMING AND THE FINISH

Although good timing in the start is a major key to establishing good timing throughout the entire approach, it is also important to maintain good timing at delivery for proper leverage at the line. Sometimes the timing you start with is not the timing you end with, especially when the swing changes during the approach. With a late start, you might cut your backswing short and end up early at the line or you may pull your ball back early at the start and overswing and be late in the finish. Deviating from your loose arm swing will affect the speed and height of the backswing, in effect changing your timing at delivery.

Entering the Slide

To better understand timing at the finish, let's first address the proper timing zone as you enter the slide. When you enter the slide (figure 3.8), generally the ball should be between your shoulder and your belt in the downswing to give you the proper leverage at delivery. This varies among bowlers, depending on the leverage necessary based on how much they hook the ball.

Figure 3.8 Entering the slide with the ball between the shoulder and belt in the downswing.

The more hook a bowler has, the later the timing will be. The ball will be higher in this zone, closer to the shoulder, to provide more leverage to project the ball away from the pocket to allow for how much it hooks. For a bowler who hooks the ball less, the ball will be near the center of the back or closer to the belt to play somewhat straighter and with less projection. Bowlers with extreme hook (i.e., many more revolutions) will be out of this zone, higher than the shoulder entering the slide, to have even more leverage to be able to project the ball to allow for such a hook. However, for most bowlers the ball should be between the shoulder and the belt.

If your ball is already below the belt when you enter the slide, the ball is at the finish too early (figure 3.9a). If your ball is still above your shoulder, the ball is at the finish too late (figure 3.9b). The exception is a bowler who has such a strong hook, he or she needs to project more away from the pocket to allow for the hook. This bowler will be above the shoulder entering the slide.

Figure 3.9   Improper timing at the slide: *(a)* early timing entering the slide; *(b)* late timing entering the slide.

Posture and Leverage

If your timing is early at the finish and the ball beats you to the line, your shoulders will end forward of your knee, creating weak leverage at the line (figure 3.10a). If you have late timing at the finish, you will tend to be too upright as a result of excessive leverage at the line (figure 3.10b).

When your timing is early, you lack leverage at delivery. This makes you weak and compromises your power and projection. When your timing is late, you have excess leverage and you will either project the ball too far or compensate by pulling the ball down to try to get it back into time.

Figure 3.10 The effect of improper timing on the finish position: *(a)* early timing; *(b)* late timing.

Keep in mind that your timing at the finish will change as a result of working on your start. Because you have had a certain feel to your timing before working on it, you may end up trying to make adjustments to your swing late in the approach to make the timing feel the way it did before you worked on it. Once you create a better start, you will also need to develop new muscle memory for the different feel at the finish.

The difference leverage makes can be demonstrated and felt by attempting to lift a chair from two positions.

Demonstrating Leverage: Lifting a Chair

Use a chair with a back you can lift it from. Try lifting the chair from a weakened leverage position, bending far forward at the waist, with your shoulders forward. It will be hard, if not impossible, to do. Now, try lifting it from an upright body position. You will feel how much easier it is to do with good posture. Just as you have (hopefully) learned to pick up something heavy using your legs, rather than bending forward and straining your back, so it is with using leverage to create a strong body position when you bowl.

Making Changes: Developing Proper Timing

When you change your timing entering the slide, it is important that you learn to relax your swing as you adapt to the new timing. However, your arm may tighten up and pull the swing down, either because it used to have to, to catch up when you were late, or because it is trying to re-create the timing it is used to.

Consider the common issue of pushing the ball late in the start. When you have a late start, you will either cut the backswing short or, if you do let it fully swing, you will have to pull the ball to get it to catch up. So, when you make a change to your start, which requires a lot of focus and repetition, and learn to move the ball sooner, you may be fixing your timing, but you will likely still pull the ball to the finish out of habit. It requires patience and understanding to realize that you really are making the fix but that your body simply hasn't acclimated to it yet. The best way to get your body used to the change is to keep repeating it so that your body can adjust and adapt to it. You will eventually stop pulling the ball down at the finish to compensate for the previously poor timing. If after a lot of repetition you are still pulling the ball, then you just have give a little extra focus to relaxing the swing into delivery because the need to pull has been fixed.

Sometimes it is just a matter of undoing the old muscle memory that you had developed prior to improving your technique. This is especially true if you have bowled a certain way for a long time and are working on changing. Just stay the course and you will begin to see the changes come together.

As you make corrections in your timing, especially in the start, you must be patient until your body gets acclimated to how the change feels and you learn to just relax to let the swing feel different at the finish. You may not see the desired result at first. Stick with it. Often, I tell a student "good job" after the ball has completely missed the pins. When I can see the change coming along and recognize that the student's body just needs more shots until it gets comfortable with the new feeling, I praise the progress and encourage the student to stick with it. This is what I hope to help you do. It is a process, and it takes patience. The results will follow.

At this point, your delivery will feel different because better timing changes your leverage at the line. Whether you were used to being late and more upright or early with the shoulders forward, or whether your body can now simply balance better, expect your body to feel different at the line than it used to. Often, it will just feel better. These timing adjustments are designed to improve your leverage.

Sometimes, you have to feel different before you feel better. Do not panic or think something is wrong. It is just different, and it should be. Once it doesn't feel so odd, it will begin to feel better when done properly. If it doesn't feel different, you are not making the change.

Once you have improved your timing, you will then be able to work on strengthening the finish position itself. Whether your goal is to get lower, keep your shoulders more upright, or be more balanced, with improved timing your world will open up to enable you to then make these changes in your finish. This is addressed in more detail in chapter 6, Finish Position and Delivery.

Leverage and Accuracy

When your timing is on and your swing is loose (more about this in chapter 5, Arm Swing), you almost cannot help but hit your target. In many lessons that I give, once we work on the timing and the swing, accuracy is suddenly restored, and we haven't even focused on a target! This is because once the mechanics become sound, they are easier to repeat and the leverage at the line is much better. However, when the timing is off, it is almost impossible to hit the target consistently no matter how hard you stare at it!

Early Timing and Missing Left

When the ball gets into the swing early and beats your body to the line, your body position will be compromised. Note that because of early timing throughout the approach, the ball can be early at the finish, or you simply cut the backswing too short, causing the ball to arrive too soon at the finish. As a result of the ball reaching the line before you do, your shoulders will be too closed at the finish (the right shoulder will be ahead of the left; figure 3.11) so you will not be able to project the ball. This early timing and resulting closed shoulders forces you to miss your target left.

Figure 3.11   The right shoulder is ahead of the left shoulder, causing the ball to miss the target to the left.

Refer to the causes of early timing addressed earlier in this chapter. Once you fix relax your swing and fix your timing, making it later, you will restore your leverage at the line and be able to project the ball to your target once again.

Late Timing and Missing Right or Left

The question I missed on the Bronze Level test had to do with which way a right-handed bowler misses the target when late. Having coached for many years, when I took the test, I answered "to the left." The answer they were looking for was "to the right." I argued the point. My reasoning is addressed in this section.

Considering that you miss your target left when you are early (because the shoulders close), it follows that you will miss right when you are late because the shoulders are too open. They are too open because the ball is still behind you at the finish, and so your right shoulder is still too far back. Point taken.

The reason I answered "to the left," however, is because most bowlers, in reaction to being late, pull the ball to try to get it back into proper time. When you pull the ball, you miss your target to the left. This is not to confuse missing your target left because you are early! When you miss because you are early, you are not pulling; rather, you are in a poor leverage position with your shoulders closed and cannot project the ball. When you miss your target left because you are late, it is because you have pulled the ball. That requires force.

There is a difference between missing the target left because of early timing and missing it left because of pulling the ball. When you miss left because your timing is early, it is because your shoulders are closed up at delivery because the ball got there first. When you miss left because you pull, that is due to force. In the first case, you miss left from poor leverage; in the second, you miss left because you pulled it!

SUMMARY

Timing is the heartbeat of the approach. It is what bowlers of all levels continually work on to improve their performance. Whatever your timing tendency is, it will always be. Managing it is the key.

Adjusting your timing can be a challenging process. It takes a lot of work to feel different. Your timing affects all other aspects of the approach, including your posture, rhythm, leverage, release, and accuracy. When you improve your timing, these areas improve as well. That is why developing good timing is worth the effort.

Timing is the synchronization between the feet and the swing. In the next two chapters we'll take a closer look at footwork and the arm swing. In particular, the profound effect the swing itself has on timing is addressed in chapter 5.

Chapter 4

Footwork

The key to good footwork in bowling is to walk naturally and, in general, walk straight. You want to have a good rhythm to the line, feeling a natural increase in momentum throughout the approach. For consistency and power, you need good biomechanics when taking your steps on the approach. Starting the proper distance from the foul line is important, too, for establishing sound footwork.

Taking a four- or five-step approach to the line provides a natural swing and stride. This makes it easier to maintain good timing between the swing and the steps. If you take too few steps, you will have difficulty establishing a natural swing; if you take too many steps, you will have difficulty creating consistent timing from shot to shot.

The other key to good footwork is walking straight to the foul line. Although there are a few exceptions to this rule, in general you should avoid walking toward your arm swing. Walking in any way other than straight is considered drifting.

WALKING NATURALLY

To be smooth, you need to walk naturally to the foul line. Taking normal steps allows your body to move freely over the approach, so you can develop a constant momentum to your swing. Many bowlers take steps that are too big or try to take them too methodically, sometimes even pausing between steps. Walk on the approach just as you would walk down the street. This is the key to developing natural momentum that you can repeat from shot to shot.

Normal steps are taken from heel to toe in natural strides. When you walk, you initiate a step by first striking the ground with the heel and then transferring body weight through the middle of the foot to the ball of the foot to push off the toe into the next step (figure 4.1). This biomechanical process is the natural way we efficiently propel ourselves forward.

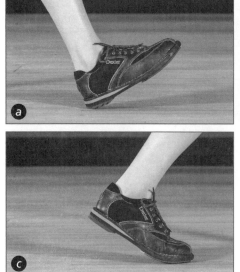

Figure 4.1 Heel-to-toe steps: *(a)* the heel strikes the ground first; *(b)* the weight rolls through the middle of the foot; and *(c)* the toes push off the ground.

The exception is the last step at delivery. In bowling, the steps leading up to the last step are to develop momentum, but you want to create a smooth delivery on the last step. The key to doing this is to slide the last step through the delivery. That is, the toe strikes first and then the heel (figure 4.2), which will eventually bring you to a stop. *Note:* This is why the soles are leather and the heels are generally rubber in performance shoes.

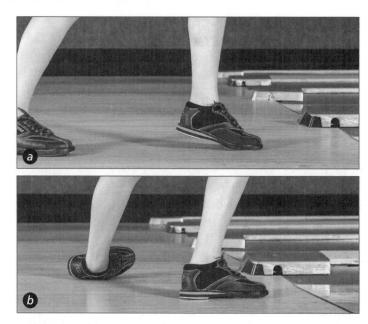

Figure 4.2 Slide step: *(a)* the toe strikes the ground first; and then *(b)* the heel strikes the ground.

BOWLING SHOES

Bowling shoes are available for rent at bowling centers. These basic shoes are sanitized between rentals. Rentals are a couple of dollars, so if you bowl on a regular basis, purchasing a pair of shoes may make economical sense, and you will have the added bonus of getting to wear the same pair of shoes every time you bowl.

Bowling shoes come in two types: recreational and performance. With house and recreational shoes, the soles of both the right and left shoes are identical (i.e., slide soles) to accommodate both right- and left-handed bowlers. On performance shoes, one shoe has a rubber sole and the other has a slide sole to provide traction in your push-off step and slide in your last step. A right-handed pair of shoes has rubber on the right shoe and a slide sole on the left. A left-handed pair of shoes has rubber on the left shoe and a slide sole on the right (figure 4.3).

In the bowling shoes market, you get what you pay for. Performance shoes are available at various prices based on features. Premium performance shoes typically provide a stronger base of support and are more comfortable than less expensive bowling shoes. When you spend even more, performance shoes have interchangeable soles and heels, using Velcro, so you can modify your footing at delivery depending on the approach.

High-end performance shoes are great if you bowl in different bowling centers because they help you achieve the same slide on the last step regardless of the type and texture of the approach. Decide on your budget for bowling, keeping in mind that when you spend more, you get more. As in any sport, good shoes can be a great investment.

Figure 4.3 Bowling shoes: *(a)* recreational shoes; *(b)* performance shoes for a right-handed bowler; *(c)* performance shoes for a left-handed bowler.

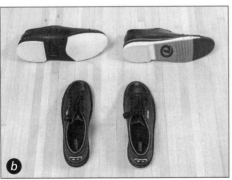

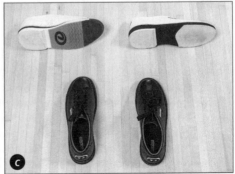

It is important to note that a slide step is not defined by *how much* you slide. Rather, it is defined by the foot angle of the toe striking before the heel. It is critical to achieve this angle as you enter the last step.

The slide step allows your body to deliver the ball more smoothly and engage the thigh muscles for power. When you plant your heel first, it is a very abrupt finish and you are jolting your knee joint. The joint is stressed sometimes to the point of injury. As a joint, the knee does not generate power, but muscles do. When you slide, you engage the quadriceps muscles in the thigh, which actually generates power. So sliding your last step not only creates a smoother delivery but also helps you avoid injury to the knee and leads to a more powerful and fluid finish.

For a smooth motion to the foul line, take strides that are natural in both size and mechanics. The strides during the approach should be similar in size to the strides you take while walking. Walking naturally keeps your body comfortable, allowing you to repeat the same motion from shot to shot.

Walking unnaturally can occur because your swing is muscled, your timing is off, or you are feeling overly aggressive about knocking down the pins and shift your body weight too far forward. Whatever the cause, it will affect your footwork.

When you are working on your game, it is easy to become mechanical as you think through changes you want to make. This can be a good thing, especially while you are working on timing changes. However, at a certain point you need to get out of mechanics mode and back into motion mode and start to walk naturally again.

When you are in the process of, say, fixing your timing, you often have to feel mechanical just to get the proper technique down. I tell my students not to worry about the feel at that point, just get it correct! It takes a lot of thought to re-create muscle memory. Although your timing is actually getting better, it does

---

Making Changes: Learning to Walk Naturally

Stand the proper distance from the foul line. (Refer to chapter 2 to determine the approximate spot.)

Trust your natural stride even if the foul line looks too close. If you are used to starting way back on the approach, you may feel awkward at first when you move up. You may feel cramped for space. It is OK if the first couple of tries feel uncomfortable. You will get used to the new length of the approach.

The key is to adjust your steps so that they eventually feel more natural. The first couple of tries after moving up, you may even get a foul if your foot goes over the foul line. Once you learn to take more natural strides, however, you will finish behind the foul line. The delivery will feel more comfortable, and the approach will feel more natural.

not necessarily feel more natural, at least not yet. Keep repeating the motion until you create the change you are trying to make.

At that point, take a break and refocus on taking your steps more naturally—in other words, get out of drill mode and into motion mode to turn your mechanics into fluid motion. As you do this, focus on taking more natural steps again. Once you can relax and walk naturally again, your timing will feel great. When your timing is on, you should be able to walk easily and more naturally to repeat your shots.

DISTRIBUTING YOUR WEIGHT PROPERLY

Improper weight transfer is a common problem at the beginning of the approach. To take a natural-size step, you need to distribute your weight properly in the stance so that your balance is centered over both feet. In the stance, center your body weight evenly on the nonstarting foot so you can take the first step properly. If you lean too far forward, you will shift your weight onto the balls of your feet and have to lunge forward to catch your balance as you take your first step. This will lead to a bigger, unnatural step.

Keep your body balanced while stepping forward. If your body weight shifts too far forward before you take the step, you're likely to overstride as your footwork responds to being off balance by trying to restore it.

AVOIDING SHUFFLING STEPS

Avoid taking weak steps or shuffling to the foul line. Shuffling (sliding your foot rather than picking it up and taking an actual step) represents poor biomechanical technique. When you shuffle, the ball of the foot, rather than the heel, strikes first. This minimizes the weight transfer forward through the foot, and the body loses natural momentum to the foul line. Simply put, when you shuffle, your momentum briefly stops, which makes the approach less fluid with less momentum to match a fluid swing. Shuffle steps lack the momentum needed to propel you forward. They are, in effect, dead steps.

To sense the effects of shuffling versus stepping from heel to toe, walk with some friends and try to keep up with them while taking shuffle steps. You should notice that it is virtually impossible to develop any momentum while shuffling.

Trying to slow down to control the ball or get it to hook is a common reason bowlers start to shuffle, unaware of how much biomechanical power they are losing as a result. Picking up their feet will generate the proper rhythm for a fluid swing.

Sliding your feet as you take your steps on the approach can be a habit that feels odd to break, even though you do not walk that way normally. Get rid of shuffle steps by striving to pick up your feet and strike with the heels first to restore a heel-to-toe motion. This may feel very awkward until you get the feel of walking naturally again.

Making Changes: Eliminating Shuffle Steps

To correct a shuffle step, overexaggerate picking up your foot until you learn to take your step from heel-to-toe again. You may feel as though you are marching the first few times you do this, although you won't be. Once you get used to picking up your feet and striking with your heel first, your steps will no longer feel awkward because that's how you normally walk!

Once you start to get the hang of it, you will not have to exaggerate picking up your feet anymore and your footwork will actually feel more natural. You will also have an easier time developing momentum in your approach.

Aleta Sill is a great bowling champion. After she and I had given a clinic together, I asked her if she would like me to take a look at her game. I noticed that she shuffled during her first two steps, although she was trying to create momentum! When she was working on taking normal heel-to-toe steps, she kept saying that she felt as though she were marching. It felt that different to her to pick up her steps again on the approach, although she normally did so when she walked. Even when professionals make changes, their efforts can feel exaggerated until they become natural again.

WALKING STRAIGHT

The relationship between the stance position and the target forms an angle for the trajectory of the ball. To maintain that angle at delivery, walk straight during the approach. Walking diagonally will alter the target line.

To check for a straight walk, first be sure to line up on the approach using the proper foot. As mentioned in chapter 2, a right-handed bowler lines up with the left foot; a left-handed bowler, with the right foot. Take note of the board your foot starts on and notice whether it finishes on the same board. If it does, you are walking straight. If you finish on a board other than the one you started on, you are drifting on the lane.

Poor alignment between the stance position and the target is a common cause of drifting. If the relationship between where you stand and where you target does not form an angle that you can hit by walking straight, you will have to drift to hit your target. The line between your stance and the target (while con-

LINING UP ON THE LANE

Right-handed bowlers line up with the left foot, whereas left-handed bowlers line up with the right foot. You line up with the foot you finish on. This helps you determine whether or not you walk straight to the foul line. Whether you line up looking at your toe or the inside of your foot, be consistent. Professionals line up with the inside of the foot because it is the part of the foot that is closest to where they release the ball.

sidering how much the ball will hook) should form an angle that enables you to walk straight and produce a pocket hit. If you stand too far to the right or left of the target, you will drift from the board you start on as you walk toward the target in an attempt to hit it.

Remember that although the eyes are in the middle of the body, the arm swing is not (figure 4.4). Do not make the mistake of lining up your head to your target rather than your swing. Because the swing shoulder is several inches from the head, centering the target in the middle of the body from the stance position requires your arm to throw the ball across your body or requires you to drift to avoid doing so in order to hit the target. (A right-handed bowler would drift to the left; a left-handed bowler would drift to the right.)

Avoid standing too far from or too close to your target to avoid drifting. Stand a healthy distance from your target when you line up and make sound adjustments.

To line up your swing and keep the relationship between your stance and the target realistic, stand on a board that is at least six boards to the left (if you are right-handed) of the target (figure 4.5). This range will change based on the angle you are playing and how much you hook the ball. When you are playing a deeper line

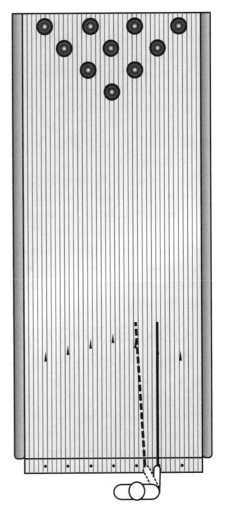

Figure 4.4 Alignment of eyes (head) to target versus alignment of shoulder to target (right-handed bowler).

on the lane (standing more inside, or past the center of the lane), you will have to line up farther than this range from your target because you have to swing the ball out more on the lane. You will turn and open your shoulders to do so, and therefore you will not have to drift to hit your target.

When you throw a hook and adjust to lane conditions, if you move your feet too much, without also moving your target, you again will be forced to drift toward the target to hit it. Try not to move your feet more than two boards or so without also moving your target in the same direction. This general rule of thumb will help you avoid getting so far from your target that you force a drift, because how you line up and make adjustments is often the culprit behind developing a drift in the first place.

You will learn more about this in chapter 8, Basic Lane Play. Chapter 9, Advanced Lane Play, provides more information on calculating your lay-down point (the board on which you lay down the ball at the foul line, as compared to the board you slide on). You will learn where to let go of the ball in relation to the target you are trying to hit.

Note: There is an exception to the rule of walking straight when the shoulders are closed to shoot spares on the left side of the lane (right side for left-handers). There will be a slight drift toward your target (away from the swing), and this is further addressed in chapter 10 and 11 on spare shooting.

CORRECTING DRIFT

Finishing a board, or even two or three boards, off your start position is not drastic, especially if you do so consistently. However, excessive drifting can be corrected with a little overcompensation.

The boards on the approach can serve as a guide to help you determine if (and how much) you have drifted, especially when you do not feel that you have. If you are right-handed, make sure you line up on the approach with your left foot because that is the foot you slide on at the finish. If you are left-handed, line up with your right foot. This is why you lined up with the slide foot in the stance; it is the only way you will know whether you drifted when you go to check.

Exaggerate walking in the opposite direction from that in which you were drifting to fix it quickly. If the drift is to

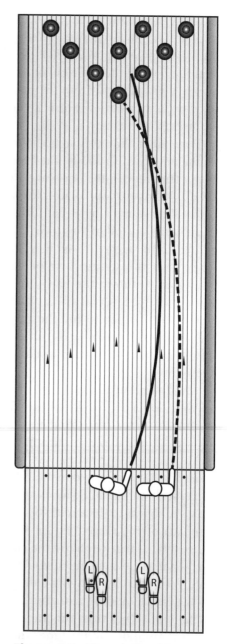

Figure 4.5 The relationship between stance and target; walk straight and adjust shoulders.

the left, trick your mind by trying to walk to the right. Although it will feel as though you actually walked to the right, you probably did not end up to the right of your starting position. Compare the starting foot position to the finishing foot position to determine the actual change.

Get into the habit of checking for drift. If you find that you have a hard time remembering to look at the end of the approach, have a piece of paper on hand to write down where you slide after each shot. You will soon learn that you will not have anything to write down if you don't look! And make sure you remember that there may be fewer dots in the beginning of the approach than at the foul line, so that you correctly identify your board numbers, both at the start and finish. (This idea can also help during target practice. Having to write down what you hit after each shot will soon train you to look at your target!)

If you really have a hard time drifting, place a towel at the end of the approach to limit the amount you can drift without hitting the towel. It's either drift less or fall! This works great because your body cares more about not falling than it does about bowling. You will avoid the towel. However, eventually you will have to learn to walk straight without it. (When placing the towel, put the edge of the towel on the board beside the board you drift toward. Depending on which way you drift, you may need to allow a couple extra boards for the width of your foot.)

Once you correct the drift, overcompensating thoughts are no longer necessary. You can then think straight and walk straight!

You have to learn to line up properly in relation to your target and make sound lane adjustments so you do not have to drift. However, you also have to drift less to be able to line up properly to your target. They work together.

Lining up better will not necessarily instantly stop you from drifting. You may need to line up better and work on your drift to create that ideal relationship between your stance and your target.

When you have been walking crooked on the approach and start to work on walking straight, you likely will find that attempting to just walk straight does not fix the problem. This is a perfect example of how overexaggeration can work to fix the problem much more quickly.

If you walk to the right, you will have to think "walk left" to start walking straighter again. In fact, it is likely that you will only walk less right in your attempt to walk left. Keep in mind that the direction in which you have drifted feels normal (or straight) for you. This is because your body has become used to the drift. You need to compensate by walking in the direction opposite to the direction in which you have been drifting just to begin to walk straighter, or less in the direction you used to walk. The more you drift, the more you have to overexaggerate walking in the other direction.

Now, trust me, you will swear that you actually walked left, but when you check, you will likely see that you just drifted less right than usual. Checking where you end up on every shot will give you the incentive you need to continue to overexaggerate your walk in the opposite direction, no matter what it feels like. With this committed and focused effort, you will learn to walk straight again!

I once worked with a student who kept saying that he wasn't sure whether he was still drifting. I kept reminding him to look. In fact, a good plan for determining whether you are drifting from shot to shot is to write on a piece of paper where you slide after each shot. When you get tired of not recalling, you will learn to look so you can write it down!

My student was saying how very awkward it felt when he started to work on it. I kept reminding him that redundancy creates comfort. He was just trying to walk straight again, like normal, but had to overexaggerate his walk in the other direction to do it. With repetition, his straighter walk began to feel normal again.

At some point, you can stop overexaggerating your walk. When you have learned to actually walk in the direction opposite to the one in which you were drifting, you will be able to just think "walk straight." I would not advise doing this until you have overcorrected several times. If you go back to drifting, you are not ready to stop exaggerating. Monitor where you are finishing to determine what your thoughts need to be for the best results. Continue to exaggerate until you fix it, and stop trying to compensate once it is fixed!

Backswing Direction and Drifting

If your arm swing comes behind your back rather than staying in line with your shoulder, often you will drift that way to walk out of the way of the downswing. This would be a drift to the left for a right-handed bowler, or a drift to the right for a left-handed bowler. This happens because your body naturally wants to avoid getting hit by the ball. If your swing comes back away from your body, you can drift in that direction. In either case, the feet tend to walk in the direction in which the ball veers out of the swing plane.

Making sure your swing comes back straight (figure 4.6) will help you walk straighter again. This is often done by making sure you push the ball straight in line with the shoulder at the start, while maintaining a relaxed arm so that it swings straight back.

Again, it is important to note that you need to line up properly to hit your target. If you stand too far or too close to the target, you will start to drift to hit it. A good lineup enables you to walk straight, while your arm swings on the desired target line.

Figure 4.6 The backswing goes straight back.

Making Proper Adjustments to Avoid Drifting

Many bowlers develop a drift because, as they make adjustments to changing lane conditions, they move their feet too much without also moving the target. To avoid this, learn to move your feet no more than a few boards unless you also move your target in the same direction. As you move deeper, you can get farther from your target to swing the ball out, but you will make up the extra distance you are from your target by opening up the shoulders.

SLIDING ON THE LAST STEP

You can learn to slide rather than plant at the line with this two-part drill that you can practice at home on an uncarpeted floor or on the bowling lane. First, stand close to the line with your right foot forward (if you are a right-handed bowler), as you get ready to slide the last step. Practice pushing off with that foot and sliding into your last step (figure 4.7). Repeat three times.

Now, still without the ball, incorporate the momentum from the approach by walking through the whole approach, sliding the same way on the last step. Repeat three times. You do not need to swing your arm to incorporate your timing during this drill. Rather, just leave your arms by your sides or put your hands on your hips so you can focus solely on sliding.

If you are on the lane, once you have completed both parts of this drill three times successfully, you are ready to bowl with the ball, attempting to slide the last step. If it is difficult at first to slide, repeat this process as many times as you have to, to develop the feel and skill of sliding.

Once you begin to bowl and slide, devote your next 10 shots to trying to slide. Worry about nothing else. Keep track of how many shots out of those 10 you

Figure 4.7 Sliding drill, right-handed bowler: *(a)* stand at the line, ready to slide; *(b)* push off with the right foot and slide on the left.

actually slid. Figure out your percentage. Repeat. Try to improve your percentage until you are sliding 100 percent of the time! Keep in mind that the critical moment is just as you are entering the slide step.

TIMING, ARM SWING, AND RHYTHM

If your swing gets quick, causing early timing, your feet will have to rush to catch up. This will lead to quicker steps as you try to keep up, which is often referred to as fast feet. Trying to fix the footwork itself does not end up really fixing fast feet because the source of the problem is the quick, early arm swing that causes the feet to have to rush. This is why trying to slow down the feet never results in a new level of performance when timing is the issue. Once you fix the swing, timing it properly and getting it to relax, your foot speed naturally will adjust.

Keep in mind that at first your new rhythm will feel like molasses compared to your quick feet! You will have to get used to it. You have not become too slow; you are simply fixing your swing and timing, which leads to calmer footwork. In fact, if you are not feeling like molasses, you are not fixing the problem! Fixing fast feet is not about trying to slow down; rather, it is about having a good swing and timing it properly to walk more naturally.

A pause in your footwork in the approach would indicate that your swing has unnaturally slowed down (as a result of contracting the muscles that should be relaxed), inhibiting the natural flow of momentum. The tight muscles clog up the arm's ability to swing freely and develop momentum. Once you relax your hand and swing muscles, momentum will be restored and your steps will again flow to keep in sync with the free swing.

You may have someone advise you to slow down. I don't give this advice. When you loosen your arm swing, you will move more briskly on the approach because of the more fluid swing. Slowing down would be counter-productive. If your timing is off, your rhythm is off, but the reason needs to be addressed. Rather than trying to adjust your rhythm, you need to adjust your timing or create a loose swing. With good timing and a loose swing, your rhythm will be right.

Making Changes: Timing and Rhythm

Because the feet tend to follow the swing, footwork most often is controlled by the swing. Once you adjust the mechanics of the swing to properly synchronize your timing, your steps will adjust, and your rhythm will feel natural again.

When you feel as though the rhythm in your footwork is off, whether it is because you hop during the approach, move too fast, or even pause, the issue usually is in the swing. That is because your feet are largely controlled by the tempo of your swing.

For example, if your swing is fast or early, your feet have to rush to catch up (i.e., fast feet). By focusing on relaxing your swing and creating better timing, you can fix the real problem and achieve a better rhythm in your footwork that you could not have done by working on your footwork alone.

PLAYING INSIDE: WALKING STRAIGHT AND ALIGNING SHOULDERS TO TARGET (90-DEGREE RULE)

A right-handed bowler who throws a hook and has to play a more inside line (toward the middle of the lane) because of lane conditions will move his feet more to the left on the approach (figure 4.8). Likely, he will have to swing the ball out more to give it room to hook back into the pocket.

Consider that the pocket is on board 17.5. When you are standing left of this, you will have to swing the ball out to allow for the hook of the ball coming back to the pocket. In this case, your shoulders will have to be open (toward the gutter) to be able to project the ball with a healthy arm swing (figure 4.9).

When you are inside on the lane and having to project the ball out, your feet often will be farther from the target than they were when you were playing more outside on the lane. The difference will be made up in the shoulders.

Note: the arm should always swing at a 90-degree angle to the shoulders. So, it is up to the shoulders to line up the same swing every time. By opening the shoulders, you can stand farther from your target and still hit it while maintaining a straight walk on the approach. By turning your body and walking straight, you can project the ball on more of an angle and maintain a swing at a 90-degree angle to your shoulders.

For many bowlers, especially those who have bowled for a long time, learning to walk straight while facing the target with the shoulders is a new concept. A long time ago, bowlers were taught to walk toward the target. However, that was when

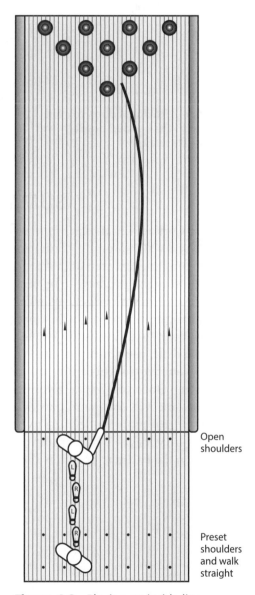

Open shoulders

Preset shoulders and walk straight

Figure 4.8 Playing an inside line.

bowling balls did not hook as much as they do now. With more hook, you must project the ball out for it to hook back toward the pocket, especially when the lane itself is dry, or hooking. This is why you need to learn to walk straight and project the ball away from the pocket. This is addressed in more detail in chapters 5, 8, and 9 on arm swing and lane play.

Figure 4.9 Shoulders open toward the gutter (right-handed bowler), and bowler walks straight.

SUMMARY

Good footwork makes it easier to repeat shots with power. You want to remain balanced and walk naturally, taking your steps from heel to toe, with the exception of sliding the last step for a smooth delivery.

To walk straight, you have to line up properly in relation to your target. If you stand too far from your target, you will have to drift toward it. As lane conditions change, making the proper adjustments with your feet and your target while adjusting your shoulders is the key to being able to continue walking straight. When you drift, your lineup is often the culprit.

When your tempo feels either too fast or too slow, focus on your swing and your timing. Once you improve your timing in the start and relax your swing, your footwork will feel more natural again. By focusing on your swing, you will fix the real problem, leading to better rhythm in your footwork that was otherwise unachievable by working on the footwork itself. The arm swing and its effect on the entire approach is the focus of chapter 5.

Arm Swing

In my many years of coaching, I have been guided by the concept that Swing is King! It has had a major impact on helping bowlers see immediate improvement in performance. Developing a good arm swing is the key to consistency and accuracy.

In this sport in which you have to repeat shots, relaxing your arm enables you to create a reliable and consistent swing. Letting the ball swing more like a pendulum allows physics to take over, which is more reliable than depending on all the muscles of your arm to work the same way, every time, from shot to shot. There is just one way to relax and let it swing.

Timing and arm swing are interrelated. In fact, developing a healthy swing and coordinating it with your footwork *is* timing. In chapter 3, which addressed approach and timing, you learned that for a right-handed bowler the right arm and right leg move together on the key step. You will soon learn that using your opposite, or nondominant, hand (the left hand, for a right-handed bowler) to create the swing is the key to moving the ball at the right time while relaxing your swing arm. We will revisit the two-step timing drill in chapter 3 with this in mind, to further develop good swing mechanics.

Finally, you need to remember that you cannot physically outperform a bad ball reaction. To be able to trust your relaxed, natural swing, you have to have a good ball reaction with respect to lane conditions. Your relaxed swing has to be rewarded with good results for you to stay loose and trust the ball!

RELAXING AND LETTING IT SWING NATURALLY

A loose swing begins with a good stance and start. Make sure your grip pressure is light and the muscles in your swing arm are relaxed in the stance. It is difficult to have a loose swing when the muscles in your arm start out tight. To help your arm relax, use your opposite hand to support the weight of the ball. With your nondominant hand supporting the ball's weight, the muscles of the dominant hand and swing arm can stay relaxed because they don't have to engage, or tense up, to support the weight of the ball.

Push-Away

Use your opposite hand and arm to start the swing. Not only should you use your nondominant hand to bear the weight of the ball in the stance, but you should also use it to push the ball out on the key step to start the swing. Use your entire nondominant arm to push the ball out to a position from which it will then swing from the shoulder (figure 5.1).

At the end of the push-away, the ball is extended out with both arms with the weight still predominantly supported by the nondominant hand. This movement of the arm initiates the swing, and the ball needs to be pushed out only as far as the nondominant arm can naturally push it out.

At this point, the nondominant arm is extended, but the dominant arm is still relaxed and still has a slight bend in the elbow. By maintaining a bend in the swing arm, you allow the push-away to move in a continuous arc into the swing as part of the swing itself. *Note:* Do not fully extend or lock the swing arm in the push-away. The elbow of the swing arm should stay bent, while the nondominant arm supports and pushes the ball away.

Once you put your hand in the ball and place it in the desired position in the stance, you can use your swing hand for leverage to hold it, but the muscles of your nondominant hand and arm should support the weight and push the ball into the swing. I often am amazed at how the positioning of the nondominant hand on the ball helps a bowler develop better timing in the start.

Try putting your nondominant hand slightly behind, under, and to the side of the ball with the weight primarily in the fingers and the thumb (figure 5.2). Your palm does not necessarily need to be on the ball. I have found this to be an effective position not only for supporting the ball, but also for pushing it farther so that it doesn't drop too early into the swing.

Figure 5.1 Pushing from the shoulder, elbows forward: *(a)* right-handed; *(b)* left-handed.

Figure 5.2 The position of the nondominant hand on the ball in the stance: (a) right-handed; (b) left-handed.

Many bowlers obsess about how they position their bowling hand in the stance, as if the way it starts is the way it will finish at release. For many reasons, this is rarely the case. I concern myself much more with how functional the nondominant hand is, because of its profound effect on timing and swing, the major factors in a solid approach and overall performance.

Making Changes:
Positioning the Nondominant Hand

The position of the nondominant hand on the ball depends on the bowler. Some bowlers put the palm on the ball. Others distribute the ball's weight over the fingers. Using the fingers and thumb to support the ball rather than placing the entire palm on the ball may make it easier to get enough of a push away from the body to get the ball to swing freely. The hand, especially the fingers and thumb, should be beside and slightly under and behind the ball rather than on top of it. The supporting hand won't be able to bear any of the ball's weight if it is on top of the ball.

Initially do not worry so much about the position of your bowling hand in the stance because it will change during the swing anyway. Too many bowlers worry that how they hold the ball in the start will be the position of the hand at release. This is rarely so. It is more important to get your swing loose at this point. However, if you really like to hold your swing hand in a certain position, just be creative about how your get the fingers of your nondominant hand to infiltrate the ball and truly support the weight of it to allow your swing arm to relax.

Backswing

Once you push the ball with your nondominant arm as you start the next step, your nondominant hand begins to withdraw support so the ball can swing from the shoulder out of your nondominant hand. The ball should naturally drop down to your side with this step, bypassing any need to use the muscles of your swing arm, thereby creating a pendulum effect (figure 5.3).

To develop a continuous, fluid arc in the start, envision that there is a bicycle tire in front of you and that you are letting the ball swing around the perimeter of the tire, rather than letting it fall too soon or pulling it back through the spokes. Many bowlers have a tendency to either drop the ball out of the nondominant hand too quickly or pull the ball back into the swing. Letting the ball fall out of the nondominant hand following the imaginary perimeter of the tire allows the ball to move through a continuous, fluid arc into the swing. Proper positioning of the nondominant hand on the ball and its timely withdrawal will help you achieve this feel and improve your timing on the approach.

Stay loose throughout the swing. The ability to relax under pressure is all a part of being an athlete. You want your swing arm to be passive (relaxed) rather than active (tense). Once you push the ball out with your nondominant arm, let it swing from your shoulder, rather than engage the muscles of your swing arm. Visualize this: the nondominant hand is there to create the swing, and the swing arm is just along for the ride. The athleticism is in being relaxed. Some have a natural ability to relax, but others have to develop it. The development of a state of relaxation starts with awareness.

Figure 5.3 The ball drops down naturally to the side in a pendulum motion: *(a)* right-handed; *(b)* left-handed.

Follow-Through

With all of the momentum from the approach, your arm should naturally follow through at the finish if your swing is loose. Follow through from the shoulder to let the ball finish on the intended path. Your follow-through, or lack of it, says a lot about how relaxed and natural your arm swing really is!

When you follow through, your upper arm should come up (figure 5.4), rather than just your forearm. This is how you finish the swing, from the shoulder. I hear some give the advice to "answer the phone" at the finish. The problem with this is that you end up following through from the elbow, rather than from the shoulder. The ball swings from the shoulder, not the elbow!

Once you follow through, typically your arm will drop right back down if your arm swing is relaxed. You do not have to hold up your arm after the follow-through. Stay relaxed and let momentum allow your arm to naturally fall back down.

LEARNING TO RELAX

The ability to repeat shots is not about tightening up perfectly to control the entire shot. Rather, it is about being relaxed enough to come close to making the same shot each time. You are like a basketball free-throw shooter in a preshot routine who is trying to get relaxed so he can repeat what he has practiced so many times.

Figure 5.4 Follow-through. The upper arm comes up: *(a)* right-handed; *(b)* left-handed.

Learn to relax your arm. Many lessons I give focus on how to start out more relaxed in the stance and develop a good start. Many bowlers think they are relaxed, but they really are not. Becoming aware of the tension in your arm is a good place to start.

Early in a lesson, I take the bowler's swing arm at the wrist, lift up the forearm, then let it go. (See the drill Are You Relaxing in the Stance? in chapter 2.) This does catch the person off guard. When I let go, the arm should just drop. Rarely does it. While the bowler looks at me strangely, with his arm still stuck in the air, I explain that it could not possibly be relaxed or it would have fallen. (Often this happens even after I've explained that he needs to be relaxed!) Once the bowler is aware of the goal, we try it again and again to try to achieve the relaxed state that allows the arm to fall.

Are you still not sure whether you are relaxed in the stance as you are about to make a shot? Try this before you take your first step: squeeze your hand and intentionally tighten the muscles of your swing arm and shoulder; then relax them to feel the difference. Take that relaxed feeling into the swing. This has helped many bowlers to feel the difference between being tight and being relaxed before making a shot.

Develop full use of your nondominant hand and arm. In the stance, most bowlers have the weight of the ball in the swing arm, because they are used to trying to swing the ball rather than just letting it swing. You should use your nondominant hand to fully create the push-away of the ball so that your upper arm is relaxed and swings like a lever from your shoulder. To achieve this, you need to support the ball with your nondominant hand until the end of the push-away. When the ball is farthest from your body, your leverage is at its weakest point and so the ball feels the heaviest to you. At this point, it is critical that you keep the weight in your nondominant hand to avoid tensing up the muscles of your swing arm.

It is common to shift the weight of the ball into the swing arm at this point, rather than keep it in the nondominant hand. Often, this is when the swing arm first tries to take control. When the swing arm tightens up, it either pulls the swing back (early timing) or resists swinging down into the next step (late timing).

Tense and Relax

If you are not sure whether your arm is tense in the stance, you can teach yourself what it feels like when you are tight and when you are loose by squeezing and relaxing your muscles in the stance. First, squeeze your hand and tighten up the muscles of your arm and shoulder. Then release the tension. Notice the difference and take particular note of the feeling when the muscles are relaxed. This is the feeling you want in your stance and throughout the swing.

Furthermore, it is good practice to pay attention to your grip pressure during the swing from time to time to see whether any tension originates from excessive grip pressure throughout the swing. Relaxing is both a talent and a skill to be developed to create a better swing. Identifying tension at its source will help.

Making Changes: Relying on the Nondominant Hand

Learning to rely on your nondominant hand can take time. For most bowlers, the arm that swings the ball tends to get all the attention. But to develop a natural and consistent arm swing, you need to learn to give up control for the sake of accuracy. Trying to take control to create the perfect shot every time is what bowlers continually attempt to do, only to be frustrated with their lack of progress.

When you first start to work on your swing, do not worry about hitting or even looking at your target. Developing a good swing is a process, and giving up control is not easy. Once you understand that you are trying to create a pendulum, you will understand the need to become passive with your swing arm. It takes time to become consistent with this.

You need to truly use your nondominant hand to create the swing and relax the muscles of your swing arm to allow the ball to swing naturally. For some, this is difficult. Learning how to relax is the key.

DEVELOPING A STRAIGHT ARM SWING

In addition to having a loose swing, you also want a straight swing that stays in line with your shoulder (figures 5.5 and 5.6). Your arm should always swing at a 90-degree angle to your shoulders. Your swing does not actually decide where the ball goes, because its job is always the same: to swing perpendicular to the shoulders. Rather, it is up to your shoulders to line up your arm with the target so it can swing naturally in the proper plane to hit your target on every shot.

Figure 5.5 Right-handed bowler's straight swing: *(a)* front view; *(b)* back view.

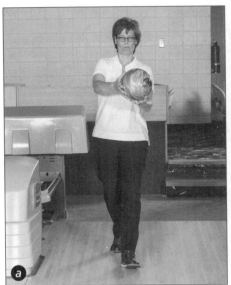

Figure 5.6 Left-handed bowler's straight swing: *(a)* front view; *(b)* back view.

In the push-away, push the ball straight in line with your shoulder. Remember that your shoulders face the target to line up the swing to hit it. Therefore, your push-away should remain at 90 degrees relative to your shoulders, no matter which way you are facing (figures 5.7 and 5.8).

You may face different angles on the approach, whether it is to line up for a strike ball at various angles or to shoot a spare on either side of the lane. Your

Figure 5.7 Straight (90-degree) swing with the shoulders facing the target, right-handed bowler: *(a)* closed (toward spare); *(b)* square; *(c)* open (inside strike shot and spares).

Figure 5.8 Straight (90-degree) swing with the shoulders facing the target, left-handed bowler: *(a)* closed (toward spare); *(b)* square; *(c)* open (inside strike shot and spares).

shoulders may be square to the foul line, open, or closed, but the swing always remains perpendicular (at a right angle) to the shoulders.

Pushing the ball in a direction other than straight forward at 90 degrees in the push-away can cause the arm to swing out of alignment with the shoulder. This leads to a backswing that either comes back behind the body or moves away from the body, which leads to problems in the direction of the downswing, causing inaccuracy.

For example, pushing the ball away from the body can cause the ball to swing in behind the back (figure 5.9). This can cause the downswing to swing out toward the gutter or outside the target at delivery.

Pushing the ball toward the middle of the body can cause it to swing away from the body in the backswing. This can cause the downswing to come across the body, causing you to miss your target to the left.

This cause and effect between the direction of the push-away and the direction of the downswing is assuming that the bowler has made no muscular correction to the swing to get it back into alignment. Bowlers often subconsciously compensate in an attempt to realign the downswing after an errant push-away.

To fix a swing that is out of alignment, you will have to overexaggerate pushing the ball in the opposite direction to get the swing back to straight. If, for example, you have been pushing the ball to the right, you may need to think "push it to the left" to combat the muscle memory you have developed to push it right in order to push it straight again. Simply thinking "push it straight" most likely will lead you to continue pushing it to the right, because of the overpowering strength of muscle memory that made you feel as though pushing it to the right *was* pushing it straight.

Figure 5.9   *(a)* Pushing the ball out away from the body *(b)* causes the backswing to go behind the back.

Note: when you work on getting the ball to swing back straighter, your downswing may still make the old adjustments it did to realign the swing when it was crooked. Be patient. Continue to create a straighter backswing and repeat it many times until your downswing learns what to expect so it can acclimate to the new swing position and just learn to swing back down naturally again.

SYNCING THE ARM SWING AND THE FOOTWORK

As your swing becomes more effortless, you will be able to bowl longer because you are no longer expending energy tightening up and trying to force the ball. For a time you may teeter between trying to control it and letting it happen. Although it is human nature to want to control the swing, you will find that letting it happen creates more consistent results. You will learn that the less force you apply, the more natural and repeatable your swing will become. They key is to get your natural swing in sync with your footwork.

Good timing involves coordinating the arm and leg on your dominant side to move at the same time. However, moving the limbs on the same side together on the key step can be difficult because it is not the way you naturally walk. When you walk, your opposite arm and leg move together for natural balance. Personally, I think this is why almost everyone tends to have timing issues in the start. For this reason, it makes sense to apply a natural walking movement to bowling.

When you use your nondominant hand to push the ball away, you are coordinating the hand and foot on opposite sides to get the swing started for better timing and a better swing. Your nondominant hand will get your swing arm into position with the foot on the dominant side. This resembles how you feel when you walk and makes timing adjustments feel a little easier to manage. You will see this as you revisit the two-step timing drill you first attempted in chapter 3, this time using your opposite hand to create the swing.

Let's revisit the two-step drill from chapter 3 and incorporate swing mechanics. In chapter 3, you worked on pushing the swing out with the key step ("out on one"), using the same side of your body. Because it is unnatural to move the arm and leg on the same side of the body together, this two-step drill should be easier to do by coordinating your nondominant hand with your dominant foot, just as you do when you walk. It makes sense to apply this natural movement to bowling.

In chapter 4, you worked on taking your steps heel-to-toe. Be sure you do this when performing this drill again, especially on the second step. Rather than shuffle, take two heel-toe steps.

Now when you do this drill, the timing, footwork, and arm swing are all involved, which makes the drill even more effective. Use your nondominant hand to push the ball out, relax your swing arm to let the ball just drop on the next step, and pick up that step to take it from heel to toe. Do all of this while maintaining your posture. This is an exceptional drill that covers half of the approach, making it very worthwhile to do as often as you are willing to do it!

Two-Step Timing With Swing Mechanics

Starting with your right foot (the left foot if you are left-handed), take only two steps to combine the "out on one" motion with the "down on two" motion. Focus on synchronizing the timing of your nondominant hand with your dominant foot on the first step. Use the nondominant hand to push the ball out. Relax the swing arm and let the ball swing naturally. Maintain good posture. Take heel-to-toe steps. When you stop on the second step, the ball should be down by your side and your posture should be upright.

This drill is challenging for many bowlers. Once out on one, if you then have trouble completing this drill with the ball down by your side, focus on when you withdraw the support of the nondominant hand. Wait until the second step leaves the floor to withdraw your hand to perfect the timing of the drop. This requires pinpoint concentration because the rhythm will feel quite different.

AVOIDING TIGHT SPOTS

Many bowlers tighten up during the swing, especially at certain key points such as when the swing changes direction. The ball changes direction twice during the swing: first in front of you and then behind you (figure 5.10). The first change occurs at the end of the push-away, and the second, at the height

Figure 5.10 The ball changes direction twice in the swing: *(a)* at the end of the push-away and *(b)* at the height of the backswing.

of the backswing. Tightening up is typically the result of trying to control the shot, help the ball swing, or hit the target.

These "tight spots" (where bowlers tend to tense up) also happen to be the heavy spots, when the ball is heaviest because it is farthest from the bowler. Having the proper fit and ball weight is essential to be able to relax and let the ball swing through these spots without having to labor to do so.

Much like the Are You Relaxed in Your Stance? drill in chapter 2, in which you tested how loose your arm is in the stance, I often take a student's arm and swing it to the top of the backswing and then let go. Often, the arm just stays there in the air behind the student. If it were relaxed, it would just drop. The arm should be relaxed throughout the swing.

Have someone lift your arm to your backswing without the ball and see if you can let it drop when your partner lets go. That will help you realize the feeling of being relaxed at that point in the swing. You can also do this with the ball in your hand. Have your partner hold the ball up for you while you relax your arm in the backswing.

It takes strength to let a heavy object swing through a full arc! Excessive ball weight or a poor ball fit will make it difficult for you to relax and let it swing

Making Changes: Adjusting Timing

Understanding what to expect with your timing is important. Adjusting your timing will affect the way you feel at the finish. Although you will have created a good motion into the backswing, on the downswing you may try to pull the ball to finish so the finish feels the way it used to feel. Understanding the adjustment to your timing at the beginning of the approach and how it will improve your leverage at the finish is critical to being patient with your swing at delivery. This is called swing patience.

If you believe that everything (your body and the ball) should be at the delivery together, you will rush your swing to achieve that feel. Understanding that you should be there slightly ahead of the ball will help you develop patience in your swing. How you believe it should be is how you will end up doing it. Your mind may have to be reprogrammed to create the proper physical movement and timing at the line.

When you do not understand how your timing will change, and why, you subconsciously may want to help the swing re-create the same old timing that you had. If you were early, you will likely continue to pull your swing down to re-create the early timing that you have had. Unlocking your thoughts to create a different picture is necessary to change your swing.

Once you understand that your body just has to get used to the new feeling, your downswing should begin to relax again. Just continue to let the ball drop into the backswing; your downswing will eventually acclimate, and you will begin to see great results on the lane!

through these points. Besides making you tighten up and squeeze, a poor ball fit makes the ball feel heavier than it actually is. It is often the culprit when you cannot seem to relax, no matter how hard you try.

BACKSWING AND SWING PATIENCE

A common question is, How high should my backswing be? The answer: Whatever height your natural, loose arm swings to! However, once you loosen up your arm and let the ball swing, your timing will likely change. When the height feels different, you may be tempted to muscle the swing back down to release so that your timing in the finish feels as it always has.

You do not have to swing the ball back. It may feel like the ball merely drops to your side, but the backswing will end up about shoulder high due to the natural momentum of your approach and the weight of the ball. To prove this to yourself, have a friend take a picture of your backswing. Be sure to relax and let the ball drop out of the push-away. Once you relax your arm and let the ball swing on its own, it will naturally achieve the proper height in the backswing. *Note:* your swing will be 3-4 feet higher than it feels. If it feels shoulder-high, it is way up there, affecting your timing in the finish.

If your backswing has been cut short as a result of tension, when you do relax and have a full swing, your timing will feel different at the line. You will feel as though you are more ahead of the ball. This is good. When your body is there ahead of the ball, what you can now do with all this time is relax your swing and use your legs for balance and power at the finish (more on this in chapter 6). But when you do not realize that feeling ahead of the ball is a good thing, you may want to pull the new, higher backswing right back down to get the timing to feel as it used to at the finish. This is a subconscious reaction to create the feel of your old timing and muscled swing.

Developing patience in the downswing is a must. When you can relax your full swing and wait for the ball to swing back down naturally to the finish, you can develop a stronger delivery by using your legs for power and leverage. It takes time to get the legs in position at delivery, which is why you need to be patient with your swing.

Although it will feel different at first, once your swing is in better time with your feet and you no longer have to muscle the shot, you will begin to feel much better because of the reduced strain on your body. Your motion to the line will flow with ease and feel effortless. This is because you are more efficiently using your body to bowl, rather than trying to overuse your arm muscles.

Because a lot of the tension in the swing starts with excessive grip pressure, you need to learn to relax your hand a bit, especially at the top of the swing. Pay attention to your grip pressure at this point. When I notice that a student is squeezing the ball, I tell her to pay attention to her grip pressure at that point in the swing. Right after the shot, I ask her to replicate that grip pressure onto my arm so I can monitor her progress. Then we repeat the process. Just about every time, the grip pressure lightens and the ball doesn't fly off! By paying attention to your grip pressure during the swing, you can learn to achieve the proper pressure to create your best arm swing.

Learning to relax your hand at the top of the swing may depend on whether you can trust that the ball is going to stay on your hand. If the ball fits properly and you are using enough tape, it should!

Consider the power of centrifugal force at work. As you develop momentum in the swing as you approach the line, this force is working to keep the ball on your

Don't Lose the Nickel

This drill will help you relax your grip pressure but keep the ball on your hand. Standing still, practice your swing with a nickel on your open hand. Begin your swing with momentum by first pushing it away to create a full pendulum swing, letting the hand come back and through as it would with the momentum of the approach. With enough natural swing force, the nickel will stay on your hand, even when your open hand is on top of the nickel at the top of the backswing. I have done this drill many times with bowlers to their amazement. It helps them learn to trust that the ball will stay on the hand, without the need for excessive grip pressure.

hand. Just as you can swing a pail of water enough to keep the water in it when it is upside down, so it is with the bowling swing. Your swing needs to be resistance free to keep moving so it can develop enough force to keep the ball on your hand naturally at the top of the swing. Relax your muscles so there is no resistance!

LOSING CONTROL

Trying too hard to make the ball go to the target is a common problem. Let's face it, it's human nature to want to control, but the key to consistent bowling is to develop your technique and trust it. Trying to steer the ball is the worst thing you can do! Ironically, you have to lose control to get control.

Many bowlers fall into the trap of trying to steer the ball rather than trusting it to naturally swing toward the target. They teeter on the fence between control and trust. Developing trust is often a challenge. I coach many bowlers who are at a point of frustration with how they've been bowling. Many express that their new, looser swing feels out of control and that they want to go back to muscling and trying to control it. So, I ask them, "How was that working out for you before?" A brief thought, followed by the realization that they are on the lanes with me quickly puts the point to rest.

At the finish, if your swing is loose, you will naturally follow through from the shoulder at delivery. Bowlers who try to control or steer the ball often cut the follow-through short or do not follow through in line with the shoulder. Trusting your swing to get the ball to the target is the key. If you are truly relaxed, after the follow-through your arm will naturally fall back down.

ADJUSTING YOUR SHOULDERS TO LINE UP YOUR SWING WITH THE TARGET

Turn your shoulders to line up your swing. You need to face the target so that your swing automatically lines up with it. To do this, turn your shoulders so that your swing can remain at a 90-degree angle to your shoulders and you can hit the target.

Keep in mind that when your shoulders are square (parallel) to the foul line, or when they are open, you are facing the target but walking *straight*. Your shoulders will be square when you play outside or straight down the lane to your target. Your shoulders will be open on your strike shots when you play inside on the lane at an angle to project the ball out and on your spare shots to the right side, if you are right-handed, or to the left side, if you are left-handed. The amount you open your shoulders depends on the angle you are playing on the lane. The exception to walking straight is when your shoulders are closed to face a spare on the other side, which is addressed in chapter 11, Advanced Spare Shooting.

Just remember that the angle of the swing to your shoulders *never* changes. It is up to your shoulders to align the swing to your target line. Adjusting your shoulder angle is the key to a consistent swing alignment from shot to shot, leading to better footwork, spare shooting, and lane adjustments.

Keep in mind that this principle of maintaining the same swing is very important when you change angles to shoot spares. Again, your arm swing remains perpendicular to the shoulders for all shots, so this will help you make more spares. Proper spare angles are addressed in chapters 10 and 11.

MAINTAINING PROPER GRIP PRESSURE WITH BOWLER'S TAPE

A proper ball fit is essential to a healthy arm swing. Letting the ball swing freely throughout the entire arc requires a gentle grip pressure and relaxed arm. Often, tension in the arm begins with excessive grip pressure.

Once the holes are drilled into the ball, you need to be able to adjust the size of the thumbhole because your thumb will fluctuate in size as you bowl. All thumbs fluctuate, for a variety of reasons (e.g., as a result of the food you've eaten, temperature, humidity, or how much you are bowling). Bowlers who do not think their thumbs fluctuate simply use too much grip pressure to be able to tell!

Many years ago I authored a monthly instructional column in a national bowling magazine and had the opportunity to choose my topics. The importance of using bowler's tape was one of my very first choices! I know how important it is to be able to maintain the proper grip pressure, and I see how it helps bowlers' swings every day. I thought it would be one of the best tips I could give for bowlers to see immediate improvement. In fact, I recently wrote another tip for a magazine article, and again it was on using bowler's tape!

When you begin using tape, you have to become more sensitive to your grip pressure to know when you need to put tape in or take it out (figure 5.11). Ideally, you should be able to tell whether you need to adjust the tape the second you put your thumb in the ball, rather than having to wait to see how it comes off your hand at release. Strive to achieve that feel.

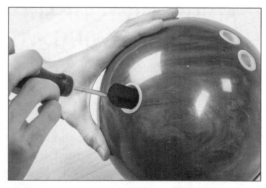

Figure 5.11   Use bowler's tape to maintain proper grip pressure.

The thumbhole should be snug, which means different things at different skill levels. Professionals have very snug thumbholes (some have to practically force their thumbs into them), but those are the players who do not grab the ball at all at release. They can't, or they would hang up in it! This is definitely a learned feel. After all, it is a fact that if you can get the thumb in, it can come out; it is just a matter of keeping a light grip pressure. Strive to be able to handle a tighter thumbhole. If you are just learning to use tape, the fact that you can even tell you need another piece is a sign that you have matured as a bowler!

Having a piece of tape in the hole does not mean that you never add to it or remove it. You should be constantly putting tape in and taking it out, as your thumb changes. This fluctuation may be random, or you may notice a trend in what your thumb tends to do as you bowl. It may shrink or it may swell the more you bowl. In any case, use tape as needed!

Once you learn to use tape properly (see chapter 1) to regularly adjust the ball to your hand, you will be able to maintain a constant grip pressure from shot to shot, as your hand naturally fluctuates in size. This will enable you to develop a constant grip pressure, leading to a consistent and accurate arm swing. The alternative is to grip the ball more or less from shot to shot, which will hinder your swing.

Finally, become proficient at using tape efficiently so that you are comfortable using it in competition. The fear of holding up league play or feeling clumsy when you use tape are not justifiable reasons to avoid using it and missing out on all of its benefits to your swing. Get comfortable adjusting the tape so you can maintain a constant grip pressure from shot to shot.

ARM SWING AND BALL REACTION

You cannot outperform a bad ball reaction! Once your swing is relaxed, if you still do not hit the pocket, you need to either adjust your angle when you throw it straight or, when you throw a hook, line up properly for lane conditions. When you throw a hook, if you do not line up properly for the lane condition, your ball will not react properly. You will begin forcing the ball to try to make it work. (Most often, this happens subconsciously!)

Bowlers typically fail to adjust to lane conditions because they do not realize they need to, they don't know how to, or they like to play in their comfort zones. The message: if you cannot relax, question your strategy! Often poor strategy causes the bowler to tighten up the swing and force the shot. Most bowlers believe that the problem is with their form rather than the ball's reaction on the lane.

I personally learned this lesson while bowling in the 1995 Sam's Town Invitational. I was on the Ebonite Pro Staff at the time, and our ball rep, Doene Moos, was watching me and realized I had to make an equipment change. I was in match play and was convinced that my poor execution was my fault. Doene gently tried to persuade me to change balls. I was irritated and resisted because I knew I wasn't executing well; *I just had to loosen up my swing.* I believed that if I could just loosen up, I would bowl better. Finally, and reluctantly, I tried the ball he suggested in the next match.

On the first ball, I struck. The next shot, I struck. Then I struck again. With each shot, my swing was getting looser. I started to feel better in my execution. In fact, I proceeded to throw the next nine strikes to shoot 300 that game! I went on to use that ball to win this Major tournament title! It would not have happened if not for Doene getting me out of my own way.

If you do not line up properly for the lane condition, you will have a tough time scoring, even when you are throwing the ball well. Many bowlers I coach develop a good swing, starting to roll it consistently in the lesson, but then when they do not see the ball hook, they think they have to put more on the ball. Rather than allowing them to revert back to forcing the shot, I advise them to continue to roll it well and move on the lane—in this case, to find more friction for the ball to naturally hook. When they do, the light then goes on in their heads that the problem was one of strategy, not performance.

Adjusting to the lane is addressed in chapters 8 and 9. Notice that this chapter refers often to these chapters on lane play (basic and advanced). Suffice it to say that when you line up on the lane properly, the good ball reaction and room for error you create reinforces your loose arm swing because what you are doing is working! You *will* be able to relax if your lane play strategy is effective. Bowling is not about being perfect; it's about creating room for error. *You cannot physically outperform a poor reaction on the lane.*

ARM SWING AND BALL SPEED

Consider that your natural swing *is* your natural ball speed. Too often, I see bowlers try to manipulate ball speed to the demise of their own swings. Speed control is a very tricky thing. Even some professional bowlers do not have speed control! So, if you are working at all on your swing or timing, I suggest that you attempt to change your ball speed as a last resort.

When you believe you have to change your speed, try to figure out why. If your ball is sliding too much, instead of slowing it down, consider moving into more friction, or try using a more aggressive ball. Maybe even improve your roll. Often, the illusion of excessive speed is really a matter of not using a strong enough ball or having weak ball roll.

Professional bowlers have good speed and a strong ball roll. If your roll happens to be weak and you try to bring your speed down, you have just given yourself low speed and a weak roll, just the opposite of professionals. And, in most instances, the swing has tightened up to do so. Why lessen, when you can strengthen? (Release is discussed in more detail in chapter 7.)

If you think you need to throw harder, try moving into the oil, throwing a weaker ball, or changing your release (more advanced). Often, this will fix your reaction. Besides, when you try to force your speed, you usually end up muscling the ball, engaging the pec muscles of the chest. By design, the motion of the pecs leads to pulling. If you engage these muscles in the swing, you will pull the ball, missing your target to the inside.

This is not to say that there are not techniques to alter ball reaction. Matching your overall rhythm in the approach and raising or lowering the ball in the stance to create more or less swing arc are plausible techniques. These can be effective as long as you know how to do this without changing your timing or tightening up your swing.

You may find that it is easier to adjust to the lane and use a different ball or add surface to the ball you intend to use to create more friction on the lane, or polish a ball to create less friction. Using the proper equipment is very important for conquering lane conditions. Much as a golfer has different clubs to hit different distances, bowlers need bowling balls that hook at different lengths and to varying degrees. Let necessity dictate. If you continue to have to force your reaction or feel as though you need to change your game for the conditions you bowl on, consider adding a ball to your arsenal that will fit the need.

SUMMARY

A good arm swing is the key to consistency, accuracy, and good rhythm. A good swing will make you, and a bad swing will break you! Many students feel as though they are far off track, doing so many things wrong. Often, many of these symptoms seem to magically disappear with a better swing! Rather than chase the symptoms that stem from a poor swing, develop a good swing. Use your nondominant hand to support the weight of the ball in the stance and to push the ball away on the key step to get the ball out to a place from which it can swing freely and consistently.

Using good swing mechanics to create a pendulum swing is to the key to repeating your shots. However, this takes trust! Learning to just let the ball swing can be challenging. Because it is human nature to want to control the outcome, we often find it easier to use force than technique. Developing good, reliable technique requires strength, training, and discipline. You need a strong mental game to trust. Therein lies your challenge.

You can rely on physics, but you cannot rely on all of the many muscles of your arm working the same way over and over. You cannot expect your swing to be the same from shot to shot if you engage different muscles in your arm to varying degrees when you bowl. Think about it. You could tighten up different muscles, to different degrees, at different points throughout the swing, creating infinitely random results! However, there is only one relaxed swing. A pendulum is reliable and consistent.

Bowling is a game of power and repetition. To achieve both, relax your swing so you can use physics to repeat your shots. Allow the weight of the ball and the momentum from your approach to create your swing as you learn to walk by your own pendulum. When it begins to feel effortless, you are on the right track. Ironically, you have to lose control to get control.

Sometimes, what you *don't do* makes you better. For many bowlers, improvement is a matter of trying better, or *easier*, rather than trying harder! It's human nature to want to control the ball, but the very tension that creates will make your efforts erratic. Tension often starts in the grip. Pay attention to your grip pressure, and learn to relax your swing from start to finish.

Keep in mind that many professionals work on their starts practically every day to get their timing down. With good timing and swing mechanics that enable you to repeat shots, you are now ready to learn to develop power by using your legs in the finish to deliver the ball without compromising consistency and accuracy.

Now, relax and let it swing!

Chapter 6

Finish Position and Delivery

The goal of the approach is to get to the finish consistently and create power. With good timing and a loose swing, you can create leverage and generate power at the finish. Bowling is all about being consistently powerful. Achieving this balance is the key.

To establish a strong, leveraged body position at the finish, you need to use your legs to generate power and maintain balance at the line. Using your legs for power while maintaining a loose swing for consistency (and accuracy) is how you strike this balance.

Having good balance at the line helps you use your body efficiently for a consistent execution. Balance does take strength. The more overall strength you have, the easier it will be to develop a strong, leveraged finish position at the line. To achieve such a position, you will need to consider both your side and back views when you deliver the ball.

Finally, with all the momentum from the approach and a loose swing, your arm should follow through as you deliver the ball. This motion is natural to a loose arm swing and will improve your ball roll. To help you conceptualize getting everything into position at delivery, I refer to times on an imaginary, upright clock around your body (your head at 12:00). This visual is used from the back view position.

FINISH POSITION AND LEVERAGE

The two views of the body in the finish are the side view and the back view. (See figure 6.6 on page 90 for a back view of the finish with the trail leg behind and hips low for power and balance.) To develop a solid finish position, you must understand it from both perspectives. A good finish position enables you to exercise good leverage at release while developing power throughout the delivery.

For proper leverage, maintain good posture in your finish position. From the side view, this means that you should be able to form a vertical line from your head to your knee (figure 6.1). As in a proper squat when picking up a heavy box using the legs rather than the back, your shoulders should not come forward in your finish position. Keep your chest up and your weight on the quad muscles of the thigh. This will give you proper leverage at release.

Finally, with all the momentum you developed throughout the approach, your swing should naturally follow through at delivery. Specifically, the upper arm, not just the forearm, should come up to follow through at the finish. Some bowlers believe that if their hand comes up, they are following through. However, because the swing originates from the shoulder, the upper arm, which is attached to the shoulder, should follow through. The follow-through (or lack of it) says a lot about the looseness of the swing. A loose swing continues through at the finish from all the momentum of the approach. The arm will naturally fall back down if it is relaxed.

FINISH POSITION AND POWER

A good delivery that uses the legs for power is initiated with the trail leg (the right leg for a right-handed bowler, the left leg for a left-handed bowler). The trail leg functions in three key ways: to create power, to clear a slot for the swing, and to maintain balance. Being balanced is a sign that you are using your body efficiently to deliver the ball.

Figure 6.1   Good posture at the finish position: *(a)* right-handed; *(b)* left-handed.

Creating Power

As your leg moves over to get behind you, it creates torque that transfers through your hips and core to your shoulder and swing. This natural process of transferring the power from the lower body to the upper body can be seen in many sport motions. Take a batter in baseball, for example. The power in the swing comes from the initial step the batter takes as the pitch approaches, allowing him to transfer his weight and create torque throughout his body to impart power to the shoulders. The equivalent motion in bowling is the movement of the back leg behind at delivery.

Clearing a Slot for the Swing

In addition to creating power, the back leg moves over and clears a slot for the swing to stay in line with the shoulder and swing straight (figure 6.2). This also allows the ball to stay close to the ankle for accuracy.

It is important to note here that from the back view, the shoulder will drop down, contrary to what many expect. This is how the leg is able to get over for power while the ball is released from a position close to the ankle (figure 6.3). Many years ago bowlers were told not to drop the shoulder. That was when the balls were significantly weaker than they are now. That outdated advice should be replaced with the current advice to let the shoulder drop! Doing so allows the back leg to finish further over, creating a more powerful execution from the legs.

Developing your finish position may be more easily accomplished by creating a visual to model. A single image can take the place of multiple thoughts,

Figure 6.2   The trail leg clears a slot for the swing, shoulder dropped: *(a)* right-handed; *(b)* left-handed.

making it easier to get into the proper position. The back view of the finish position, using the clock for reference (refer to figure 6.6 on page 90), can be especially helpful. The photos in figure 6.6 are single images of all the text that explains a strong finish position!

Figure 6.3 The release point: the ball close to the ankle and the shoulder dropped (right-handed bowler).

Maintaining Balance

Finally, the back leg serves as a counterbalance to all the momentum on the swing side of your body from the ball coming through at release. In addition, this leg is positioned to provide a solid base of support beneath your upper body for good balance.

If you have been off balance because of poor timing or a muscled swing that pulls you off balance, it is time to start balancing at the line again. With better timing and a relaxed swing, it is just a matter of expecting to balance again. It takes strength to use your legs and balance, whether it is for the first time or to get back into balance as you improve your timing and swing.

Making Changes: Old School Versus Current Game

Advancements in technology have changed the way the game is played. Bowling balls have gotten a lot stronger over the years, and so our form has had to evolve. Technology has created the need for changes in technique.

It used to be that proper technique was to keep the trail leg straight behind at delivery. Just look at a hall of famer from many years ago. Back then, because the bowling balls were not very strong, strong leverage to project them was not necessary. Those players rolled the ball directly to the pocket because they barely hooked. If you have been bowling for a very long time, you have probably noticed that your form has had to evolve to keep up with the changes in equipment.

Furthermore, in today's game, the shoulder *is* dropped so that you can get that back leg over and create the leverage to project the ball. The need to keep the shoulder up is a myth I have to dispel often as the game has changed from years ago. You do want your shoulder to drop!

To develop your balance and finish position, start by using a wall for support. Get into a good balanced finish position beside a wall. Once you get the feel for the proper position, strive to hold it without the support of the wall. Go back onto the lane, up to the foul line, and get into the same solid, balanced finish position. Just hold the position at the line as you did by the wall to get accustomed to this feeling of balance.

When you can balance in a finish position at the foul line, walk through the approach without the ball, learning to balance while in motion. Work at this, with a focus on your posture and legs, until you master it.

Now, pick up your ball and assume this balanced finish position while bowling. Try holding your balance at the line until the ball hits the pins. Your body is learning the control required to be solid and balanced at the line. This will also have a training effect, making your legs stronger as you hold the position longer. Balance takes strength!

Getting into a good finish position requires strength and a touch of flexibility. For some, it comes naturally. For others, it requires more exertion than they are used to. Frankly, for many it is a lot like exercise; it is just easier *not* to do it! The position of your front leg at the finish is a lot like the position of a leg in a squat position. The knee is bent, but not past the toe. The core is upright, balancing over the legs.

The Wall: Finish Position

Part 1

Without the ball, find a wall and stand beside it, far enough away so that your nonswing, or balance, arm can extend out to put your hand again the wall for support. Put your back (trail) leg into position, around 8:00 (if right-handed) or 4:00 (if left-handed) and feel the weight of your body on the thigh of your slide leg. Remember to maintain your posture or you will not feel the weight on your thigh. Hold this position with your arm up as it would be in the follow-through at 1:00 (right-handed) or 11:00 (left-handed). Feel the balance from your legs as it will feel in the finish as you deliver the ball and follow through.

If you want to get lower, and are strong enough and flexible enough to do so, stand farther from the wall and stretch your back leg farther, to 8:30 (right-handed) or 3:30 (left-handed). This will create even more knee bend on your front leg. A good trick to get low is to tuck the laces of your trail foot toward the floor (again, if you are flexible and strong enough to do so). This will give you an even deeper knee bend. Once you get the feel for this full-body position, move away from the wall and onto the lane at the foul line. Now get into the same position you were in beside the wall, only without the support. Hold the position until you are in control of your balance. *Note:* Position your leg over as far as you can and maintain good balance. Based on strength and flexibility, your trail leg can range from 7:00 to 8:30 (right-handed) or 3:30 to 5:00 (left-handed).

Part 2

On the lane at the foul line, still without the ball, learn to enter this position while adding some motion. Stand back far enough to allow enough room to take a step. Start with your trail leg forward (the step before the slide) and your arm behind you in the backswing. From this position, push off with the trail leg and slide into the last step. Finish with the trail leg at 8:00 (right-handed) or 4:00 (left-handed) or so to get into the same position you were in by the wall. Finish with your arm up at 1:00 (right-handed) or 11:00 (left-handed). Repeat until you can do this and hold your balance at least three times in a row.

It is more challenging to get into this position once in motion and without the support of the wall to maintain your balance.

Part 3

Still without the ball, add momentum to the drill by walking through the whole approach a few times to learn to finish in this position and balance after being in motion. *Note:* Go only as fast as you can while maintaining your balance. When you can get into position and balance successfully at least three times in a row without the ball, you are ready to attempt to bowl and finish in this position.

Once you can balance and hold your position when you bowl, learn to keep it by holding your balance until the ball hits the pins. This will develop your strength and endurance so you can balance and get your hips low at the line every time.

Note: although your focus throughout this entire drill is on your legs, keep in mind that when you finally go to bowl, your timing and swing will affect your ability to balance. If your timing is off or your swing is tight, it will be hard to balance, no matter how much you focus on your legs. Once in motion, all that you have worked on to this point is involved!

Following Through

Be sure to follow through with the swing! Your follow-through says a lot about your arm swing and how relaxed or unrelaxed it is. A good follow-through even improves ball roll. If you find that you are cutting your swing short, you are decelerating a swing that should be accelerating at delivery from all the momentum in the approach, if it is relaxed.

To get a feel for following through, stand at the foul line with your slide foot forward and your back leg out of the way behind you. With the ball, stand still and create a full swing and release the ball. Starting with the push-away, let the ball swing back and down. Release and finish with a follow-through, all in one fluid motion. There should be no disruption to the flow of energy in the swing at the release point. Repeat until you can follow through without a hitch and recognize how it feels. Then you are ready to bowl and finish your swing with a good follow-through at 1:00 (right-handed) or 11:00 (left-handed).

TIMING AND FINISH POSITION

Poor timing leads to posture and balance issues at delivery. With early timing, the shoulders tend to drop forward at delivery (figure 6.4). This creates a lack of leverage or a weaker body position at delivery. With late timing, the body tends to come up as a result of excessive leverage at the line (figure 6.5).

There is a mentality to proper timing at delivery. From the following choices, choose the correct statement about proper timing at the finish:

a. The ball should be there before you.

b. You should be there before the ball.

c. You and the ball should be there together.

Many choose C, which was the answer years ago when equipment was weaker and bowlers rolled the ball more directly to the pocket. Although timing does vary among bowlers based on style, this question pertains to the sequential motion of the body to create power and balance at delivery.

The correct answer is B, but keep in mind that we are talking about split seconds. Remember that in baseball, the step for power *precedes* the swing of the bat. A batter wouldn't step and swing at the same time. Also consider a baseball pitcher, who winds up with his legs *before* actually throwing the ball from the shoulder. It wouldn't make sense to wind up and throw at the same time. Again, the pitcher does this to create torque throughout the body, initiating power from the legs, the strongest muscles in the body.

Figure 6.4 Early timing causes the head to be in front of the knee at delivery.

Figure 6.5 Late timing causes the body to rise up as a result of excessive leverage.

I typically ask my students to reflect on what the ideal timing will be at the finish. When we have worked on their timing and swing in the start, but they are having difficulty maintaining that timing through the finish, we have to discuss proper timing so they understand it well enough to execute it. Implementing this different sense of timing can be particularly challenging because it feels different from what they are used to.

Bowlers who have been early but have corrected their timing in the start often pull the ball from the backswing to the release simply because they subconsciously expect the ball to be there sooner, as it was when their timing was early. Often, they have to rewire their thoughts about how the timing at the finish should be so they can understand what they are now trying to feel for proper leverage. It is critical to understand this timing and relax the downswing enough to get into the proper finish position and balance.

ARM SWING AND BALANCE

With a loose swing, you should be able to balance at the line. Too often, bowlers try to force the shot and literally *pull themselves off balance.* This usually happens when the bowler is too impatient to wait for the swing, is trying to throw the ball too hard, or simply forces a ball reaction that is not there naturally. Lane play adjustments are covered in chapters 8 and 9. The trail leg is strong enough to counter all of the momentum from a loose swing and the weight of the ball, but will be challenged to counterbalance all of the extra force of a muscled swing that pulls the shot.

However, this process also works in reverse. *What your legs don't do, your arm will tend to make up for.* If, for example, you are just being lazy and not using your legs, your arm will detect the lack of power coming from the legs and try to make up for it. As a result, your arm ends up forcing the ball to try to create power that wasn't transferred to it naturally. Your legs need your arm to be patient and relaxed, but your arm needs your legs to work so it can relax!

A lack of balance is most commonly caused by either poor timing or a forced arm swing. Again, bowlers too often pull themselves off balance. If you are off balance, check your timing and relax your swing. From there, make sure you work on using your legs to balance!

Often, the culprit behind a muscled swing is a poor ball reaction on the lane. Bowlers subconsciously tighten up when they sense they do not have any room for error on the lane. This is tricky because, typically, bowlers blame themselves for throwing the ball badly, when the reason they are doing so may be poor strategy on the lane. Step back and assess whether you could make an adjustment that would give you more room so you can relax your swing. Sound lane play strategy is addressed in chapters 8 and 9.

BACKSWING AND FINISH POSITION

Swing height and swing patience are critical to establishing a strong finish position. If you do not have a full backswing, you will have a hard time kicking your trail leg into position. Your swing needs to be high enough to allow time for your leg to move into position before the swing arrives at delivery. In some lessons, I see a lazy trail leg. When we work on making the timing later and create a fuller swing arc, often I notice that the leg starts to move over into the proper position, simply because the bowler has more time. Sometimes this happens without my even mentioning the leg! Again, this demonstrates how the sequential motion of the body from the bottom up works.

For some, this happens naturally. Others have to make a concerted effort to position the back leg. With bowlers in whom this happens naturally, I then work on strengthening the position of the trail leg to get the hips as low as possible for even more power and better leverage. The further over the leg goes, the lower the hips at delivery.

BALANCE AND SWING PATIENCE

It requires swing patience to be able to create leverage and use your legs. It is very common to want to steer the ball to the target at the finish or to create power using the swing itself. Using the smaller muscles of your arm is just easier than using the larger muscles of your legs. But, for consistency and power, develop swing patience and wait for the legs to create power at delivery.

Making Changes: Developing Swing Patience

When you have been used to pulling your swing because you have been out of sync or lazy about using your legs for power, you need to develop swing patience going into delivery. Swing patience is learning to wait for the downswing to fall to the release point rather than pulling it there.

Sometimes it is difficult to do nothing when you are so used to doing too much, as in pulling the swing down. Focusing on what to wait for will help. Waiting for your legs to get into position before you deliver the ball will help you learn how to be patient, and *passive*, in the downswing.

When your legs work, your arm does not have to create the power. Giving your swing "legs" it can count on to generate power and balance at delivery is the key. When you use your legs consistently, the swing will relax and be part of the natural sequence of delivering the ball, without trying to be the source of power. As a result, you will become much more consistent, powerful, and accurate.

Your arm will naturally feel the power that is transferred from the legs and then throughout the body to create torque and provide power to the swing. From there, just follow through, using the power generated from the legs and throughout your body. Your swing will feel more effortless because you are using your body so much more efficiently. Rolling a heavy ball down the lane will not feel so strenuous when you use your entire body, and not just your arm, to do it.

GETTING LOWER: HIPS VERSUS SHOULDERS

A strong finish with good balance can become even stronger. To get into your strongest position, stretch that back leg even farther to 8:00 or 8:30 (right-handed bowler) or 3:30 to 4:00 (left-handed bowler) (figure 6.6). The farther over your back leg gets, the lower your hips will get. I refer to finish positions at the line as good, better, and best. In a good finish, the right-handed bowler's trail leg finishes at 7:00. In a better finish, the trail leg finishes around 7:30 to 8:00 to create more knee bend. In the best finish, the trail leg gets all the way over to 8:30 so the hips are even lower at delivery.

A trick to create more knee bend to get into your lowest position is to invert your foot and get the laces of your trail foot on the ground. This takes a great deal of strength and some flexibility. As you get that leg farther over, your hips will come down and you will have more knee bend. The greater the distance between your feet, and the more you can tuck your trail foot to get the laces down, the lower you will get.

Figure 6.6　The trail leg stretched over, laces down: *(a)* right-handed; *(b)* left-handed.

Do not confuse getting low with dropping your shoulders forward! Keep your posture upright, but bend your knees. Like a squat, your chest is up and your core should be over your legs. Getting your hips low is a function of the movement of your trail leg. The chair drill in chapter 3 is a good one for working on this point.

FINISH STRONG

For almost all bowlers, creating a stronger finish position takes a lot of effort. For one thing, it will feel very different from what you are used to, especially if your timing has changed. Second, it takes more strength to finish with your hips lower to the ground. Commit to working on your finish, and you will become a better bowler.

Once my students understand *how* to get lower, helping them get lower at the line becomes more about coaching than instructing. I always say it's like doing a bowling squat at the foul line when finishing. Getting lower while supporting the weight of your upper body requires strength, and it is exercise to get into a stronger and balanced position at the line. Just as a trainer pushes a client to get lower in a squat, I try to encourage my students to get lower in their finish positions. Frankly, it is just easier *not* to do it! It is exercise.

SUMMARY

As in life, when we have leverage, we are naturally strong! When we do not have leverage, we try to use force. Using force is far less productive than using leverage, especially in bowling, because proper bowling technique requires a balance between power and repetition.

The more you develop your technique, the more you will achieve this balance for improved performance. You may feel as though you are doing less, but that is the magic of leverage! As I often say to my students, using force is easy, but developing technique is a greater challenge because it requires strength and discipline. It also improves scores.

Ironically, the less muscle force from your arm you use and the more technique you apply, the more athletic you look and feel! It feels more effortless to bowl because you are using your whole body to throw the ball, not just the muscles of your arm. And when you are not forcing the swing but rather using your body to get into a strong, leveraged position, you *are* stronger. However, using the big muscles of your whole body to develop technique is much harder than using the little muscles of your arm to create force.

Getting into a stronger position does take strength. Improving your fitness level can help you achieve greater levels in your bowling game, as in any other sport. Whether you are looking to develop better balance, get into a lower position at the line, or consistently make good shots over longer periods of time, you may want to improve your fitness level to enjoy better results on the lanes.

Chapter 7

Release

Some bowlers roll straight, and some bowlers have a hook release. In a hook release, the hand imparts side rotation, which makes the ball curve. The amount and type of hook varies from bowler to bowler. Some hook the ball more than others do. Most right-handers hook the ball to the left, which is a standard hook release. However, some hook the ball to the right, which is a reverse hook.

Some bowlers have a hook release (i.e., they impart rotation to the ball), but the ball does not actually curve because of the type of ball they use. For example, imparting a hook release to a plastic ball may result in the ball rotating but not hooking, because of the lack of friction the cover is able to create on the lane oil. For a ball to curve, two things need to be present: a rotation of the hand at release and enough friction for the ball to grab the lane.

The type of release you have will affect where you line up and target on the lane. Chapter 2 provided some basic guidelines on where to stand. Upcoming chapters address adjusting for the hook release and lane conditions.

When you roll a straight ball, you target just to the right or left of the center arrow, depending on whether you are right- or left-handed. When you roll a hook with a ball that actually grabs the lane and curves, you need to adjust your target more outside, starting around the second arrow or so, to allow for your hook. In chapter 8, you will learn how to take lane conditions into consideration when you throw a hook.

The equipment you purchase and the way your bowling balls are drilled should be determined with your type of release in mind. This varies depending on whether you roll a straight ball, hook, or reverse hook.

RELEASING THE BALL

In a sound release, the thumb comes out first and the ball rolls off the fingers. This process should be smooth and easy to do. For this to be the case, the ball must fit properly and you must maintain proper, not excessive, grip pressure. Remember, using tape in the thumbhole will help you adjust the ball to your hand so you don't have to grip it to keep it on your hand!

Rolling a straight ball or creating a basic hook is adequate for a bowler just beginning to establish an average approaching 100 or even a bowler averaging around 120 to 130. The key to raising your score is accuracy in hitting around the headpin so that you leave spares you can get. Raising your average is a matter of getting just another spare or a few more each game. However, a straight ball deflects more when it hits the pins. This makes it hard to strike, and it can lead to more difficult spare combinations.

Developing a hook will help the ball hit the pins with more drive and pin action to leave better pin counts. Also, developing a curve will give you a little more room for error hitting your target and still get the ball to hit the headpin. When you develop a hook release, eventually going to a fingertip grip will further improve the roll on the ball to create even more pin action when the ball hits.

If you already hook the ball and have an established average, you may need to improve your basic hook release to improve your roll. This will enable you to create more room for error at your target and leave easier spares, or just help you strike more.

Once your basic hook release is established, making a change to it can be a very tedious process. It is much easier said than done. A bowler's release is very reflexive; it comes naturally. It is one of the most difficult things to change. Strive for small changes that will make a big difference. Just a slight, almost undetectable visual change in hand position can be the difference it takes for you to carry all 10 pins and strike when you hit the pocket!

IMPROVING BALL ROLL FOR CARRY

Many bowlers tell me they just don't throw enough strikes to raise their score or average. Before we focus on fine-tuning their release, I remind them that if their average is under 189, the reason they aren't raising their average is not that they don't strike enough; it's that they don't spare enough.

Think of it this way: if you left a single-pin spare and made it in every frame you bowled, you would average 189! So, until you average 189, every pin leave is a chance to improve your average!

The point is that you do not have to get too fancy, too soon. Improving your roll to increase your strike percentage and your effectiveness on various lane conditions is a tedious process and can only be developed when the time is right for you to commit to it. However, when you are getting your spares and when you have developed your basic hook release but need to manipulate your ball roll to either become more effective to carry more strikes or conquer various lane conditions, you need to understand ball roll.

Ball Roll in a Hook Release

There are two basic components to the hook release: forward roll and side roll. You achieve forward roll when you stay behind the ball. You achieve side roll when you rotate, or turn, your hand at release. Forward roll gets the ball to grab the lane and hook sooner, creating a smoother reaction on the back end. Side roll gets the ball to skid more and delays the hook, potentially creating a stronger reaction on the back end.

Too much of either roll, however, leads to a weaker ball motion. That is, imparting all forward roll would lead to a straight ball (figure 7.1*a*). Additionally, excessive side turn would lead to a ball that just skids too long without grabbing the lane (figure 7.1*b*). With either, you would not see very much hook (or curve) from the ball.

A healthy combination of forward roll and side roll creates the ideal release (figure 7.2). Many bowlers have to work on creating less or more of either type of roll. If the ball is going straight because you are behind the ball too much, you need to learn to create more side turn to make the ball change direction and hook. In this case, you need to rotate your hand at release to develop more side roll so the ball can hook.

If, however, if you are turning the ball so much that it is just skidding all the way down the lane, you need to learn to stay behind the ball longer before

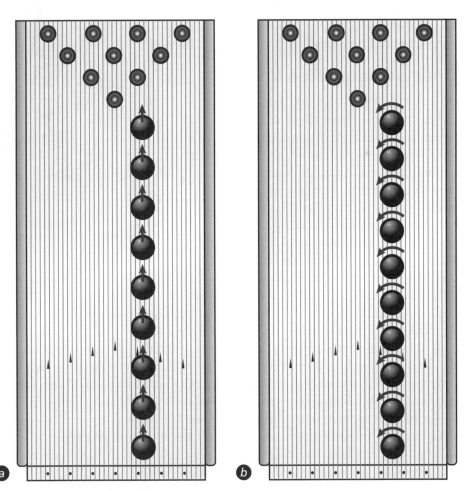

Figure 7.1   *(a)* All forward roll creates a straight ball with no reaction. *(b)* Excessive side roll at release creates a ball that spins too long down the lane.

you turn it. In this case, staying behind the ball to create more forward roll will enable to the ball to grab the lane and hook sooner.

Note: At times, excessive side turn can result in spinning the ball. When the ball is spinning, such a small portion of it is actually touching the lane; although you can see it revolving, it is really just sliding down the lane and not moving toward the pins. Liken this to a top that just spins in place. Spin and roll are not the same thing. When you have too much turn, or excessive spin, you need to learn to stay behind the ball more before you rotate it, so that you turn through it and create some forward roll, rather than just turn or spin around the side of it.

Understanding Side Roll

When you turn the ball, it has more potential to hook later down the lane, because side roll stores energy, which delays hook. But if this reaction is delayed too long, the ball will run out of time to hook. This is especially true if you are bowling on a lot of oil. In this situation, more turn does not create more hook! On oiler conditions, the ball naturally slides; too much side roll only further delays reaction. On

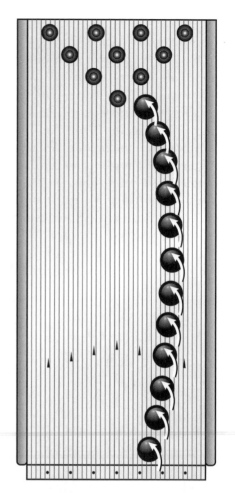

Figure 7.2   The ideal release: a good combination of forward roll and side roll.

oily conditions, you will be more effective when you get the ball to hook sooner, rather than create more side roll. Do not make the mistake of trying to get it to hook more on the back end. Again, getting it to grab sooner is the key—more turn does not necessarily translate into more hook!

To reiterate, forward roll gets the ball to grab and change direction sooner on the lane. Side roll gets more length and delays hook. On oily lane conditions, your strategy is not to try to turn and lift the ball more; doing so will only further delay ball reaction. Instead, create more forward roll by staying behind the ball longer to get it to hook sooner (figures 7.3 and 7.4).

Conversely, on drier lanes, when the ball tends to grab and hook too soon, side roll will help it skid more and react later (figure 7.5). And, when the lanes require you to move inside and deliver at an angle more away from the pocket, this delay effectively stores energy so the ball can react more on the back end. This helps the ball hook back and drive more into the pins from such an angle.

Figure 7.3 Stay behind the ball longer to create more forward roll.

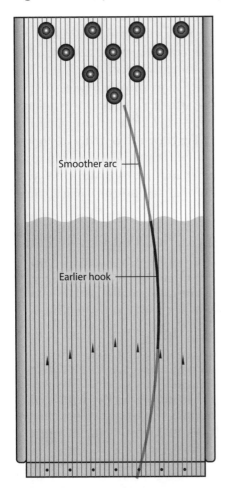

Figure 7.4 On an oily lane, more forward roll will create an earlier hook.

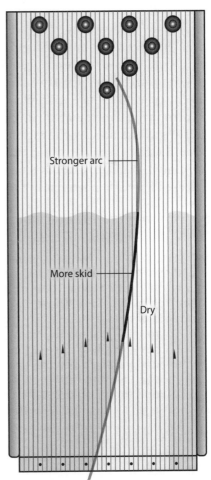

Figure 7.5 On a dry lane, use side roll to get the ball down the lane farther before it reacts.

Adjusting Roll

Once you learn to go from a straight ball to a hook, your basic release develops. Once you have developed a hook release, your tendency to roll the ball a certain way is very strong. Trying to change your release can be one of the most tedious things you work on in your game. It requires patience. Overcoming weaknesses in the release takes a lot of hard work, and the change often seems slight compared with the amount of effort you put into it. However slight changes make a big difference.

Do not expect to be accurate when you are working on your release. Let the ball go where it may, especially at first. It will require all your effort just to change your roll, and this will unintentionally affect your swing. So cut yourself some slack and compromise on accuracy when you are working on your release.

Consider the common fault of turning the ball too much. Trying to stay behind the ball can be a very demanding task, mostly because of how we are put together. When you just stand in a relaxed state, by default your hands face your body. Just opening your hands to face your palms forward requires effort, even without a ball in your hand. When you then put a heavy load on it, such as a bowling ball, the effort becomes even more challenging.

Overexaggerating to stay behind the ball more moves to a whole new level when trying to change your release. As someone who has fought this tendency to turn the ball too much, I personally know what it is like to try to change the roll to stay behind the ball longer. I had to overexaggerate and actually try to just keep my palm facing forward throughout the whole release, just to keep from turning it so much. I would attempt to keep my hand flat behind the ball as I released it, trying not to turn it at all. But I always did still turn it, just slightly

---

Making Changes: Turning Too Much

It is very common to turn the ball too soon or too much. You should turn the ball once the thumb exits, rather than while the thumb is still in. Turning too soon, while the thumb is still in, leads to extra side roll, which makes the ball skid too long before it potentially hooks. (If the lane is very oily, the ball will run out of time to hook.)

Try to keep your elbow in and stay behind the ball until your thumb comes out. Once your thumb clears, turn the ball. It is not easy to determine whether your hand is behind the ball until your thumb comes out, but you will see it in your ball roll and reaction. That is your feedback.

A good trick is to think about keeping your elbow in, *leading with your ring finger* to turn the ball. This will help you turn through it, rather than around it. Also, always strive to relax your thumb so it can come out cleaner and earlier at release.

When you stay more behind the ball, you will not see as sharp of a hook on the backend. The ball will have more of an arc into the pocket. The ball may seem to go straighter only because it is actually hooking sooner. The different shape of the shot enables you to match the ball's reaction to lane conditions.

less. I was so used to turning the ball too much that I could count on turning it, even when I wasn't trying to. I remember how hard I worked to exaggerate staying behind it, only to turn it slightly less than I usually turned it. I would have sworn I was throwing a flat ball, staying straight behind it at release (because that's how it felt), but I would still see my ball hook. So, I must have turned it.

With all the work it takes to modify your hook release, it is that much more difficult to repeat it on every shot. It is easy to let your tendency overcome your work. This is not to say that you shouldn't work on developing your release; just be prepared for how much you have to exaggerate to realize any change, especially when fine-tuning it. If your work enables you to carry a few more shots here and there or be just that much more effective on a given lane condition, it will have been worth it. Be patient.

USING WRIST GUARDS FOR A BETTER RELEASE

Many bowlers whose wrists break before they release the ball will benefit from using a wrist guard. Different wrist guards have different functions. Some simply firm the wrist position, whereas others have a specific effect on ball roll. A good matchup can definitely improve performance!

When you need to stop your wrist from breaking back, a basic wrist guard with a metal backing will straighten the wrist (figure 7.6). In fact, you may already have a natural hand motion to impart rotation to the ball, but you just don't get to see it actually hook because your wrist breaks before you do it. This wrist guard would be good with either a conventional or fingertip grip. *Note:* when I put these wrist guards on my students, I take out the front piece of metal so the ball sits flush on the palm. It's the backside metal that gives the support.

Figure 7.6   Basic wrist guard.

Whereas a basic wrist guard stops at the knuckles, a longer wrist guard that extends to the second joints on the fingers offers even more support to keep the wrist firm and position your fingers lower, more under the ball at release (figure 7.7). With this kind of wrist guard, the ball will come off your thumb even cleaner, creating more revolutions at release. A longer wrist guard would be good with a fingertip grip.

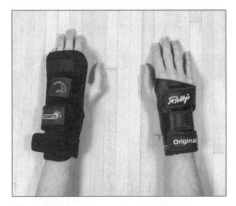

Figure 7.7   Longer wrist guard.

Other wrist guards are made of metal and offer strong support, and also have some knobs on them to make adjustments to wrist position (figure 7.8). *Caution:* Although these are excellent, it is important that you are measured and fit for your ball with these wrist guards on. They change the measurement of your span. If you commit to wearing one of these, have your ball fit adjusted for your new span. This wrist guard would be good with a fingertip grip.

Figure 7.8   Adjustable wrist guard.

Finally, one type of wrist guard has a finger guard on the index finger (figure 7.9). This is very helpful for bowlers who need to get out of a reverse hook or who are trying to develop more rotation on the ball. Something in the design naturally helps the hand rotate around the ball. Although it works instantly for some, others still need to cultivate the technique of rotating at release. Some may

Figure 7.9   Wrist guard with finger guard.

use this wrist guard to help learn rotation, whereas others end up wearing it all the time for good rotation. This wrist guard would be good with a fingertip grip.

If you can, experiment with wrist guards during a lesson or in the pro shop before making a commitment to one. At your local pro shop, ask if you can try a few shots with a wrist guard to see whether it helps before you buy it. Some are a bit uncomfortable at first, especially the ones that change your span. Just know that your span has to be adjusted if you commit to wearing a wrist guard of this type.

Some bowlers believe that they can firm up their wrists on their own, and some can. But many (who may otherwise be strong people) too often confuse the

Making Changes: Wrist Supports

Sometimes you will need a wrist support to achieve the type of roll you desire. Each wrist guard has a specific function and should be experimented with in a thoughtful manner. Good advice from your reputable pro shop professional or coach can be a guiding force. Trying a wrist guard for a few shots to learn whether it will work for you is always a bonus. Some do change your ball fit. Although you have to deal with the way it feels when you try it out, your span may be different with the use of certain wrist guards and need to be adjusted. Once you commit to a wrist guard, you should wear it during the fitting process.

muscles needed to firm up the wrist with the muscles that control grip pressure. In fact, they are a completely different set of muscles! Professionals who do not wear wrist guards have learned how to relax their grip and their arm swing, yet keep their wrists firm. However, this requires natural wrist strength and talent. When this challenge leads you to lose more than you gain, you are definitely a candidate for a wrist guard.

MULTIPLE RELEASES FOR VARIOUS LANE CONDITIONS

If you are an advanced player who has learned to adjust to lanes and has an arsenal of bowling balls to adjust ball reaction, another asset to develop is multiple releases. From your typical hand position, you can learn to minimize or maximize your ball reaction by manipulating your hand position at release. This will change the shape of the shot to help conquer lane conditions. When the part of the lane you are playing is hooking a lot, you can make your release weaker so that the ball does not overreact. Conversely, when the lanes are super oily (referred to as "tighter"), you can try to strengthen your roll to help the ball grab and hook sooner.

Starting from a neutral position with a straight wrist and your hand under the ball, try minimizing your hand position by putting your hand to the side and slightly breaking the wrist (figure 7.10). This will feel weak. It is, but it will work in an area of the lane with high friction.

Now, from neutral, try to slightly cock your hand and cup your wrist to put your hand in a stronger position at release (figure 7.11). This will help you get more behind and under the ball to impart a stronger roll to help it hook on oilier conditions. *Note:* Cock and cup your hand only about 15 percent more than

Figure 7.10   Stand in a neutral position with your hand under the ball and minimize your hand position by putting your hand to the side and slightly breaking the wrist: *(a)* in the stance; *(b)* at the release point.

Figure 7.11 From a neutral position, slightly cock the hand and cup the wrist to put the hand in a stronger release position: *(a)* in the stance; *(b)* at the release point.

usual; do not overdo it! You will not have the strength to maintain that position if you do. Also, keep in mind that most bowlers who try this manufacture the desired hand/wrist position in the stance, but go right back to their comfortable neutral position by the time the ball reaches the release point. Maintaining this position from the top of the backswing down into the release point is the key.

Keep in mind that developing multiple releases is advanced work. You will need time, patience, and repetition to develop this capacity and to become confident enough to use it and repeat it in competition. Strengthening your main release to make it more effective is hard work in itself. Developing multiple releases takes a lot of practice to master. Done properly, you can change your release to tweak your reaction on the lanes.

CHALLENGES TO A GOOD RELEASE

Many bowlers want a better release. Although this is understandable, they must also understand that good form leading up to the release has a major effect on the release itself. When you improve your approach and create better leverage at delivery, you often will see improvement in your release, for free!

Excessive Grip Pressure

Squeezing the ball creates problems in the release, which affects ball roll. Getting out of the thumbhole cleanly is really important because it helps you get the thumb out while you are still behind the ball, resulting in a better, smoother ball roll. Maintaining a light grip pressure is essential to achieving a clean thumb release.

To maintain the proper grip pressure, you have to keep up with the changes in your hand while you bowl. Using tape to adjust to the natural fluctuations in your thumb size is key. Bowlers who do not use tape simply adjust their grip pressure without even realizing it.

Rather than insisting that your thumb never changes (you'd be the first person on the planet for that to be the case!), learn to count on your thumb changing in size and expect to have to use tape in the thumbhole to adjust it to your thumb. Knowing that you even need a piece a tape is a sure sign that you are maturing as a bowler!

Steering the Ball

Trying to control, or steer, the ball at the last minute often gets in the way of what would otherwise be a good, sound release. Many bowlers teeter between the desire to control the ball and to trust the ball. I get it. I often ask my students who do this, "How's that control working out?" They often pause to think and then realize that's why they've come to see me.

Trying to Put More On It

It is important to understand that you are not always trying to do more to the ball. Rather, you are trying to create an effective roll with technique, not force. Good ball roll with sound lane play strategy is a formula for success.

Developing a strong roll does not mean that you will feel a lot of pressure on your fingers (i.e., lift). You want to get into a strong position of leverage and roll the ball off the pads of your fingers onto the lane. You are not trying to lift or squeeze the ball; rather, you want to get the ball off your hand as cleanly as possible. This creates a more predictable and controllable ball reaction, especially with the stronger bowling balls in today's game.

ROTATION VERSUS REVOLUTIONS

I have addressed the way you rotate a ball, but the number of revolutions you get is a different matter altogether. Rotation is the angle at which the ball is revolving down the lane. Revolutions are the number of times the ball rolls over its circumference on the lane. Rotation refers to angle of the roll, whereas revolution refers to the amount of action.

Bowlers often express a desire to hook, or rev, the ball the way someone they've watched hooks it. Some bowlers have natural talent and wrist strength to create more revolutions, or revs, than the average bowler. They actually load the wrist by cupping it to get their fingers under the ball; then unload it by quickly uncupping it at release. It comes naturally to them and involves God-given strength and talent. With this, they create a higher revolution rate (nicknamed rev rate), which distinguishes their release from others'. Generally speaking, professional bowlers have higher rev rates. Furthermore, men generally have higher rev rates than women do, because of the strength factor.

The good news is that bowlers with various rotations and revolution rates can compete with each other by making adjustments for how they bowl and play the lane. A bowler's game and timing are typically solidified around the release. Trying to become a different type of bowler does not work. Spare yourself the frustration and play and stay within your game. I have seen too many bowlers misunderstand this concept and ruin their swings trying to create a release (specifically, a rev rate) that is not their own.

Foam Football

This drill requires a foam-type football and a partner. These footballs come in multiple sizes. The small ones can be used by kids or those with really small hands.

Play underhand catch with a partner, creating a motion to make the ball spiral. This motion mimics the bowling release. With your hand underneath and your wrist slightly cocked around the back of the ball, toss the football underhanded to your partner, creating a perfect, tight spiral off your fingers. This motion enables you to create the proper wrist motion to turn through the ball, without overturning the thumb, to create a strong roll on the ball. Create the spiral by letting your thumb off the ball and rolling it off your fingers as you turn. It's all in the wrist motion, letting your fingers create the spiral. Your thumb is on the ball only to hold the ball in the swing. Again, as in the bowling release, the more cleanly you get your thumb off the ball, the more revs your spiral will have!

I had a student tell me he couldn't feel his fingers in the shot. I listened then watched. He was very tense, squeezing the ball. After we worked on his timing and relaxed his swing, his ball roll and projection toward the target steadily improved. He said he could feel the ball roll of the pads of his fingers. Rather than using force, he improved his leverage through better technique.

Strengthening a Weak Wrist Position

Many bowlers can create a stronger roll by putting on a wrist guard that stops the wrist from breaking back too soon. I know that some bowlers and coaches are dead set against them, often to the demise of the bowler. The goal is to bowl better and have more fun. A wrist guard is another piece of equipment to use when necessary.

Many bowlers are candidates for wrist guards; not everybody has a strong wrist. You can be a strong person, but still have your wrist break back with a bowling ball in your hand. Typically, when bowlers are told to keep their wrists firm, they often mistakenly tighten up the wrong muscles and instead create too much grip pressure in their hand. In this case, a wrist guard is warranted to improve ball roll.

Furthermore, although a wrist guard will firm up your wrist, it will not stop you from turning the ball too much. That task is left to you. The wrist guard will firm your wrist to position your fingers lower, more underneath the ball, and stabilize otherwise excessive wrist movement, but training to stay behind the ball more is up to you.

Pulling the Downswing

Your hand position will be adversely affected if you pull the ball down to the release point from the backswing. You can have the best intention to stay behind the ball at release, but when you pull down, the muscles in your chest tighten, closing down your shoulder and your hand with it. It is important to relax your arm from the backswing down to allow your hand to stay open at the release point for a stronger roll (figure 7.12).

Figure 7.12   The downswing: *(a)* pulling the swing down and closing the hand; *(b)* relaxing during the downswing and leaving the hand open.

CLEAN ROLL VERSUS LIFT

The technology of bowling balls has drastically changed over time. One notion that is greatly outdated is that the bowler should lift the ball with the fingers.

Today's bowling balls have stronger cores, or guts, on the inside, and they roll more strongly than the balls of the past did. They have the innate ability to hook more. You do not want to make your ball overreact to the point of being unable to control it, or even make it drive too hard into the pins, lowering your chances of striking.

The less resistance there is at release, or the cleaner the ball comes off your hand, the better and more consistent the roll will be and the more predictable the trajectory of the ball path will be. With this, adjusting to lane conditions becomes easier. Learn to roll the ball cleanly off your thumb and fingers, literally releasing it rather than grabbing it. That will be the difference between a smooth, predictable roll and an overactive, unpredictable reaction.

Using the strength you have, start with your wrist slightly cupped and cocked in a loaded position. Then unload it to allow the weight of the ball to transfer through your palm to your fingers once your thumb clears. Then just roll the ball onto the lane, rather than lift it into the air.

MENTALITY AND THE RELEASE

I see many bowlers who are taken by those who hook the ball a ton because they have a high revolution rate. Some even try to emulate that type of roll, but mistakenly do it with improper technique and thus never achieve it. They end up altering their swing and hurting their own performance as they try to put more on the ball. Developing your release should not require your swing to change.

All bowlers have their own type of release, largely formed by the strength and talent they were born with. The key is to develop your release to the best of your ability and let your game form around it. You will experience less frustration and find much more success, and enjoyment, when you learn to stay and play in your own game.

Fortunately, bowlers with different releases can compete with each other by making the necessary adjustment on the lane, using appropriate equipment, and adjusting angles for the way they roll the ball. Always remember that more turn is not more hook. Learning to stay behind the ball more will help you roll the ball sooner, and you will have a smoother, more predictable arc down the lane. This is especially effective when you are on more oil. The key on a heavily oiled lane is to keep the ball from sliding too much, or to say it differently, to get the ball rolling sooner. Staying behind the ball (creating more forward roll) will make it grab and hook sooner.

Many bowlers try to do the opposite and turn the ball more on oil, to hook it more. Again, more turn is not more hook. Trying to lift the ball and turn it more only delays the ball's reaction on the lane, which is counterproductive on an oily pattern! Staying behind it and rolling through it more will get the ball to hook sooner (and often more), which is more effective on heavy oil.

SUMMARY

You hook the ball with body leverage and wrist action, not with grip pressure or lift! A clean release is what professionals strive for because it makes the ball roll more predictable and effective, creating better pin carry while also making it easier to read the lane and make adjustments.

Whether you are trying to improve your main release or develop multiple releases, working on the release is a tedious process. It takes a lot of patience because it is one of the hardest things for a bowler to change. But a small change can make a big difference. It will take a lot of overexaggeration in feel just to make a small change in ball roll. Often, what you think you are doing and what you are actually doing are two different things!

You may need to alter your roll to be effective on the lane conditions, modifying your release to create an earlier or later hook. You may need a wrist support to achieve the roll you need to be effective and score on various conditions. You can be a strong person, yet still need the support of a wrist guard to achieve a stronger wrist position and better roll.

Play your game and adjust to the lane. Make sure your equipment is drilled for the way you release the ball to enhance your game. Bowlers with different releases may attack a lane condition from slightly different angles, but all can compete with sound lane strategy and good spare shooting. Chapter 8 focuses on how to line up and adjust on a typical lane condition.

Basic Lane Play

To increase your strike percentage, you want the ball to hit the pocket when it hits the pins. The 1 pin and the 3 pin make up the pocket for the right-handed bowler; the 1 pin and the 2 pin, for the left-handed bowler. Even if you don't strike, hitting the pocket typically leads to spares that are easier to pick up. Therefore, hitting the pocket is essential to improve your scores and average.

How you hit (or miss) the pocket influences the way you adjust your line, the trajectory of your shot. With reference to the pocket, when the ball hits more on the 3 pin (right-handed bowler) or 2 pin (left-handed bowler), it is a *light* hit (figure 8.1). When the ball hits more of the 1 pin (headpin), it is considered a *high* hit (figure 8.2).

You have to make adjustments on the lane depending on where the ball hits in relation to the pocket. When making adjustments on the lane, *moving inside* refers to moving toward the middle, whereas *moving outside* refers to moving toward the gutter. A right-handed bowler moves to the right on the lane when moving outside and to the left when moving inside. A left-handed bowler moves to the left when moving outside and to the right when moving inside.

If you throw a straight ball, you need to learn to adjust your angle through the target to hit the pocket. If you throw a hook, you need to learn to adjust to the lane conditions to hit the pocket. Remember, this is a game of creating room for error rather than a game of being perfect, especially as you develop a hook. Once you establish good form, strategy becomes as important as execution. This is where your game will blossom. When your strategy is effective, your swing will relax because you have more room to make a mistake but still hit the pocket. It's that simple.

But you have to be willing to expand your comfort zones and adjust. Just as improving form means getting out of your physical comfort zone, improving strategy requires expanding your ability to play different areas on the lane. Players often are stubborn, wanting to play where they are used to playing rather than playing where the lane requires them to play. Once you learn to adjust to the lane and experience the forgiveness that the proper adjustment gives you, there is no going back! Sometimes, you have to see it to believe it.

Oil is invisible, so making a good shot is the most important key to reading and adjusting to lane conditions. But you do not have to be perfect to read the lane. When you are making decent shots—say, at 75 to 80 percent of your potential— you should be reading the lane and attempting to make adjustments. Adjusting to create more room for error will make a big difference in how you score. Your swing will relax when you have a little room to miss your target and still hit the pocket. Yet, it was because your swing was relaxed to begin with that you made decent enough shots to be able to read the lane. It's a big circle.

Many have heard the adage: If you miss right, move right. If you miss left, move left—or basically, move in the direction of the miss. Although this can be a good rule of thumb for adjusting the angle when throwing a straight ball, it also works (but takes on a whole new meaning) when you throw a hook and adjust on the typical house shot (THS). The THS is the usual, basic type of oil pattern applied to the lanes during open bowling and standard league play. Bowling centers may deviate from this during tournaments or special league play. Chapter 9 provides more information on other lane conditions.

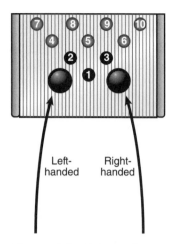

Figure 8.1 Light pocket hit. The ball hits more of the 3 pin for a right-handed bowler and more of the 2 pin for a left-handed bowler.

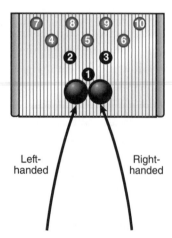

Figure 8.2 High pocket hit. The ball hits more of the 1 pin.

STRAIGHT BALL: ADJUSTING THE ANGLE

When you throw a straight ball and hit your target but miss the pocket to the right, move your feet to the right to adjust your angle through your target; this creates a different angle so you can hit the pocket (figure 8.3a). If you hit your target but miss the pocket to the left, you can move your feet to the left to create a

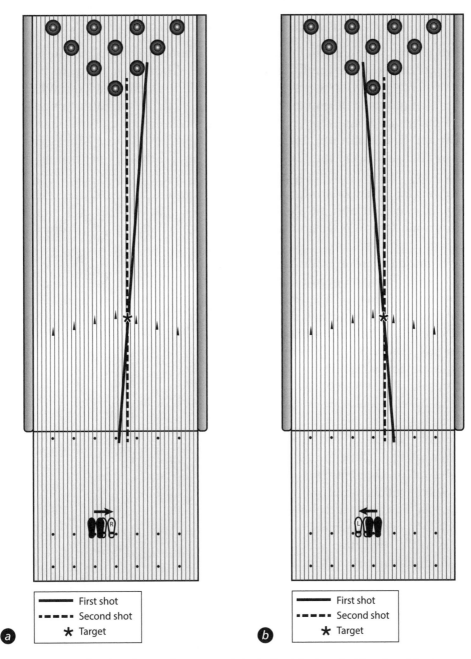

Figure 8.3 Adjusting the angle on a straight ball, right-handed bowler: *(a)* miss pocket to the right; *(b)* miss pocket to the left.

different angle to hit the pocket (figure 8.3*b*). In either case, you adjust by moving your feet in the direction you miss the pocket, but keep the target the same.

At some point, you will want to learn to hook the ball to create more room for error at the target to continue to hit the pocket as well as create more drive when the ball hits the pins.

HOOK BALL: FINDING THE OIL LINE

If you throw a hook, adjust by moving in the direction in which you missed the pocket because of the lane conditions on a THS. You adjust to the oil on the lane. In this case, you will likely move your feet and your target to adjust. When you throw a hook, adjusting to the lane conditions is the key to hitting the pocket. On the typical house shot (THS), the oil is much heavier in the center of the lane and lighter on the outsides toward the gutters, so there is more friction there (figure 8.4). On the THS, your goal is to find the oil line; that is, where the heavy oil stops and the friction starts.

On the THS, when the conditioner is first applied, it is common for the oil line to start around the second arrow, so this can be a good place to start.

To make the proper adjustment to line up on the THS, you need to understand how oil, or a lack of it, affects the ball. Oil makes a ball slide. A lack of oil creates more friction between the land and the ball, making the ball hook. The ball will slide more where there is oil and hook more where there is less oil.

To hit the pocket consistently when throwing a hook, you have to adjust to the lane condition when the ball is sliding too much or hooking too much. When it slides too much, it hits *light,* and when it hooks too much, it hits *high*—that is, if it does not miss the pocket altogether. (Refer back to figures 8.1 and 8.2.)

Typically, when the ball hits light, it is sliding too much. Because oil makes a ball slide, you are in too much oil and need to move out where there is more friction for the ball to hook. A right-handed bowler would move right; a left-handed bowler would move left (figure 8.5). Once you move outside the oil, the ball will hook again where there is more friction.

If the ball hits high on the headpin, perhaps even missing the headpin completely toward the opposite pocket, the ball is hooking too much. (This is only when a decent shot was rolled, not when the ball

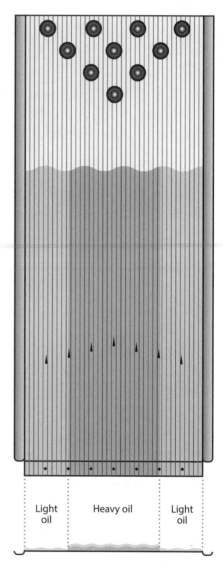

Figure 8.4 The typical house shot (THS) oil pattern, simplified.

Light oil   Heavy oil   Light oil

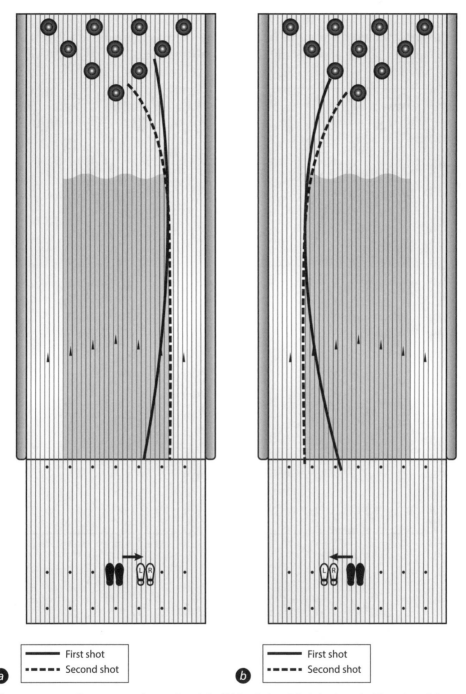

Figure 8.5 Adjustment when a hook ball hits light: *(a)* right-handed bowler; *(b)* left-handed bowler.

was pulled that way!) Because the ball hooks where there is friction, the proper adjustment would be to move inside, where there is more oil so the ball slides long enough before it hooks into the pocket (figure 8.6).

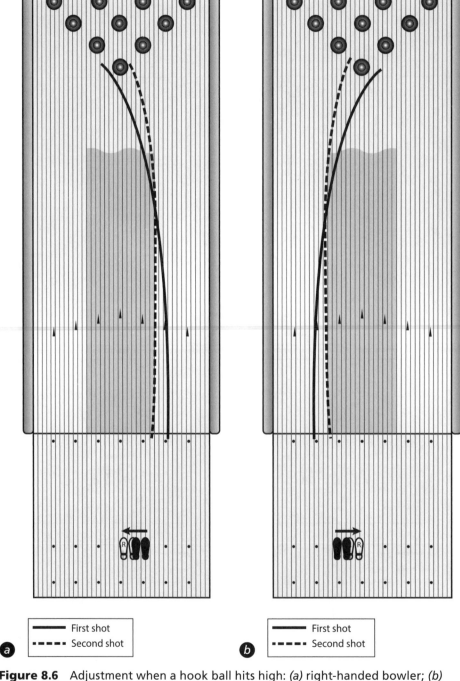

a — First shot, Second shot

b — First shot, Second shot

Figure 8.6 Adjustment when a hook ball hits high: *(a)* right-handed bowler; *(b)* left-handed bowler.

SHOT ANALYSIS

Sometimes we don't pay attention to what is going on, and so we don't have a system to analyze the shot. Focusing makes it easier to decide on the adjustment. Here are three points of analysis for each shot you take. Your observations will help you decide what adjustments, if any, you need to make. You must stay in position at the line once you make the shot so you can make all three observations.

- Watch the ball roll over the target. Did you hit your target?
- Watch the ball's reaction at the pins. Was it in the pocket or did it miss? If it missed, which way did it miss?
- Check your finish position. Did you end where you started?

Always consider how well you executed the shot before you determine your adjustment. Although you do not have to be perfect, justify any adjustment you make by taking these three things into consideration, as well as how well you threw the ball.

Whether the ball hits light or high, adjusting is about managing the friction of the ball on the lane to hit the pocket. The correct adjustment will lead you toward the oil line. If you can find and play around the oil line, you will have more room for error to hit the pocket consistently.

You have more room because, around the oil line, you have oil just to the inside of your target in the event you slightly pull the ball (miss your target inside). This oil will correct the pull, helping the ball slide rather than overhook. If you miss your target a little to the outside, there will be less oil and more friction to correct your miss and help the ball hook back to the pocket. Playing around the oil line provides a little bit of room on either side of your target to still hit the pocket and potentially strike. This has a huge effect on loosening up your swing.

Making Changes: Knowing When Oil Is the Reason

A common problem for bowlers is failing to adjust when they are rolling the ball well. Hitting the second arrow only to watch the ball miss the pocket does not necessarily mean that you threw the ball poorly. You may have thrown it well but just did not get the proper ball reaction on the lane. Do not try to be more perfect or put more on the ball; *just move.* If you are throwing well and do not move, your only alternative is to start throwing the ball poorly to force the ball to react.

Keep in mind that you cannot see the oil and that the lane conditions will change as you bowl. You have to watch the ball on decent shots and adjust accordingly. Go on the premise that oil is heavy toward the center of the lane and lighter outside toward the gutter. Let this guide your moves. If your ball slides too much, move out of the oil. If it hooks too much, move into the oil. Just because you cannot see the oil, do not think that the problem is with you or wait until you are perfect to adjust.

ZONE MOVES

The bigger your miss is, the bigger your move should be. Your goal is to line up on the lane in as few shots as possible. If your ball does not make it to the pocket at all, make a significant move. If you are a right-handed bowler playing the second arrow and completely miss the headpin, light on the 3 pin, you should move everything (you and your target) to the right and try the first arrow to get the ball to hook. If you are a left-handed bowler who is playing the second arrow and miss the headpin, light on the 2 pin, you should move everything (you and your target) to the left and try the first arrow to get the ball to hook (figure 8.7).

In these examples, the ball hits so light, missing the pocket completely, that you need to move the whole zone more outside to get the ball to hook. If the ball hooks too much at the first arrow, at least you now know the parameters. At that point, you learned quickly that somewhere between the first and second arrows would be the shot to the pocket. From there, you need only fine-tune any adjustments.

Conversely, if your ball hooks so much that it hits toward the opposite pocket, make a bigger move toward the inside of the lane. If you are playing the first arrow when this happens, move to the second arrow. If this happens when you are at the second arrow, move closer to the third arrow to find more oil to make the ball skid more.

In these examples, the ball totally missed the pocket. For this reason, you need to move the whole zone either inside or outside to adjust and hit the pocket more quickly, rather than just moving your feet a board or two. (If you move your feet a board or two, it will take too many frames before you adjust enough to hit the pocket!)

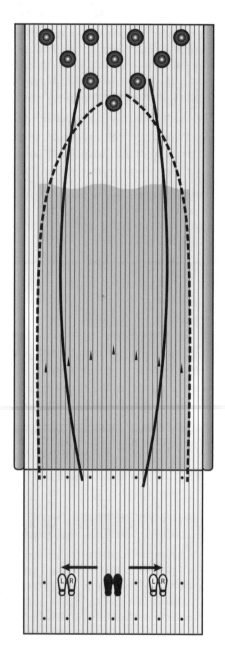

First shot
Second shot

Figure 8.7 Making a zone move to the right (right-handed bowler) or left (left-handed bowler), making the first arrow the target to get the ball to hook.

BOARD MOVES

When you are close to being flush in the pocket, common adjustments are to move your feet a board or two, sometimes even moving both your feet and your target in small increments. As a right-handed bowler who hits slightly high in the pocket, you may consider making a 1:0 adjustment to adjust to the left, the first number being the number of boards you move your feet and the second number being the number of boards you move your target (figure 8.8a). Therefore, a 1:0 left would be moving the feet one board to the left and keeping the

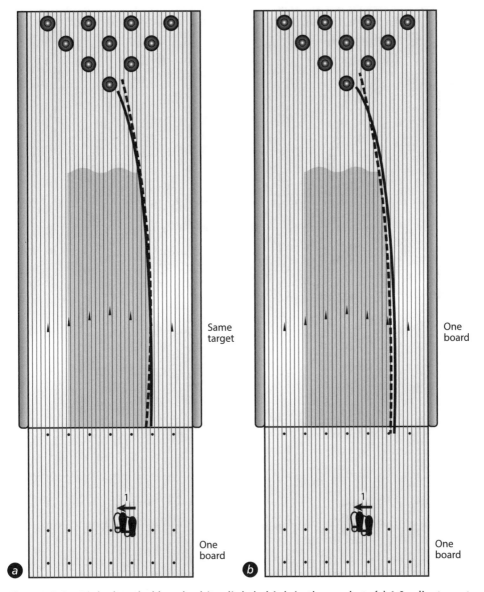

Figure 8.8 Right-handed bowler hits slightly high in the pocket: *(a)* 1:0 adjustment to the left; *(b)* 1:1 adjustment to the left.

target the same. Or you may try a 1:1 left in an attempt to go flush against the oil line. A 1:1 left would be moving the feet one board to the left and the target one board to the left (figure 8.8*b*).

A right-handed bowler who is hitting light may consider a 1:1 or 2:2 adjustment to the right, just to get out of the oil and into more friction on the lane to get the ball to hook more (figure 8.9). You may even move more, depending on how light the ball hit the pocket.

Keep in mind that on the THS there is a great imbalance between the amount of oil on the lane on either side of the oil line. The ball can hook high into the

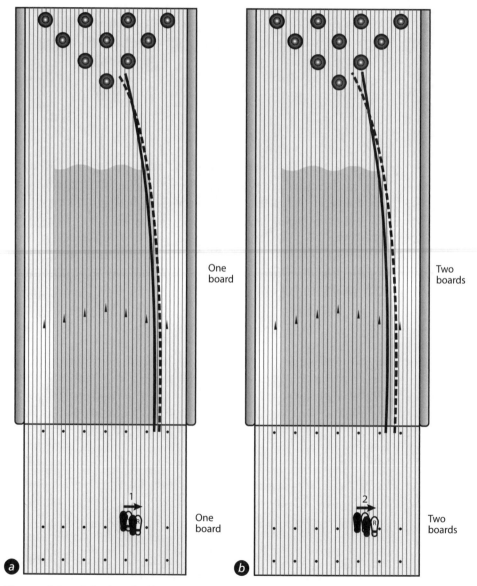

Figure 8.9   Right-handed bowler hits light: *(a)* 1:1 adjustment to the right; *(b)* 2:2 adjustment to the right.

pocket where you are currently throwing it, but a slight move may create enough slide to get the ball back flush into the pocket, because of the increased volume of oil as you move inside on the lane.

When you start moving in because the oil pattern breaks down during play (more later on how the oil disappears), common adjustments are to move in, making a 1:0, 1:1, 2:1, or 3:2 move, or moves, until you are flush in the pocket hit. Just use sense and have a reason for your move. Move incrementally to continue maintaining a healthy relationship between you and your target. This will help you maintain proper form (i.e., walking straight and relaxing your swing to hit your target). Adjusting to the lane is an ongoing process and is always about making a series of educated guesses.

All adjustments reflect your intention to adjust your line to hit the target. Do not try to force accuracy when you make subtle adjustments. Because of the forgiveness playing near the oil line provides, you should be able to miss your target slightly to either side but still hit the pocket. This mindset will keep your swing loose, helping you hit your target as you intended.

LINING UP AND ADJUSTING TO BREAKDOWN

When lining up on the lane, you need to maintain a healthy relationship between where you stand and your target. This will help you walk straight and hit your target.

Initially if you start out with the second arrow as your target, you will start approximately 8 to 10 boards over, standing on board 18 or so. The exact distance you stand over from your target will vary depending on how much the ball hooks. This distance assumes that you are releasing the ball close to your ankle as suggested in chapter 5. If you release the ball further from your ankle, include that in your calculation. (Later in this chapter, you will learn to change the distance you stand from your target as you play different angles on the lane.)

From there, you will make adjustments. Do not move your feet too far without also moving your target! When you move your feet more than two boards, consider moving your target, too. If you start to get too far from your target, you will miss the target or drift toward it to try to hit it.

Make adjustments to find the oil line when you begin to bowl, and follow the oil line as the lane breaks down during play. The lane condition breaks down because the oil is absorbed into the lane, moves, or is absorbed into the ball. On a wood lane, the oil can soak into the wood, and on a synthetic lane, the oil can move. Usually, the lane breaks down because the oil is absorbed into the balls, especially when bowlers use more aggressive performance balls that absorb oil as they hook.

Although you cannot see the oil, the key is to realize that it is not distributed evenly on a typical house shot (THS). When you move on the lane, your ball reaction will change significantly as a result of the friction factor associated with more or less oil.

When the ball hooks too much, *do not* make the mistake of trying to adjust the angle rather than taking lane conditions into consideration. When you throw a hook, lining up on the lane is about adjusting to lane conditions and using the oil pattern to create the proper ball reaction on the lane. Remember, on a THS the oil is not flat; there is more oil toward the center of the lane. Move inside to strategically use the oil to help the ball slide more or move away from the oil if you need the ball to hook more. Adjusting to lane conditions gives you more room for error.

If you adjust to the oil line to create the proper skid and best ball reaction, you will stay in the pocket and improve your chance to carry all 10 pins to strike. It's about ball reaction, not angle.

Not sure how to move? Experiment, experiment, experiment. Adjusting is about making a series of educated guesses that make sense. Some adjustments are easier than others. With experience, you will learn to make better moves. The key is to adjust. Aleta Sill never forgot the sage advice the great Nikki Gianulias gave here: "A bad move is better than no move at all!" This is great advice. Go for it! With experience, you will develop a better feel for adjusting quickly on the lane.

PLAYING THE OIL LINE AND BREAKDOWN

As lane conditions break down (which happens more quickly on the right side of the lane than on the left because there are more right-handed bowlers), you need to adjust to the oil line as it changes. If the ball starts to hook too much as you move into the oil, your angle may need to change to keep pace with the changing oil line. Bowlers who throw a hook tend to throw the ball at an angle toward the target to allow for the hook. Because they project the ball at an angle, the oil tends to break down at that angle in the front part of the lane (figure 8.10), known as *the heads*. For this reason, the initial oil line that was applied straight and parallel to the boards eventually forms at an angle on the lane. You may need to move your feet slightly more than your target to catch the evolving oil line at this angle, rather than play straight down as you did on the initial oil line.

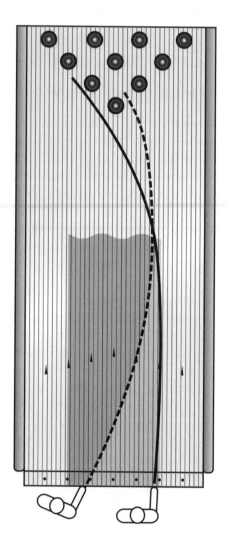

Figure 8.10   Oil breakdown in the heads.

ANGULAR VERSUS PARALLEL ADJUSTMENTS

Moving your feet and your target equally (a 1:1 adjustment) forms a parallel line to your last shot. Moving your feet more than you move your target (a 2:1 adjustment) creates a different angle toward your target.

Making angular moves requires you to open your shoulders to maintain the proper angle between your shoulders and your swing as you line up to hit the target. This becomes necessary especially as you move more inside on the lane to adjust to conditions. You cannot make an angular move without also adjusting your shoulders for the shot. Remember that you always want to maintain a swing that is 90 degrees to the shoulders.

As the lane breaks down, you may need to make incremental angular moves to get deeper on the lane to project the ball out enough before it hooks back to the pocket. As a result, you will be standing farther from your target than you were when you played more outside. *You will still be able to walk straight because the difference is made up by turning your shoulders to face your target.*

For example, if you stand on board 18 to hit the second arrow (or board 10), your line is referred to as 18-10. The first number is where you stand; the second number is where you target. Here, you are eight boards from your target. As you move in, you may be at 23-12, now 11 boards away. Or, you may get really deep, standing on board 35 and projecting to board 20. Playing 35-20, you are 15 boards from your target, but your shoulders are much more open to face the target.

Again, make your moves incrementally and open your shoulders to maintain integrity between you and your target so that you can stay in form and easily hit it.

PLAYING INSIDE ANGLES

The pocket is on board 17.5. If you are a right-handed bowler who has to stand deeper, or more inside on the lane, as you move more left of center, you will begin to create a bigger distance between you and the target than when you played more outside. This is necessary because you have to project the ball *away* from the pocket past board 17.5 before it hooks *back* to the pocket.

The way to stand farther from the target without drifting is to walk straight but *open* the shoulders to face the target. Turn your shoulders to line up your swing to your target, maintaining a 90-degree angle between your swing and your shoulders. For a right-handed bowler, open shoulders face to the right; the right shoulder is back at delivery (figure 8.11).

If you are a left-handed bowler who has to stand deeper, or more inside on the lane, as you move more right of center you will begin to create a bigger distance between you and the target than you did when you played more outside. In this case, you need to learn to walk straight but *open* your shoulders to face toward your target. Turn your shoulders to line up your swing to your target, maintaining a 90-degree angle between your swing and your shoulders. For the left-handed bowler, open shoulders face left; the left shoulder is back at delivery (figure 8.12).

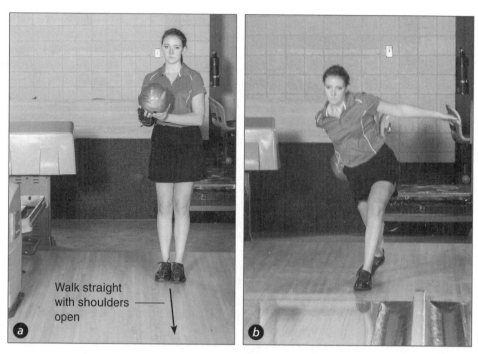

Figure 8.11 *(a)* A right-handed bowler's open shoulders face right. *(b)* The right shoulder is back at delivery. Walk straight.

Figure 8.12 *(a)* A left-handed bowler's open shoulders face left. *(b)* The left shoulder is back at delivery.

Note: When you open your shoulders, also open up your hip and foot so that you are in alignment on the swing side of your body in the stance. This will enable your spine to stay relaxed and make it easier to stay in alignment throughout the approach. You may feel as though you are side-stepping through your footwork, but that is what you need to do to walk straight yet face your target.

LANE ADJUSTMENTS AND EQUIPMENT

Besides moving left and right on the lane to adjust to conditions, you can also change balls to create more or less friction on the lane. If your ball is hooking too much at the second arrow, try a ball that slides more (or hooks less) instead of moving. Sometimes you can do both: use a ball that slides more as you move slightly on the lane.

Alternatively, you may find that when you do move away from the friction to the inside of the lane where there is more oil, you actually have to throw a stronger ball (i.e., one that rolls earlier) to handle the volume of oil you encounter on that part of the lane. However, when you play a deeper inside angle, you likely will need to change to a ball that skids down the lane and stores enough energy to finish strong enough from that angle.

If your ball is sliding too much, consider a ball with a stronger cover that can handle more oil by creating more friction with the lane. Again, you may have to change the ball *and* move outside on the lane to create enough friction for the ball to hook.

Making moves left and right on the lane to adjust to conditions is usually the first thing you do to find the oil line. However, you may like to try to stay in a particular part of the lane, commonly around the second arrow, and may need a different ball to be able to play there. Or, you may need a different ball altogether to play effectively on the lane conditions you bowl on. Another way to say it is that if you get forced way out of your comfort zone all the time with the ball you currently use, it is because it is not adequate for the amount of oil you bowl on or for the part of the lane that you have to play.

For example, if the lanes are generally very oily or the oil line is more outside (toward the gutter) than the typical second arrow shot, you may find that you have to play closer to the first arrow to create enough friction for the ball to hook to the pocket. Many are uncomfortable with this because of a fear of the gutter. Keep in mind that the gutter is still a good distance away, but the fear of throwing a gutter ball takes over and often leads to swing issues and drifting issues in the footwork. Either expand your comfort zone or add a ball that hooks more to your arsenal. Sometimes, you have to do both.

Early in my career, I did not always realize that the ball I was using was making me force the shot. I competed in a tournament and was vying for a spot on the TV show. On the last round of match play, the shot had extremely broken down and I kept moving deep inside to keep up with the changing oil line. My adjustments to move inside were working but, with just two games to go, I started bowling

Making Changes: Changing Balls

Some bowlers have different bowling balls so they do not have to move on the lane as much. That can be a perfectly fine strategy as long as it is effective. However, you typically will have to make some adjustments on the lane as well.

When the lane starts to hook where you are playing, you can try a weaker ball (one that hooks less) and stay in the same area. Or if the ball is not hooking enough where you like to play, you may consider using a stronger ball that hooks more.

For some, it's a drawback to have limited equipment for the conditions. The fewer balls you own, the more you have to adjust by moving your line to change your reaction on the lane. Sometimes, this is not enough to create the ideal reaction to score that another ball could provide.

badly. I could not strike. Hitting the pocket was getting harder. What I failed to realize was that the ball I was using was too strong and hooking too early for the conditions. Because I had been bowling well and was so close, in contention to make the cut to the top five, I thought I could just finish out with that ball. However, I couldn't score, and I missed the cut. A ball change would have given me a much better reaction and the chance to make it, with the potential to even win.

Although ball covers vary in how aggressive they are to create friction with the lane, you also can make adjustments to the surface of your ball to further alter its reaction on the lane. You cannot do this during competition, but you can have your ball's surface adjusted beforehand as you anticipate the lane conditions you will be bowling on. In effect, you can add more grit to the cover or smooth it out, to make it hook more or less. Chapter 9 addresses making surface adjustments to improve the performance of your ball for the conditions you bowl on in greater depth.

As your game improves, you need to expand your equipment arsenal to manage lane conditions. Just as golfers have more than one club, bowlers need more than one ball. Let necessity dictate.

EXPANDING YOUR COMFORT ZONE

Many bowlers try to adjust over the same arrow (namely, the second) and change angles by just moving their feet. Sometimes, however, the shot is not there but elsewhere on the lane. In some cases you may need to slightly adjust the trajectory of the shot to effectively play the oil line to get the best ball reaction. Learning to expand your comfort zone, play different parts of the lane, and adjust your line is important to being able to stay in form and score. You have to learn to follow and adjust to the oil line as it changes during play. And you have to learn to trust the shot and the fact that you have moved left or right for a reason (to find more or less friction) because the ball was either sliding or hooking too much.

When you practice, take time to play different parts of the lane. For example, practice lining up and playing the first arrow. Then, do the same for the second and third arrows. Take some time to play targets between the arrows as well. Keep in mind that you may not strike or even hit the pocket, depending on lane conditions. This is fine because neither one is your goal. Being able to line up to play different targets and areas on the lane and make good shots is your goal. You have to be willing to practice without the reward of scoring or even hitting the pocket. Focusing on your performance rather than on the outcome at the pins requires discipline.

Many bowlers are uncomfortable playing different parts of the lane. However, this definitely hinders their ability to score. Just as a golfer has to play within the fairway, the bowler needs to line up on the lane where the shot is to create the most room for error and still hit the pocket.

When she came out to coach with us at a PBI clinic, the great Carolyn Dorin-Ballard advised students, "If you really pay attention, the lane will tell you where to play. It will reveal itself to you so you can make the proper adjustments when you make good shots."

However, too many bowlers like to play where they like to play, which limits their adjustment range. Although you can try to drill equipment that will match the friction to the area that you like to play in, sometimes you just have to move to another part of the lane. You cannot always hover around the second arrow and move your feet to hit the second arrow from different angles. You have to be able to move and keep up with the changing oil line, especially when there is more play on the lane.

You may blame your execution when you are not bowling well, but the problem could be your strategy. You tighten up when you do not have a good reaction on the lanes. Remember, *you cannot outperform a bad ball reaction.* If you feel as though you are tight and fighting things, consider changing your strategy. It may be difficult to think about changing strategy when you aren't throwing the ball well, but it may make all the difference in your performance. When you are not scoring well, make a move!

If you continue to play the wrong part of the lane where you are comfortable but have no room for error, you will start forcing your reaction, which will tighten up your swing. Although you may realize that you are bowling badly, what you will likely fail to realize is that you are throwing it badly because you are not lined up properly on the lane to create some room at your target to still hit the pocket. Furthermore, adjusting may also involve making a ball change.

Once in match play while on tour, I looked down the lanes to watch a particular player who looked flawless to me. No wonder she was having a stellar year, in contention for Bowler of the Year honors.

Then it was my turn to bowl against her. Now, I got to witness her shots from behind. Although she was bowling great, I got to see how she created a little room for error and did not have to nail her target perfectly every time to hit the pocket. She was in the right part of the lane and had good ball reaction. Her lane play strategy was brilliant, giving her some room for error. I say *some,* because at the professional level, that is not much. However, it was an observation that I never forgot. Although execution is very important, the game is not about being

Making Changes:
Moving Outside Your Comfort Zone

Many bowlers have a limited area on the lane where they like to play. Often, it is the second arrow. And there is a reason for that. It is a comfortable angle to play, and on many house lane conditions, the oil line is typically right around the second arrow, or at least starts there.

However, the person oiling the lanes may set the machine for other than the second arrow. The oil line may be closer to the first arrow or between these arrows. Plus, the oil line changes based on any play on the lane. Not only does it break down during league play, but there's no guarantee that the lanes are freshly oiled when you show up to a bowling center to practice or bowl in league. Typically fresh oil is applied for league play, but you may play in a league that follows another league, with no time to reapply oil to the lanes. You may be bowling on lanes that have already been bowled on so the conditions are already somewhat broken down. Expect to have to adjust, and you will never be disappointed!

Because oil is clear and virtually invisible, it can be a tough sell to convince a bowler that the oil actually is controlling the ball. Rather than move, many bowlers stay in the same place and start forcing the ball so that it hooks more or less. If not done consciously, this often happens subconsciously. Furthermore, many bowlers do not move on the lane because doing so is out of their comfort zone. Sometimes it's easier to think that the problem is you rather than accept that you have to move out of your comfort zone to adjust, especially when you cannot even see the oil!

Moving Out

You have to trust yourself when you play closer to the gutter if you are going to move out. That can be daunting for many, but it may be where you get the best reaction. If there is too much oil where you are playing, no matter how well you throw the ball, it will not hook enough. Making that move out can make all the difference in hitting the pocket with ease.

When first learning to move out toward the first arrow, many bowlers pull the ball or drift away from the gutter, out of fear of throwing a gutter. It is just a matter of learning that the line is similar to that of playing the second arrow; there just happens to be a gutter nearby. Nothing will stop you but fear itself. By practicing playing the outside, you will become proficient at it. I recommend practicing there from time to time even if the shot isn't really there, just to get used to it.

To push my students who need it, I have them play between the gutter and the first arrow to help them overcome this fear and learn they can do it. Once they do, playing the first arrow doesn't seem so bad.

Moving In

If the ball is hooking too much, you need to move in toward the oil, away from friction. To do this, make *incremental* board moves as you adjust when the lane breaks down. Do not move your feet more than three boards without also moving your target in the same direction. Too often, I find a bowler drifts toward his target because of the way he lines up or especially the way he makes adjustments. To move inside, he might move his feet five boards but leave the target the same. Starting on board 25 and still targeting the second arrow will cause you to either miss your target or, more likely, drift toward it to hit it.

When you move in, you have to trust the ball to come back when you throw it at more of a trajectory out and away from the pocket. This can be especially challenging the deeper you move inside. Again, you cannot see the oil, so the tendency is to pull the ball to help it to the pocket. Remember that the reason you had to move is that the ball hooked too much where you were playing, because the oil disappeared. Therefore, trust that it will hook back!

This is particularly important when you are standing to the left of center on the approach. The pocket is on board 17.5, so when you are starting deeper than that on the lane, you need to open your shoulders and project the ball past board 17.5 to allow for it to hook back to 17.5. If you try to throw too directly, or pull the ball, the ball will hit high or even miss the pocket altogether toward the opposite pocket.

As you move in, turn your shoulders to line up your swing to your target. Keep in mind that you may have to also make an equipment adjustment to fine-tune your reaction so that your ball has the proper energy to strike from this angle!

perfect. In fact, you'd rather be loose than perfect. It is about playing smart enough to create some room so that you can relax your swing and get the ball off your hand cleanly enough to carry all 10 pins to strike.

I say in lessons, "When you are throwing the ball well but have a poor ball reaction on the lane, if you do not adjust, the only alternative is to start throwing the ball badly!"

SUMMARY

Scoring well is a function of making decent shots, lining up properly on the lane to hit the pocket, and picking up spares. Additionally, using the right equipment to create good ball reaction will further enhance your ability to score.

Bowling is not a game of perfection. It is a game of creating room for error. The smarter player does this. Take a bowler who averages 175 who plays the lane smarter versus a 190 bowler who plays the lane poorly. In a match, the smarter player will most likely win because of all the room for error at the target. Her swing will loosen up while the other bowler's will tighten up to force reaction. Remember, swing is king!

On that note, in league, make sure you are prepared for your warm-up shots so that you can gather as much information as possible to line up to the pocket. Show up early enough to have your equipment ready, with the proper amount of tape in each thumbhole for the current size of your thumb (don't wait until it swells up for the hole to fit). You need your best swing during practice to read the lanes quickly. If you have a hard time loosening up in so few shots, stretch or bowl practice games. Your goal is to line up to hit the pocket in the fewest shots possible with your best swing.

If your ball is not hooking enough, move out into the drier part of the lane. If it is hooking too much, move into the oil to get it to slide more. Learn to be comfortable playing different parts of the lane to be successful at scoring on various conditions and adjusting as the lane conditions break down. If the shot is at the first arrow and you play the second arrow, you will have to force your reaction. You may also consider a ball change as you adjust to the lane. *When you line up properly and get good ball reaction, you can stay in form and score.*

Let necessity dictate your equipment needs. If you are constantly forced to play either way over to the left or the right because of your ball reaction, consider getting another ball, one with a different amount of hook, to accommodate the conditions you bowl on.

Your adjustments are an intention to modify the shot to create a better ball reaction on the lane. Do not try to be perfect. Often a small adjustment will be enough to see a big difference in reaction. Trust yourself.

You'd rather be loose than perfect. Sometimes you have to question your strategy when your swing is not loose. If you play where you will have more room and you have a good ball reaction, you will loosen up, strike more, and score. At least you'll be in the pocket to leave spares that are easier to get, a big key to improving your average, and the focus of upcoming chapters.

Chapter 9

Advanced Lane Play

At one time, oil was applied to the lanes as a conditioner to protect the wood surface from the friction created by the ball. As lane surfaces have evolved, so has the purpose of applying oil to the lane. The oil is now applied in specific patterns as part of the sport to challenge a bowler's prowess to adjust strategically to play the lanes effectively and score. The way the oil conditioner is applied to the lanes has become known as the lane conditions.

The development of various lane oil patterns has led to an entire array of lane conditions that affect scoring, ranging from patterns that help recreational bowlers score better to more difficult patterns that challenge the competitive bowler's shot-making skills. Although the THS (typical house shot) lends itself to higher scores, the more difficult sport and challenge patterns create a greater challenge to score. Oil is applied more uniformly in volume across the lane (instead of the larger amount of oil in the middle like on a THS), creating a flatter lane condition. Because of this, they are often referred to as flatter patterns.

Sport and challenge conditions were actually created to restore the integrity to the relationship between the quality of shot making and scoring. A typical drop in average when playing the flatter conditions as compared to the THS can be about 25 pins!

The major difference between the THS and the sport and challenge patterns is the ratio between the units of oil in the middle of the lane and those on the outsides (figure 9.1). What makes the sport and challenge patterns more difficult is that the ratios are much smaller; that is, the oil is dispersed much flatter across the lane. You do not get the forgiveness that an imbalance of oil provides (as addressed in chapter 8). So, hitting the pocket on flatter patterns is much more difficult.

Whereas the ratio of oil from the inside to the outside of the lane on the THS can be 8:1 or 10:1, the flatter patterns can be as low as 2:1. These ratios are slightly different among the various patterns, but this will give you an idea

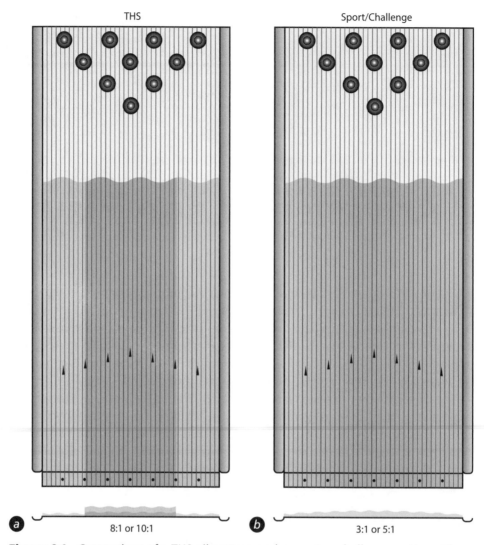

Figure 9.1 Comparison of a THS oil pattern and a sport or challenge pattern. The difference is the ratio of the amount of oil in the middle of the lane to the amount on the outsides of the lane.

of how much less oil there is in the middle of the lane in the flatter patterns as compared to the THS.

Without extra oil in the middle and friction to the outside to help your ball slide or hook more, the flatter patterns require a different strategy to play. You must more accurately deliver the ball at a consistent trajectory to a point down the lane, called the *breakpoint*.

You may not know exactly what the lane conditions will be ahead of time. However, you may be told whether you will be bowling on a THS or a sport or challenge condition. Your league or tournament association may or may not

LANE PATTERNS IN USE

Kegel Navigation Series patterns are created by this industry-leading lane conditioning machine manufacturer and are used voluntarily by some United States Bowling Congress–sanctioned leagues and in various competitive tournaments. The USBC uses custom-designed patterns specific for the centers used in their domestic competitions. The World Tenpin Bowling Association (WTBA) uses a bank of 12 standard patterns designed by the WTBA Technical Committee for its international competitions. (This is what Team USA competes in.) The Professional Bowlers Association (PBA) uses its own challenge patterns in its tournaments. Organizations often have themed names that they apply to their lane oil patterns. For example, Kegel commonly names its patterns after streets (e.g., Route 66), and the PBA names some of its after animals, such as the Shark and Scorpion. The WTBA uses world cities, such as Sydney and Los Angeles.

The defining characteristics of the various lane patterns include the distance and the volume of oil. These variables influence the angle to play and the type of equipment to use to hit the pocket. With less room to make a mistake, bowlers must rely on better shot making to make adjustments.

provide this information. Some special leagues and tournaments highlight these patterns and identify the type of patterns you will be competing on before you sign up. Other organizations choose not release this information.

If the specific pattern you will be bowling on is identified, the information on that pattern can be researched online; a lane graph may even be provided. Lane graphs are technical readouts that show the application of the oil on the lane. On tour, we were often given lane graphs. With all the information that a lane graph provides, we would pay particular attention to both the distance and the volume of the oil.

BREAKPOINT

On a sport condition, the oil is spread across the lane more evenly so the distance of the oil, or how much back end friction there is for the ball to hook, determines how far out to project the ball to hit the pocket. The projection point is referred to as the breakpoint.

The breakpoint (figure 9.2) is defined as the farthest point out the ball goes before it hooks back, or breaks, toward the pins. On flatter patterns, you need to be able to consistently project the ball to a breakpoint down the lane. Your ability to project the ball on a consistent trajectory will be tested! You will not have the room to miss your target and still hit the pocket as you would on the THS.

Let's look at how the distance of the oil affects reaction and your success in hitting the pocket on lanes that are oiled more flat. Finding the proper breakpoint is a function of knowing the distance of the oil. On a longer pattern, your breakpoint will be closer to the pocket. On a shorter pattern, your breakpoint will be farther from the pocket (figure 9.3).

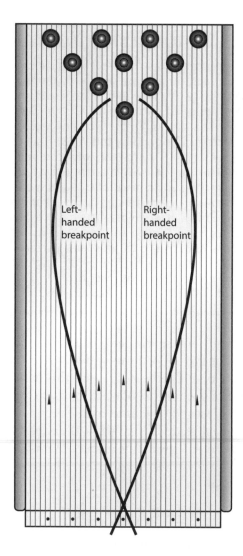

Figure 9.2 Breakpoint.

Consider that the lane is 60 feet and the pocket is on board 17.5. If the lane is oiled 40 feet, the ball has 20 feet of dry back end on which to hook. On a lane that is oiled 34 feet, the ball has 26 feet of lane on which to hook back to the pocket once it gets out of the oil. That is 6 more feet on which to hook. Therefore, in the first example of the longer oil, the breakpoint is closer in, or closer to the pocket, because the ball has less time to hook on the back end and reach the pocket. In the second example of the shorter oil, the breakpoint is farther out, away from the pocket, because the ball has more time to hook to the pocket. In either case, you need to project the ball to the proper breakpoint to allow for how much distance the ball has remaining to hook back to the pocket on the back end of the lane.

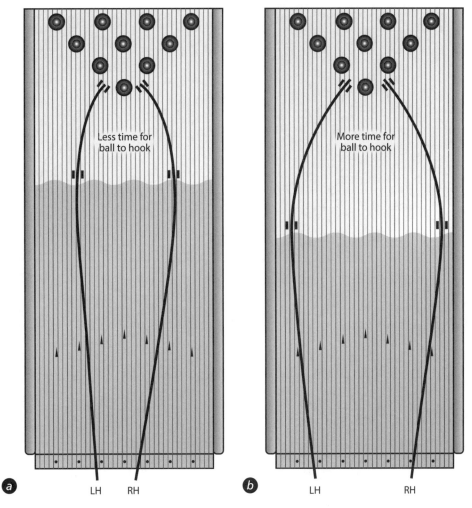

Figure 9.3 Long and short oil breakpoints: *(a)* a longer pattern with a breakpoint closer to the pocket; *(b)* a shorter pattern with a breakpoint farther from the pocket.

DETERMINING THE BREAKPOINT: THE RULE OF 31

An equation was developed to determine your approximate breakpoint, based on the distance of the oil pattern. You take the distance of length of the oil pattern and subtract the number 31 to figure out your approximate breakpoint at the end of that pattern. This is just an approximation. The surface of the lane itself, the type of oil applied, and the balls used during play will all affect the breakpoint.

For example, if the lane is oiled 42 feet, subtract 31 and your breakpoint will be around the 11 board, approximately 42 feet down the lane (the end of the oil pattern where your ball breaks; figure 9.4). You will have about a three-board

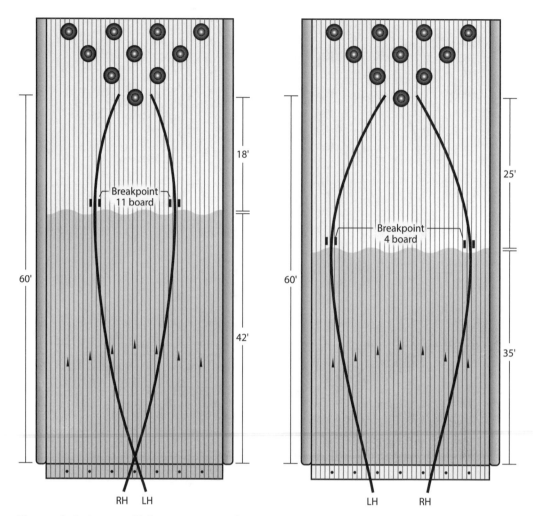

Figure 9.4 Longer 42-foot pattern and breakpoint for right-handed and left-handed bowlers.

Figure 9.5 Shorter 35-foot pattern and breakpoint for right-handed and left-handed bowlers.

area to hit at the breakpoint and still hit the pocket. So in this example, your breakpoint area is around the 10 to 12 board. Figure 9.5 shows a shorter 35-foot pattern and breakpoint.

Breakpoint and the Pocket

On a flatter oil pattern, you will hit the pocket when you hit the breakpoint, and you will miss the pocket when you miss the breakpoint. The direction you miss your target will also be the same direction you miss the pocket. If you miss your target right, it will miss the pocket to the right. If you miss left, your ball will go left. *Note:* This is unlike the THS, where you can miss your target to the outside and it actually hooks back to the pocket! On flatter patterns, the way you miss the pocket is a true reflection of how you missed your target.

If you miss the pocket to the light side, you missed your breakpoint to the outside (figure 9.6). If you miss the pocket to the high side, you missed your breakpoint to the inside (figure 9.7). Therefore, you have to adjust your angle to get the ball into the breakpoint, rather than move on the lane as if are trying to find more or less friction on either side of a heavy oil line like on the THS.

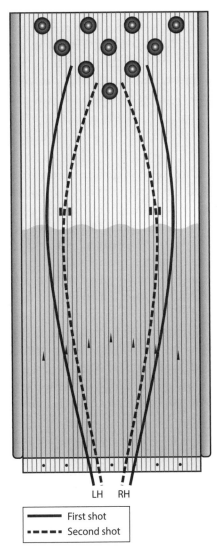

LH   RH

	First shot
	Second shot

Figure 9.6 Missing to the outside and angle adjustment.

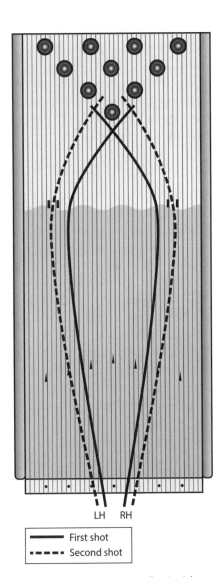

LH   RH

	First shot
	Second shot

Figure 9.7 Missing to the inside and angle adjustment.

Opposite Reactions

On the THS, you could miss your target to the outside; however, with all the friction out there, your inaccuracy can still land you in the pocket, or you could even hit high. Similarly, if you pull your shot inside, the ball can actually slide more and hit the pocket light.

Such is not the case on sport patterns. On a flatter pattern, your ball reacts to more truly reflect the direction you miss your target. The direction you miss your target is also the direction you miss the pocket. Again, these conditions were created to give you a truer read on your consistency and accuracy, or perhaps your inconsistency and inaccuracy.

Because the ways you miss your target in both of these scenarios are so diametrically opposed, your adjustments will be different on the THS than on sport patterns. Because of this, those who have bowled on the THS for years will find their moves on the sport patterns counterintuitive, seemingly against their gut instinct compared to how they learned to move based on the way the ball missed the pocket.

Opposite Adjustments

When the ball hits the pocket light (or altogether misses it in that direction) on a flatter pattern, realize that the ball simply missed the breakpoint to the outside. Therefore, the move would be to adjust your angle to bring your breakpoint in. On the THS, you would be light because the ball slid too much in the heavy oil that's in the middle of the lane, so you would make the opposite adjustment to move to the outside and find more friction for the ball to hook. (See chapter 8.)

Conversely, if the ball hit high, or heavy on the headpin, or missed the headpin completely to the other side, then the ball missed inside the breakpoint. Therefore, the move would be to adjust your angle to move your breakpoint out. On the THS, when the ball hits high, you would typically move in toward the middle to find more oil to make the ball slide more. On a flatter lane pattern, the correct adjustment involves adjusting the angle of your trajectory to adjust the breakpoint, rather than adjusting to find more or less oil on either side of an oil line, as you would on the THS. On flatter patterns, throwing a hook becomes about adjusting your angle to hit your breakpoint.

Again, the breakpoint will be closer to the pocket when the lane is oiled a longer distance, and farther from the pocket when the lane is oiled a shorter distance. The adjustment is to modify your breakpoint, whether you have to make a better shot or slightly adjust your angle by moving on the lane.

You may also have to make a ball change to properly adjust your reaction on the lane. If the ball is hooking too early, you may need to throw a weaker or shinier ball to get it to skid longer. Or, if the ball is sliding too long, change to a stronger, duller ball to create more friction and earlier hook on the lane.

Finally, you may alter your release to get the ball to hook sooner or slide longer. If you need the ball to hook sooner, stay behind it more to create a stronger roll through the ball. If you need more length, create more side roll to get the ball to skid down the lane. If the lane is really dry and the ball is just hooking too much to get it to the breakpoint, try a weaker wrist position to cut down the hook. Often staying behind the ball longer will get the ball to roll sooner in the midlane to create more room at the target to hit the pocket. (See the section Multiple Releases for Various Lane Conditions in chapter 7.)

LINING UP

Often, bowlers stand too far in or too far out to hit the breakpoint. Understanding your lay-down point, or where you set down the ball at the foul line, will help you line up better to project your ball to the desired breakpoint.

Lay-Down Point

The lay-down point (figure 9.8) is the board on the lane on which you deliver the ball at the foul line. It is the distance from your ankle to the center of the ball. Because the ball is just under 9 inches wide, it is about four and a half or five boards from the outside of the ball to the center of the ball. (A board is 1 inch.) If you are 1 inch from your ankle at release, add that to 5 and you would then be laying the ball down approximately six boards to the right (right-handed) or left (left-handed) of where you slide (figure 9.9). For example, if you are close to your ankle and the inside of your slide foot ends on board 20, you would be laying the ball down on approximately board 14.

Incidentally, professionals line up with the inside of the slide foot in the stance because it is the closest point from which the ball is released. Releasing the ball close to the ankle plays a major role in leverage and accuracy. In a properly aligned swing, you release the ball 1 or 2 inches from your ankle.

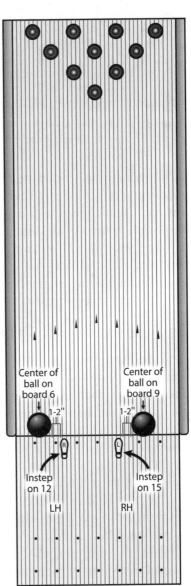

Figure 9.8 Lay-down point.

Figure 9.9   The lay-down point is approximately six boards from where you slide: *(a)* right-handed; *(b)* left-handed.

Knowing your lay-down point is instrumental when initially lining up to hit a desired breakpoint to avoid making an obvious mistake where to stand on the approach. I have seen many bowlers who know that their breakpoint down the lane is board 10 but stand on 15 to hit it. The problem is that they would be laying down the ball on approximately board 9, trying to project the ball out to a breakpoint of 10 even though the 10 board is inside the 9 board! This just doesn't make sense unless they plan to make a bad shot and pull the ball every time instead of projecting the ball when throwing a hook.

Lay-Down Point: Target to Breakpoint

Because bowlers are so used to trying to play up an oil line, many line up improperly from the start on flatter patterns. When the ball does not hook on the THS, the strategy is always to move out into the dry part of the lane. On flatter patterns, however, that reaction is not there.

Strategically use your lay-down point as you consider where to target at the arrows to then project the ball toward your breakpoint. You do not have to be perfect from the start, just in the ballpark so you can make adjustments. For example, if the pattern is 44 feet, using the rule of 31, your approximate breakpoint would be at about the 13 board. Let's say you have a small arc. Maybe you are going to project the ball three boards to your breakpoint. At the arrows, your target would have to be inside the breakpoint to allow for this projection. If you are going to swing the ball three boards to the breakpoint, your target might be around the 16 board at the arrows.

To determine where to slide (figure 9.10), consider your lay-down point to finish the math. If your lay-down point is six boards from your ankle, add six boards from your target (the 16 board), which puts you at the 22 board. If you

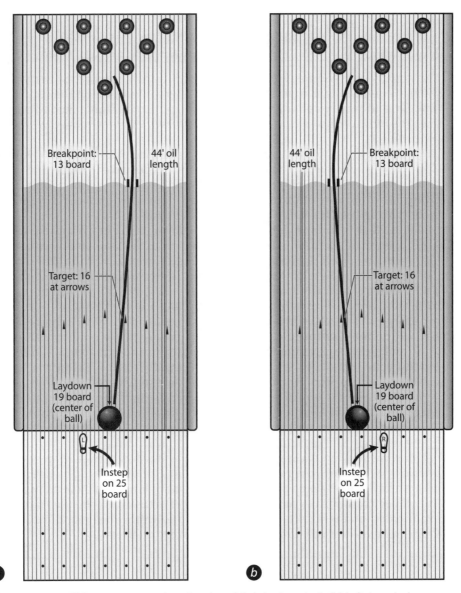

Figure 9.10 Slide to target to breakpoint: *(a)* right-handed; *(b)* left-handed.

were playing straight down the lane, you would slide on board 22. But, to finish the calculation, remember that you are projecting the ball from your target to the breakpoint, about three boards in our example. You have to allow for those three boards of projection to determine where to slide to create the proper angle from your lay-down point to your target. Adding those three boards would put you at approximately the 25 board in the stance. This is an imperfect approximation due to the actual dimension of the lane and other variables. The distance you are from your ankle, your release, the ball you use, and your speed will all affect this calculation.

Making Changes: Adjusting to Sport and Challenge Lane Conditions

The adjustments you need to make on a sport and challenge pattern may seem counterintuitive, especially if you are used to bowling on the THS. You now have to learn to adjust to hit a breakpoint rather than adjust to an oil line. The moves to adjust to an oil line are different from the moves to hit the proper breakpoint.

Further complicating matters is that you cannot see the oil pattern to know what you are bowling on. You have only the shots you make to determine how to make adjustments to play the lane. Although you need to have a loose arm swing, it is difficult to relax your swing simply because you have less room for error than on the THS. It can become a vicious cycle.

Ball reaction is huge on flatter patterns. Being able to get the ball into a roll at the right time is critical to create room for error at the target for room to still hit the pocket. It is easy to blame yourself when strategy might be the culprit.

You will need a lot of patience to bowl on these conditions. You must adjust your mentality to scoring conditions. For example, when you are on a long oil pattern and have to play a line that is tight (close) to the pocket, you may experience deflection, making it hard to carry when the ball hits the pocket. This will be the case for you and just about everyone else! Expect to have to grind and pick up spares until the shot opens up. In addition to this, you must expand your comfort zones to be able to play different areas of the lane. When you line up properly and get good ball reaction, that is when you score.

When it comes to equipment, let necessity dictate. If you constantly don't have enough reaction to get to the pocket on heavy oil or your ball hooks too much on drier, flatter patterns, you may need to develop your arsenal, like a golfer who has different clubs in the bag.

What further complicates matters is that as bowlers are learning how to bowl on flat patterns, their varied and often uninformed strategies affect the way the lane breaks down and can make the conditions even more difficult as the oil pattern becomes spottier. Professionals who are more educated and experienced on these patterns tend to break down the lane more uniformly than amateurs who are just learning how to play on them.

Given lane oil length and all the variables that affect the breakpoint itself, you need to get in the ballpark and fine-tune adjustments from there. Use your reaction on the lane to guide your moves from this point. Again, your goal is to get lined up in as few shots as possible; this serves as a way to start out close.

EQUIPMENT AND VOLUME OF OIL

Whereas the *distance* of the oil determines the breakpoint on flatter patterns, the *volume* of oil dictates what type of ball to use. The cover and type of core of a bowling ball create approximately 75 percent of its reaction. Pin placement, or the position of the core in relation to your track, fine-tunes the ball's reaction. Therefore, having the proper ball, one with the right cover and core, to begin with is far more important than having the right pin position, but in the totally wrong ball for the conditions.

Because this is largely a game of managing friction to get the ball to hit the pins with the right energy to strike, the cover plays the most significant role in ball reaction.

Whereas you adjust your angle by moving from side to side on the lane, you adjust the distance at which the ball hooks and the shape of the hook with your equipment and your release. In some cases, you can also manipulate your speed, but that takes a lot of practice to be able to do it consistently. As I always say, even some professionals do not master speed control. Therefore, you may consider adjusting your speed as a last resort, especially if you have any timing or swing issues that may be further aggravated by any attempt to adjust your speed.

If you are on a heavy volume of oil, use a stronger cover to cut through the oil and get the ball to hook sooner rather than slide too much. If you are on a light volume of oil, use a weaker cover, perhaps a pearlized cover, to get the ball to skid long enough before it hooks.

In a stronger, more aggressive cover, the coverstock is typically solid. This creates more friction on the lane to grab the lane sooner. Balls that slide more and react later on the lane are more pearlized. Pearlized balls skid longer and save reaction for the back end. Furthermore, some pearlized balls are weaker than others in overall hook to match up properly to lane conditions. Neither is necessarily better all the time. The volume of oil and the friction created by the ball on the lane determine if the ball will hook at the proper distance.

There are different surfaces on bowling balls, just as there are different tires for vehicles. Some tires have a lot of tread, and others have less; you need to match the surface to conditions. You would not want to use tractor tires with chains on dry pavement. Nor would you want to use bald tires on slick conditions. So it is with bowling balls and lane conditions.

Again, bowling is a game of managing friction to get the ball to hit the pocket with the proper energy to strike. Therefore, given the conditions, you need to make adjustments to the cover of your ball as necessary. These are called ball surface adjustments.

Surface adjustments are made to further manipulate your ball's reaction to improve your scoring. Adjusting the surface of your ball is a huge factor in creating the best ball reaction for the conditions. Again, bowling is about properly managing the friction the ball makes with the lane to achieve the best reaction to strike.

When I was bowling on tour, making surface adjustments to bowling balls was always the key to scoring. We traveled with bowling ball spinners and all the abrasives needed to adjust bowling ball surfaces between and before each block of bowling. We could do this ahead of time, including during warm-up practice, but not during play. We rarely used bowling balls the way they came out of the box from the factory. Adjusting the surface is standard practice for fine-tuning performance.

Making Changes: Adjusting the Ball Surface

Altering the surface of the ball (figure 9.11) helps you fine-tune its reaction on the lane. The ball comes from the factory with a certain finish on the cover, but you can get it to hook earlier or skid longer by adjusting the surface, sanding it with an abrasive. Abralon pads have become the chosen abrasives and range from 180 to 4000 grit. Most commonly used are 1000 to 4000. Sanding the ball with a lower grit pad will get it to react (hook) sooner, and therefore be smoother on the back end. Sanding it with a higher grit pad (4000) will smooth out the surface and get it to skid down the lane and react later. A good pro shop will be able to adjust the surface of your ball.

You also can shine a ball's surface with polish to get it to skid the longest, which is effective on dry lanes. The proper surface adjustment fine-tunes your reaction for the conditions you are bowling on.

Adjusting the surface is best done on a ball spinner. This is a standard piece of equipment in the pro shop, and so are various grit Abralon pads. Some bowlers who own multiple bowling balls invest in their own ball spinners and pads, because it makes economical sense for all the adjusting they do, and it is convenient. Nevertheless, if you are in your warm-up practice in league or in a tournament, you have until the first shot of competition to have the surface altered. You may run into the pro shop and have them sand your ball with the appropriate grit to achieve the reaction you need.

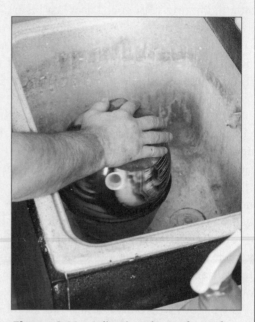

Figure 9.11 Adjusting the surface of the ball.

You may also find that you like a ball at a certain grit. With use, however, the surface will change. When you notice that the reaction is compromised, it's time to have that surface refreshed with that grit Abralon pad to restore performance.

You must sand the entire ball. Again, you cannot sand a ball during competition, once scoring begins. You can, however, adjust it during practice or warm-ups. Be sure to check the rules that govern the league or tournament.

To sand the ball, with the ball in the spinner and the motor on, spray the ball with water using a spray water bottle, and then apply even pressure with the Abralon pad. Continue to spray as you sand the ball. Turn the motor off, turn the ball to expose the other side, and repeat. To polish the ball, squirt the polish on the ball before you turn the spinner on, cover it with a dry towel, turn the spinner on, and then evenly apply the polish with the towel. Repeat on the other side of the ball.

During breaks, we would adjust the surfaces of the balls we thought we would be using for the next block of games. During warm-ups to competition, all of the bowling ball company representatives would be behind us, ready to adjust any of our surfaces as we thought necessary, to finish fine-tuning our ball reaction as we saw fit.

If the ball was sliding a little too much, we would adjust the surface with a more abrasive pad to create more friction so the ball would grab sooner. If we wanted it to slide more, we would use a less abrasive pad to smooth out the finish and get the ball to skid more. We just had to remember how we had last prepared our surfaces to be able to advise on what we needed to make the ball roll sooner or later. We had only about 10 minutes to do this during warm-ups; altering the surface this way during competition is against the rules.

BALL REACTION

When you are not hitting the pocket because of poor ball reaction, usually it is because you are not controlling the midlane. The key is to note when the ball changes direction. Too many bowlers look for the backend reaction, thinking it will solve their issue, but discovering *when* the ball hooks really is the key.

You will typically miss the pocket light when the ball does not hook soon enough in the midlane (figure 9.12). It might appear as though your ball is not hooking enough on the back end; however, more likely it is not hooking early enough to change direction sooner in the midlane to make its way earlier toward the pocket.

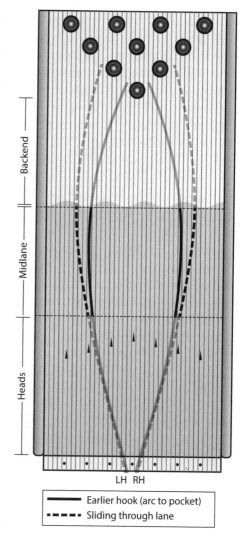

Figure 9.12 Midlane hook versus sliding.

Manipulating Release

Because controlling the midlane is the key, how you manipulate your release is equally important. As with ball surface, more back end reaction is not always the solution.

When a ball is not finishing, the problem is often that it slid too long. Although you see that the ball is not hooking on the back end, it is likely that it did not hook soon enough. If you try to turn the ball more to create more hook on the back end, you will only perpetuate the problem by further delaying your ball's reaction.

Because you really need to get the ball to roll sooner to change direction to the pocket earlier on the lane, you actually need to stay behind it longer to create more forward roll. More roll and a stronger cover with more friction are the key here, not a ball with more back end or putting more turn on it at release. Trying to create more backend to hook a lane that is not hooking much does not produce the desired results.

A ball that slides too long is a common problem. Conversely, you actually could be in a situation in which your ball is too strong for the conditions. In this case, the ball is using its energy way too soon for the amount of oil on the lane, causing it to start hooking and lose so much energy that it has nothing left to give on the back end of the lane. This is called *roll-out*.

Sometimes detecting whether the ball is sliding too long or rolling out early is more easily determined when you totally miss the pocket one way or another. However, when you are in the pocket and you are not carrying, it is not always easy to tell the difference between a ball that is sliding too long or one that is rolling out. In the first case, the ball does not use up its energy soon enough; in the latter case, it uses up its energy too soon, or rolls out and just dies at the pins. In either case, the ball's energy is just not right to strike. You can change the ball or your release to fine-tune the ball's reaction into the pocket.

Some bowlers are limited by the equipment they have to conquer conditions. You may need a stronger ball to get into a roll sooner to handle more oil. Or, you may need a weaker ball to handle the lighter volume of oil on the lane, adjust to lanes that break down quickly, or simply stay in an area you like to play.

If you do not have additional equipment, you have to make other adjustments, such as in your release or perhaps your speed to do the best you can to strike. However, be advised that release adjustments, and especially speed adjustments, are advanced concepts that are not easily mastered. When striking becomes difficult, it is a sign that you need more equipment to handle the conditions you are bowling on. You may need to develop your main release or multiple releases to effectively change the ball's reaction on the lane.

You have to play within your means, and I always say, "Let necessity dictate." If you are finding that you are frequently on a condition that you are not able to score well on, that is a sign that you need another ball. At that point, discuss this need with a reputable pro shop operator to determine how to fit another piece of equipment into your arsenal.

Cover and Core

Bowling is a game of managing friction when it comes to lane play. The cover of the ball, both the composition of the material and the preparation of the surface, is the most influential variable affecting how it rolls. In addition, the type of weight block, or core, inside the ball also influences its dynamics as it rolls down the lane. The cover and the core of the ball together determine the majority of the ball's reaction.

The two basic types of cores are symmetrical and asymmetrical. A ball with a balanced, symmetrical core has a smoother, more predictable roll. A ball with an imbalanced, asymmetrical core creates more overall hook on the lane.

It may seem that all bowlers would want an asymmetrical core for more hook, but that is not necessarily the case. Bowlers who already have a high revolution rate in their release may not want the extra reaction of a ball with an asymmetrical core. Bowlers with low ball speed may not want too much reaction either, unless the lane is heavily oiled.

The radius of gyration (RG) is a number to explain how the mass of the weight block is distributed inside the ball. RG ratings typically range from 2.48 to 2.60. The lower the number is, the more the mass is distributed toward the center and the earlier the core will get into its roll. The higher the number is, the more the mass is distributed toward the outside (or cover) and the later the core begins to roll. Sometimes balls are referred to as having shorter, center-heavy cores (low RG) or taller, cover-heavy cores (high RG).

The best analogy to understand symmetrical and asymmetrical balls is that of an ice skater who brings her arms in toward her body to spin faster; then extends them away from her body to slow down or delay the spin.

Using a ball with a lower RG makes sense when the lane is oily because it will get into a roll sooner, helping the ball to grab and cut through the oil. Using a ball with a higher RG makes sense on medium to dry lanes, when you need length to get the ball down the lane.

Given all of the variables involved, including release, ball speed, and lane conditions, consult with your pro shop professional, who can match you up with the right type of ball with the proper drilling.

Axis Point

Although the composition of the ball itself, its cover and core, has the most influence on the way it reacts, its reaction can further be fine-tuned by where the holes are drilled in relation to the weight block. Laying a ball out to put the holes in a strategic spot for the way you release the ball will create specific dynamics to the core's reaction to influence its roll down the lane. Identifying your axis point of rotation is key.

The pin on the ball is the top of the weight block inside (figure 9.13). It provides the ball driller with clear information about the position of the weight block within the ball so he can put it in a strategic position in relation to your axis point to achieve the desired reaction for the way you bowl. The pin is typically positioned

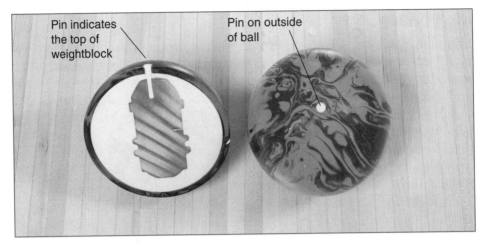

Figure 9.13 The pin and weight block inside the ball.

a calculated number of inches from your axis point to influence the way the ball rolls for your release.

Every ball released rotates on an axis. The track is the part of the ball that actually touches the lane as it rolls. Identifying the track is essential to finding the axis point of rotation (figure 9.14), which is an imaginary line perpendicular to the track around which a bowling ball rotates during its path down the lane. The axis is a measurement of the point that the ball rolls around going down the lane.

The axis point can be determined by a qualified pro shop operator,

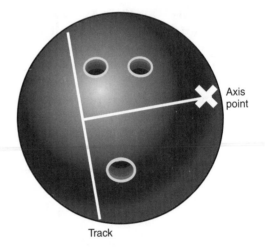

Figure 9.14 The track of the ball in relation to the axis point of rotation.

who uses this information as a guide when drilling equipment. Once located, it is defined using coordinates from the center of your grip. Once found, it is documented and used to lay out your new bowling ball and position the holes strategically to achieve a precise ball reaction on the lane. Keep in mind that you can change the layout of a ball by plugging it up and having it redrilled to create a more desirable reaction.

Knowing your axis point is not necessarily important when laying out your first entry-level performance ball. However, when you begin to develop your arsenal to fine-tune your performance, you will want your equipment laid out with reference to your unique axis point. If your pro shop technician downplays the relevance of this, consider finding a more qualified technician.

Pin Up or Down

Once the position of the weight block is determined in relation to your axis point, the height of the pin must be considered when laying out the ball. The height of the pin has a secondary influence on ball dynamics.

When the pin is up (figure 9.15a), or above the finger holes, the ball gets more length going down the lane before it reacts and hooks toward the pins. Because of this stored energy, the reaction is a little stronger at the breakpoint. Use a ball with the pin up when the front of the lane is hooking to create more length and a more angular back end reaction into the pins.

When the pin is down (figure 9.15b), or below the finger holes, the ball rolls sooner and has a smoother reaction at the breakpoint. Use this drilling when you want the ball to roll sooner and be smoother on the back end. These are very fine adjustments. Remember, the cover and core are the biggest factors that determine a ball's reaction on the lane. These are simply guidelines. For further guidance, ask a qualified professional to individualize a strategic plan for you.

As you develop your game and become more competitive, your equipment arsenal will begin to play a more significant role in your performance. When you bowl in multiple leagues, leagues with challenge conditions, or tournaments, you will need to develop your equipment to strategically adapt to those conditions. Because you cannot change your ball surface during play, sometimes you will need multiple balls with various surfaces prepared to conquer the conditions.

In golf, clubs get the ball to travel different distances; in bowling, balls hook earlier or later on the lane. Just as a golfer has multiple clubs to hit various distances, competitive bowlers need multiple bowling balls to hook differently and at different distances on the lane, to conquer various lane conditions and the way they break down during play.

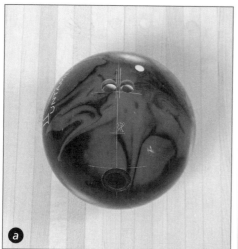 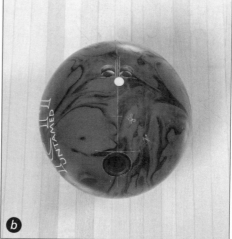

Figure 9.15 *(a)* Pin up. *(b)* Pin down.

SUMMARY

When you hook the ball, adjusting to the lane conditions is key. On the THS, your goal is to find and play the oil line. However, on sport patterns, in which the ratio of oil in the middle to oil on the outsides of the lane is much lower, the key is to be more accurate and project the ball to the proper breakpoint to hit the pocket consistently. A better swing will create a consistent trajectory toward the target to hit the breakpoint.

The longer the oil is, the closer to the pocket you will play. The shorter the oil is, the farther out your breakpoint will be from the pocket. Remember the rule of 31. If the lane is oiled 44 feet, your approximate breakpoint will be the 13 board. Consider your lay-down point to strategically find a starting position on the approach to get into the proper part of the lane; then fine-tune your adjustments from there.

Although the primary key to adjusting to the lane is to make a decent shot, develop your equipment arsenal as necessary to better adapt to and conquer lane conditions. Sometimes you will need a stronger ball to create more reaction; other times you will need a weaker ball to manage the friction. Developing the skill to modify your release will help you tweak your ball reaction on the lanes.

Bowling is a game of friction. The more friction there is on the lanes, the less friction you need on the ball. The less friction there is on the lane, the more friction you need on the ball, to cut through the oil. Adjusting your bowling ball surfaces is the key to managing the friction and the ball's reaction on the lane to create more room for error for your swing.

Do not forget to adjust your mentality for the scoring conditions. It is not uncommon to average 25 pins less on a difficult sport pattern as compared to the THS. Because more bowlers are just learning how to play on these conditions, the way the lanes break down can make conditions even tougher.

Always strive to stay around the pocket, especially on tougher conditions, to leave spares you can pick up. Making spares is the key and is the focus of the next two chapters.

Chapter 10

Spare Shooting

Good spare shooting is critical to good scoring. Making spares is the key to improving your average or maintaining a higher average. Good spare shooting consists of two variables: making good shots and playing the proper angles. Shooting cross-lane creates more room for error than shooting straight at the spare directly down the lane. This will lead to an increased percentage of spare conversions without requiring you to be perfectly accurate.

To be a consistent spare shooter, you must have a system for changing your angles to make spares. Not only will a systematic method help you make more spares, but also, if you miss one, you will be able to make a more calculated adjustment to pick it up the next time.

A good strategy for picking up spares is to follow a four-step process:

1. Identify the pin(s).
2. Calculate the angle adjustments.
3. Align your shoulders.
4. Make a good shot.

Although no adjustments are set in stone, it is important to be systematic in calculating them. This will help you to make spares more often and to strategically recalculate when you miss one. Following a process will help you determine why you missed a spare (i.e., whether it was execution or angle). In this chapter the spare system is presented separately for right-handed and left-handed bowlers.

IDENTIFYING THE PINS

The first step is to identify the pin(s). You need to know which pins are standing to be able to calculate what you are shooting at. Learn to memorize the pins by their numbers (figure 10.1). They are numbered from front to back, left to right.

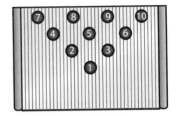

Figure 10.1 Pin numbers.

CALCULATING ANGLE ADJUSTMENTS

You need to know your pin numbers so you can identify which ones you are shooting at and calculate the proper adjustment. To get to know your pins by heart, practice naming the pins that other bowlers leave before they shoot at the spare. A real bowler always names the pins from lowest to highest in number. For example, the 2-4-5 versus the 4-2-5. You will get to know them in no time!

Once you identify the pins and which side they are on, you can calculate the proper adjustment to make the spare.

Spares are divided into left-side spares (pins standing to the left of the headpin; figure 10.2a) and right-side spares (pins to the right of the headpin; figure 10.2b). The 1 and 5 pins are not noted on either side because you will throw your strike ball to pick them up.

Right-handed bowlers will make adjustments off their strike line to shoot spares on the left side, and left-handed bowlers will make adjustments to shoot spares on the right side. Right-handers will shoot spares on the right cross-lane from the left side of the approach, and left-handers will shoot spares on the left from the right of the approach.

The proper adjustment for where to stand and target follow for both right- and left-handers are presented in more detail later in the chapter.

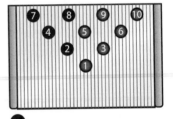

a

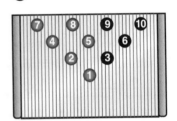

b

Figure 10.2 *(a)* Left-side spares; *(b)* right-side spares.

ALIGNING THE SHOULDERS TO YOUR TARGET LINE

Because you always want your arm to swing at a 90-degree angle to your shoulders, it is important to adjust the shoulders to face your new target line (figure 10.3). This will ensure that you maintain the same execution. Adjusting the shoulders toward the pins at which you are shooting is the key to a consistent arm swing from shot to shot and picking up your spares.

On the same note, you have to adjust the amount you turn your shoulders based on your ball reaction. If the ball hooks a lot, do not turn your shoulders as much (figure 10.4a). If it hooks very little, turn your shoulders more directly at the spare (figure 10.4b).

Make sure that you adjust your shoulders for the spare angle. You want to set up your swing so you can follow through at a 90-degree angle, so it is up to your shoulders to create that line. Because you do not want to change your swing, make sure it lines up properly with the target by adjusting your shoulders.

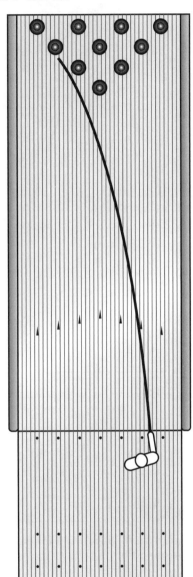

Figure 10.3 Aligning the shoulders to the target line.

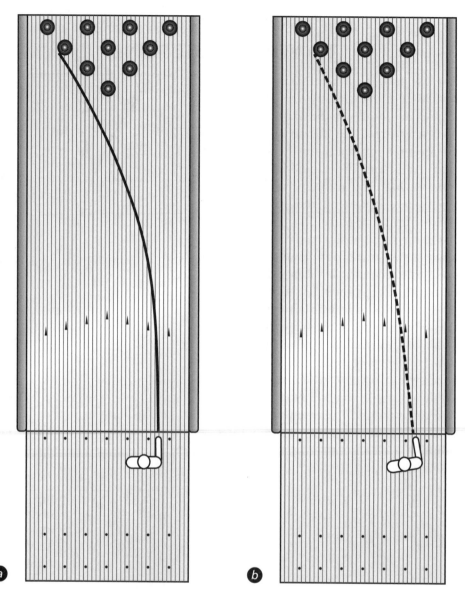

Figure 10.4 Shoulder alignment based on ball reaction: *(a)* ball hooks a lot; *(b)* ball hooks a little.

MAKING A GOOD SHOT

Once you identify the pins, make the proper adjustment, and turn your shoulders, you are prepared to make the spare. Now you just need to make a good shot, using the same mechanics you used on the strike ball. You are simply executing from a different angle.

Keep it simple. If you follow the system, not only will you make more spares, but you also will be able to troubleshoot when you miss them. Make just one more spare each game and improve your average 10 pins!

RIGHT-HANDED BOWLER

In this section, spares are divided into left-side and right-side spares, depending on which side of the headpin the pins are left standing. For spares on the left, a right-handed bowler shoots cross-lane, adjusting the feet to the right from the strike line. For spares on the right, a right-handed bowler also shoots cross-lane but from the left side of the approach. Single-pin spares are addressed first, followed by multiple-pin spares.

Left-handed bowlers may skip this section and go directly to the section for left-handed bowlers that follows.

Single-Pin Spares

For pins on the left, in this basic 3-6-9 spare system, you move to the right on the approach from your strike position. That is, note where you stand and target for your strike ball and adjust your angle for these spares from your strike line (figure 10.5). You will move your feet to the right and maintain your strike target. How much you move your feet to the right depends on how far over the pin is to the left. *Note:* your strike line (and target) may differ from the target line used in the illustrations. Be sure to adjust from your strike line.

For pins on the right side, in the original 3-6-9 spare system, a right-handed bowler was traditionally taught to move left, incrementally from the strike line. However, we will depart from that strategy and develop an independent position for the corner pin (10 pin) and make the remaining adjustments from there for the rest of the pins on the right side.

This is important to do because there is an optimal angle for shooting the 10 pin to gain the most room for error to pick up the spare. If you simply move to the left a designated number of boards from your strike line (12 boards was suggested in the original system),

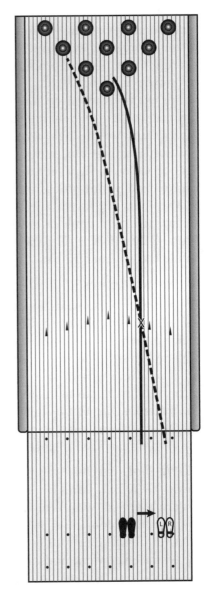

Figure 10.5 A right-handed bowler moves to the right from the strike position to pick up a left-side spare.

often you will not end up at the optimal angle to shoot the 10 pin. This is especially true when you are playing farther right on the lane for your strike ball.

Left-Side Spares: 2/8, 4, and 7 Pins

To pick up spares on the left, adjust your angle off your strike line. From your strike position in the stance, move your feet to the right, using the same basic strike target, thereby adjusting your angle toward the spare. In shooting cross-lane, the more left the pin is, the more right you should move.

There are three columns of pins left of center. The first is the 2/8 pins, then the 4 pin, and then the 7 pin. Taken from the basic 3-6-9 spare system, a good starting point is to move your feet to the right in three-board increments per column of pins. So you will move approximately three, six, or nine boards to the right, depending on how far left the pin is (figure 10.6).

For example, when you leave the 2 or 8 pin, you would move your feet approximately three boards to the right from your strike position. For the 4 pin, move approximately six boards to the right. For the 7 pin, move approximately nine boards to the right.

Keeping your target area virtually the same, angle your shoulders toward the target line and then make a good shot much as you would throw your strike shot.

Right-Side Spares

For the right-side spares, you must first establish your angle for the 10-pin shot. To pick up the remaining spares on the right, adjust your angle off your 10-pin shot. The other pins on the right side of the lane can be broken down into two columns based on their relationship to the 10 pin. For these spares, you move your feet to the right from the 10-pin shot, keeping the 10-pin target.

10-Pin Shot To create the optimal angle to shoot the 10 pin, stand far left on approximately board 35, with your target between the third and fourth arrows at about the 17 or 18 board (figure 10.7). (Remember, a right-handed bowler counts the arrows from right to left on the lane.) Although there is

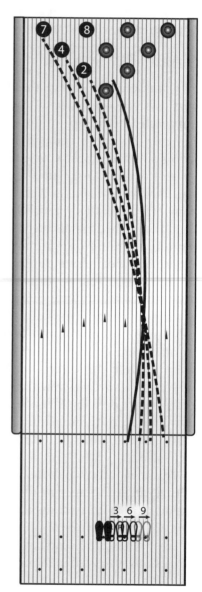

Figure 10.6 Converting the left-side spares, right-handed bowler: 2- or 8-pin spare, 4-pin spare, and 7-pin spare.

always a dot on board 35 at the foul line, there may not be a dot on board 35 at the beginning of the approach.

Turn your shoulders to face the pin. Walk straight to the foul line, with your shoulders open, to end on the same board you started on to maintain your angle.

Improving your the corner pin shot is addressed in more detail later in this chapter in the section Troubleshooting the Corner Pin Shot.

6 Pin and 3/9 Pins There are two columns of pins to the left of the 10 pin: the 6 pin and the 3/9 pins. When shooting at these pins, keep the same target as for the 10 pin (between the third and fourth arrows; figure 10.8).

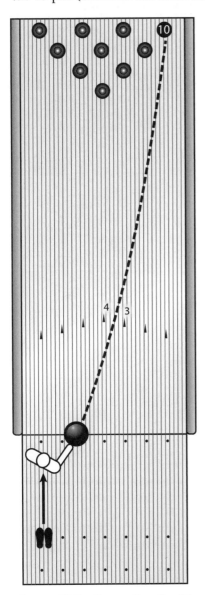

Figure 10.7 Converting the 10-pin spare, right-handed bowler.

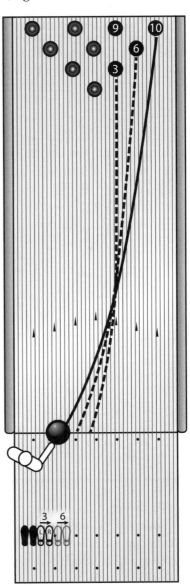

Figure 10.8 Converting the 6-pin spare and the 3- or 9-pin spare, right-handed bowler.

OPTIONAL 3-PIN SHOT FOR A RIGHT-HANDED BOWLER

Some right-handed bowlers see the 3 pin (or 9 pin) and view it close to a pocket shot and so choose to shoot it from the strike line. That is certainly an option. If you move from your strike line to shoot it, you will move left with your feet and keep your target the same (figure 10.9). Move three to five boards left. It may be as many as five boards, depending on conditions, because when you move left and throw a hook, your ball will swing out to the dry area where there is more friction, and you have to allow for how much it will hook.

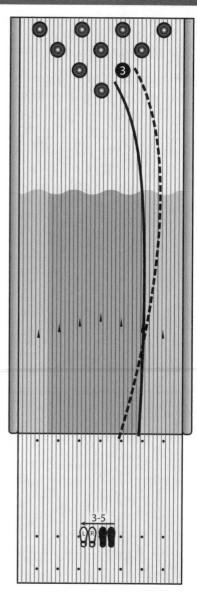

Figure 10.9 Moving from the strike line to hook at the 3 pin, right-handed bowler.

For the 6 pin, move your feet three boards to the right from where you stood for your 10-pin shot. For the 3 or 9 pin, move your feet six boards to the right. (There is not a nine-board move from this side, because you would end up back at the headpin, which is a strike shot.)

Remember, the adjustment for these pins is not made based on their relationship to the headpin. Instead, it is made based on their relationship to the 10 pin.

Multiple-Pin Spares

When you leave two-pin spares, adjust so that the ball goes between the pins. When you leave three pins or more, you have to consider which is the key pin (i.e., the one closest to you, toward the front of the rack).

Left-Side Spares

To pick up spares on the left, adjust your angle off your strike line. When you leave two pins, move to the right from your strike position, keeping your same strike target and adjusting the number of boards to an amount between the number you moved for either pin separately.

4-7 Spare   Calculate your move so that the ball hits both the 4 pin and the 7 pin. Because you would move six boards to the right to pick up the 4 pin and nine boards to the right for the 7 pin, move to a number between the two, or seven and a half boards to the right, to pick up the 4-7 combination (figure 10.10).

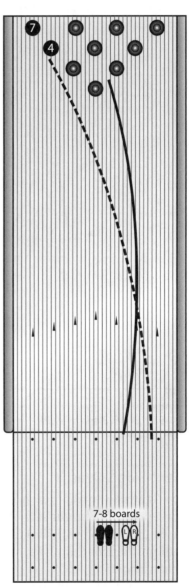

Keep in mind that you will convert more spares when the ball contacts more pins, rather than counting on the domino effect of the pins. When you leave three- and four-pin clusters, choose the pin you are actually trying to hit, or the key pin.

2-4-5 and 2-4-5-8 Spares   If you leave the 2-4-5-8, the key pin is the 2 pin. Let's clarify this point. Ideally, on a good shot, the assumption is that your ball is hitting the pin slightly to the right of center. That would mean that the outside of the ball would naturally hit the 5 pin. Therefore, you would move about three boards to the right, as you would typically move for the 2 pin (figure 10.11).

2-4, 2-4-5-7, and 2-7 Splits   In all three of these combinations you are trying to hit the 2-4, even in the case of the baby 2-7 split when the 4 pin isn't there. You would move three boards to the right for the 2 pin and six boards to the right for the 4 pin. Because you are trying to put the ball between the 2 pin and the 4 pin, you would move approximately four and a half boards to the right to pick it up this combination (figure 10.12). Note: the 2-4-7 is not a likely spare leave for a right-hander, but a 2-4-5-7 is.

Figure 10.10   Converting the 4-7 spare, right-handed bowler.

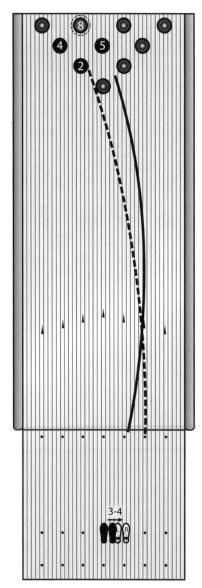

Figure 10.11 Converting the 2-4-5 or 2-4-5-8 spare, right-handed bowler.

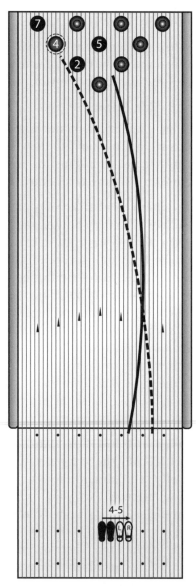

Figure 10.12 Converting the 2-4, 2-4-5-7, or 2-7 split, right-handed bowler.

Right-Side Spares

For right-side spares, you need to adjust your angle off your 10-pin shot. The other pins on the right side of the lane can be broken down into two columns based on their relationship to the 10 pin. You move your feet to the right from your position for the 10-pin shot, using the 10-pin target between the third and fourth arrows.

When you leave two pins, you move to the right from your 10-pin position, moving your feet a number of boards that is between the number you moved for either pin separately.

6-10 Spare Calculate your move so that the ball hits both the 6 pin and the 10 pin. For spares on the right, you start from the 10-pin position (approximately board 35). Because you would move three boards to the right to pick up the 6 pin, you would move one and a half boards to the right for the 6-10 combination (figure 10.13). Keep in mind you started from the 10-pin position.

3-6, 3-6-10, and 3-10 Splits All three combinations come down to trying to hit the 3-6, even in the case of the baby 3-10 split when the 6 pin isn't there. You would move three boards to the right for the 6 pin and six boards to the right for the 3 pin. To put the ball between the 3 pin and the 6 pin, you would move four or five boards to the right from your 10-pin position (figure 10.14).

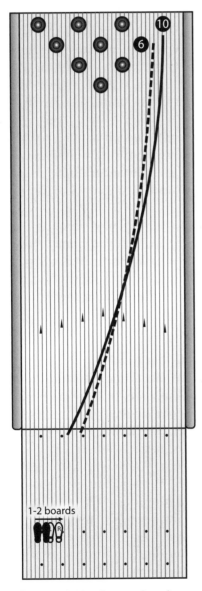

Figure 10.13 Converting the 6-10 spare, right-handed bowler.

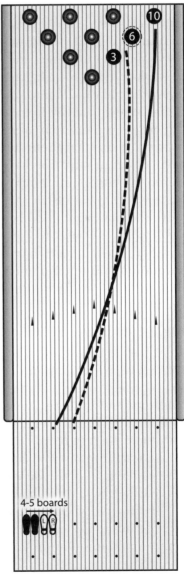

Figure 10.14 Converting the 3-6, 3-6-10, or 3-10 split, right-handed bowler.

LEFT-HANDED BOWLER

In this section, spares are divided into right-side and left-side spares, depending on which side of the headpin the pins are left standing. For spares on the right, a left-handed bowler shoots cross-lane, adjusting the feet to the left from the strike line. For spares on the left, the left-handed bowler also shoot cross-lane but from the right side of the approach. Single-pin spares are addressed first, followed by multiple-pin spares.

Right-handed bowlers may skip this section.

Single-Pin Spares

For pins on the right, in this basic 3-6-9 spare system, move to the left on the approach from your strike position. That is, note where you stand and target for your strike ball and adjust your angle for these spares from your strike line. Move your feet to the left and maintain the same strike target. How much you move your feet to the left depends on how far over the pin is to the right. *Note:* Your strike line (and target) may differ from the target line used in the illustrations. Be sure to adjust from your strike line.

For pins on the left, in the original 3-6-9 spare system, a left-handed bowler was traditionally taught to move right incrementally from the strike line. However, we will depart from that strategy and develop an independent position for the corner pin (7 pin) and make the remaining adjustments from there for the rest of the pins on the left.

This is important to do because there is an optimal angle for shooting the 7 pin to gain the most room for error to pick up the spare. If you simply move to the right a designated number of boards from the strike line (12 boards was suggested in the original system), often you will not end up at the optimal angle to shoot the 7 pin. This is especially true when you are playing farther left on the lane for your strike ball.

Right-Side Spares: 3/9, 6, and 10 Pins

To pick up spares on the right, adjust your angle off your strike line. From your strike position in the stance, move your feet to the left, using the same basic strike target, thereby adjusting your angle toward the spare. In shooting cross-lane, the more right the pin is, the more left you should move.

There are three columns of pins right of center. The first is the 3/9 pins, then the 6 pin, and then the 10 pin. Taken from the basic 3-6-9 spare system, a good starting point is to move your feet to the left in three board increments per column of pins. So you will move approximately three, six, or nine boards to the left, depending on how far right the pin is (figure 10.15).

For example, when you leave the 3 or 9 pin, move your feet approximately three boards to the left from your strike position. For the 6 pin, move approximately six boards. For the 10 pin, move approximately nine boards to the left.

Keeping your target area virtually the same, angle your shoulders toward the target line and then make a good shot, much as you would throw your strike shot.

Left-Side Spares

For left-side spares, you first must establish your angle for the 7-pin shot. To pick up the remaining spares on the left, adjust your angle off your 7-pin shot. The other pins on the left side of the lane can be broken down into two columns based on their relationship to the 7 pin. For these spares, you move your feet to the left from the 7-pin shot, keeping the 7-pin target.

7-Pin Shot To create the optimal angle to shoot the 7 pin, stand far right on approximately board 35, with your target between the third and fourth arrows at about the 17 or 18 board (figure 10.16). (Remember, a left-handed bowler counts

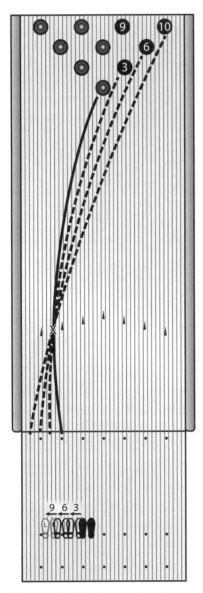

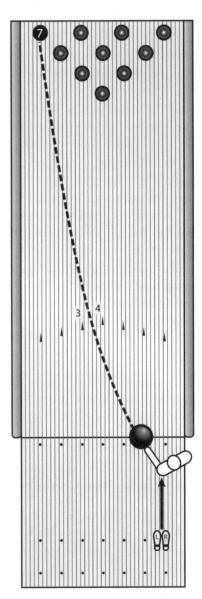

Figure 10.15 Converting the right-side spares, left-handed bowler: 3- or 9-pin spare, 6-pin spare, and 10-pin spare.

Figure 10.16 Converting the 7-pin spare, left-handed bowler.

the arrows from left to right on the lane.) Although there is always a dot on board 35 at the foul line, there may or may not be a dot on board 35 at the beginning of the approach.

Turn your shoulders to face the pin. Walk straight to the foul line with your shoulders open to end on the same board you started on to maintain your angle.

Improving your the corner pin shot is addressed in more detail later in this chapter in the section Troubleshooting the Corner Pin Shot.

4 Pin and 2/8 Pins There are two columns of pins to the right of the 7 pin: the 4 pin and the 2/8 pins. When shooting at these pins, keep the same target as for the 7 pin (between the third and fourth arrows; figure 10.17).

For the 4 pin, move your feet three boards to the left from where you stood for your 7-pin shot. For the 2 or 8 pin, move your feet six boards to the left. (There is not a nine-board move from this side, because you would end up back at the headpin, which is a strike shot.)

Remember, the adjustment for these pins is not made based on their relationship to the headpin. Instead, it is made based on their relationship to the 7 pin.

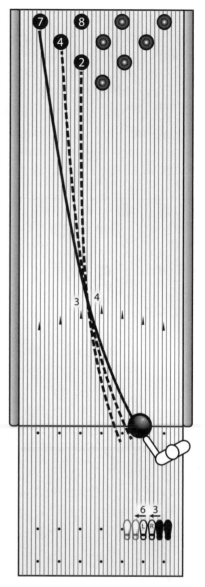

Figure 10.17 Converting the 4-pin spare and the 2- or 8-pin spare, left-handed bowler.

Multiple-Pin Spares

When you leave two-pin spares, adjust so that the ball goes between the pins. When you leave three pins or more, you have to consider which is the key pin (i.e., the one closest to you toward the front of the rack).

OPTIONAL 2-PIN SHOT
FOR A LEFT-HANDED BOWLER

Some left-handed bowlers see the 2 pin (or 8 pin) and view it close to a pocket shot and so choose to shoot it from the strike line. That is certainly an option. If you move from your strike line to shoot it, you will move right with your feet and keep your target the same (figure 10.18). Move three to five boards to the right. It may be as many as five boards, depending on conditions, because when you move right and throw a hook, your ball will swing out to the dry area where there is more friction, and you have to allow for how much it will hook.

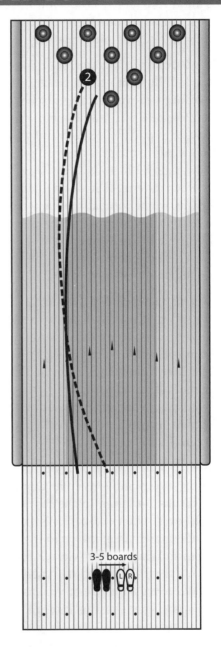

Figure 10.18 Moving from the strike line to hook at the 2 pin, left-handed bowler.

Right-Side Spares

To pick up spares on the right, adjust your angle off your strike line, keeping your same strike target. When you leave two pins, move to the left from your strike position, adjusting the number of boards to an amount between the number you moved for either pin separately.

6-10 Spare Calculate your move so that the ball hits both the 6 pin and the 10 pin. Because you would move six boards to the left for the 6 pin and nine boards to the left for the 10 pin, move seven and a half boards to the left to pick up the 6-10 pin combination (figure 10.19).

Keep in mind that you will convert more spares when the ball contacts more pins, rather than counting on the domino effect of the pins. When you leave three- and four-pin clusters, choose the pin you are actually trying to hit, or the key pin.

3-5-6 and 3-5-6-9 Spares If you leave the 3-5-6-9, your key pin is the 3 pin. Ideally, on a good shot, the assumption is that your ball will hit the pin slightly to the left of center. That would mean that the outside of the ball would naturally hit the 5 pin. You would therefore move about three boards to the left, as you would typically move for the 3 pin (figure 10.20).

3-6, 3-5-6-10, and 3-10 Splits All three of these combinations come down to trying to hit the 3-6, even in the case of the baby 3-10 split when the 6 pin isn't there. You would move three boards to the left for the 3 pin and six boards to the left for the 6 pin. To put the ball between the 3 and 6 pins, you would move approximately four and a half boards to the left to pick up this combination (figure 10.21). *Note:* The 3-6-10 is not a likely spare leave for a left-hander, but the 3-5-6-10 is.

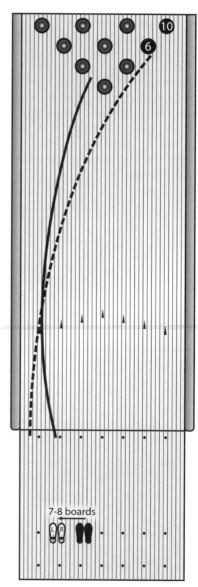

Figure 10.19 Converting the 6-10 spare, left-handed bowler.

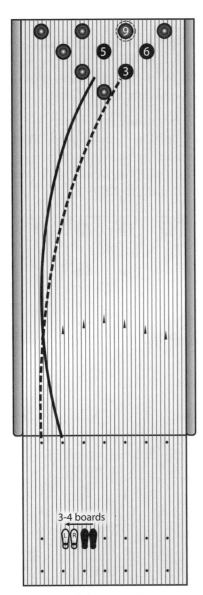

Figure 10.20 Converting the 3-5-6 or 3-5-6-9 spare, left-handed bowler.

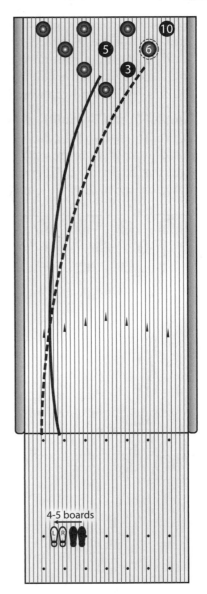

Figure 10.21 Converting the 3-6, 3-5-6-10, or 3-10 split, left-handed bowler.

Left-Side Spares

For left-side spares, you need to adjust your angle off of your 7-pin shot. The other pins on the left side of the lane can be broken down into two columns based on their relationship to the 7 pin. You move your feet to the left from your position for the 7-pin shot, using the 7-pin target between the third and fourth arrows.

When you leave two pins, you move to the left from your 7-pin position, moving your feet a number of boards that is between the number you moved for either pin separately.

4-7 Spare Calculate your move so that the ball hits both the 4 pin and the 7 pin. For spares on the left, you start from the 7-pin position (approximately board 35). Because you would move three boards to the left for the 4 pin, you would move one and a half boards to the left for the 4-7 combination (figure 10.22). Keep in mind you were starting from the 7-pin position.

2-4, 2-4-7, and 2-7 Splits In all three of these combinations you are trying to hit the 2-4, even in the case of the baby 2-7 split when the 4 pin isn't there. You would move three boards to the left for the 4 pin and six boards to the left for the 2 pin. To put the ball between the 2 pin and the 4 pin, you would move four or five boards to the left from your 7-pin position (figure 10.23).

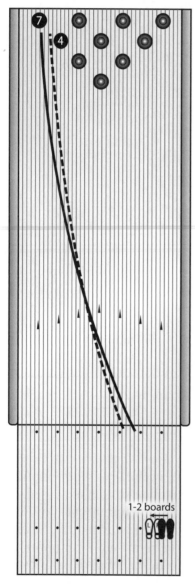

Figure 10.22 Converting the 4-7 spare, left-handed bowler.

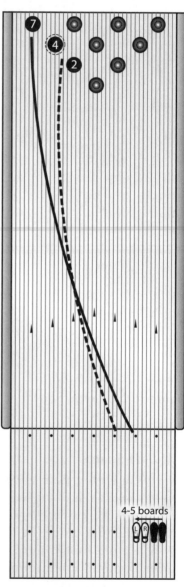

Figure 10.23 Converting the 2-4, 2-4-7, or 2-7 split, left-handed bowler.

TROUBLESHOOTING THE CORNER PIN SHOT

For a right-handed bowler, the 10 pin is the corner pin shot. For a left-handed bowler, it's the 7 pin. Let's face it, most bowlers have strong feelings about the corner pin, and that probably includes you. Leaving it seems to evoke more emotion than leaving any other pin. Maybe this is because it is daunting, all the way over by the gutter all by itself. Maybe it is because it is one of the spares you leave the most. In either case, many bowlers express a mental block when it comes to the corner pin. Let's dispel the myth that the reason you miss it is strictly mental. There are three important things to do to pick up the corner pin: maintain the correct angle, keep the swing loose, and create proper ball reaction. Most bowlers who claim that their problem is a mental one are not doing one or more of these three things.

Maintaining the Proper Angle

To shoot the corner pin, stand on approximately board 35, and open your shoulders to face the pin. Be sure to walk straight to end on the same board you started on, but keep your shoulders facing the pin throughout the approach. If you walk toward the target, you will lose your angle. Again, your target is between the third and fourth arrows. The straighter you walk, the more room for error you will have and the bigger your target will be to get the spare.

It can be a challenge to learn to walk straight, yet face the pin. The right foot, hip, and shoulder should be uniformly open the same amount, so there is no twist to your spine (figure 10.24). Done properly, you almost feel as though you are *side-stepping* with your feet to walk straight, but continue to face toward the pin. Make sure you check your foot at the finish, so that you can tell if you end up where you started, around board 35.

A common problem is facing the pin and walking toward it or walking straight but with the shoulders facing the same direction. *You want to walk straight, but face the spare.*

For the corner pin, make sure you are walking straight rather than drifting toward the pin. Again, line up your shoulders to face the spare and make sure you end where you started. The straighter you walk, the better your angle will be and the bigger your target will become to make the spare!

Figure 10.24 Maintain body angle toward pin, walking straight.

Having a Loose Swing

Again, swing is king! Tightening up is a major reason bowlers miss the corner pin (or any pin). Whether they are trying to steer the ball or throw it hard or just lack confidence, the swing is commonly the culprit. Learn to relax and trust it. The alternative just isn't working!

Creating Proper Ball Reaction

When you walk straight, have a loose swing, and hit your target area, watch your ball as it heads toward the pin. Does it suddenly hook at the very end to miss it? In this case, the first two variables appear to be in check. The problem is *ball reaction*. You do not correct ball reaction by changing your angle; rather, you want to achieve a different ball reaction. Some choose to change the release, to flatten the hand to kill the rotation so that the ball hooks less. Although this certainly is an option, you need to be proficient to do this, yet maintain your hook release on your strike ball.

Another option is to use a plastic ball that does not hook. This is a very popular solution because you can execute the way you do on your first ball, but the plastic ball will slide more. This helps bowlers who try to force the shot to get the corner pin, knowing that the strike ball likely will hook too much to get it.

Ideally, a plastic ball should be the same weight and fit as your strike ball. This makes the transition between using your strike and your spare ball seamless. Only in extremely dry conditions will you have to use your plastic ball *and* kill your rotation to keep the ball from hooking at the corner pin.

Using a plastic ball for the corner pin can instantly improve your average. Chapter 11 describes a spare system in which you use a plastic ball for all spares. When using this system, your new plastic ball could end up being one of the balls you use the most!

Note: Be careful about just trying to throw the ball harder, because usually you will pull the ball. Getting the corner pin comes down to angle, swing, and ball reaction. If you are doing all three of these well but continue to miss the spare, work on that mental game!

Making Changes: Using a Plastic Ball

It is a good idea to use a plastic ball for spares if you are not good at flattening out your roll to keep your strike ball from hooking at spares or if you can't go back to hooking your strike ball once you flatten out your roll for a spare. The whole idea is to be able to release the ball about the same as you do on your strike ball, but the ball won't hook because it is plastic.

That is not to say that plastic balls never hook, because they can. If you roll the ball very slowly or if there is a lot of friction on the lane, even a plastic ball can hook. However, on most conditions they don't, and they certainly hook less than performance balls do.

If your plastic ball is hooking, you need to flatten your roll in addition to using the plastic ball. Extreme circumstances call for extreme measures!

Practicing the Corner Pin Shot

Practice getting the corner pin on a full rack. Be mindful of the three factors—proper angle, loose swing, and ball reaction—when you troubleshoot a miss. Keep practicing. Once you begin to figure it out, commit to getting it three times in a row. If you miss, start over. The worst that can happen is that you get more practice. When you become proficient, increase it to five times in a row. Each time you pick it up, you are becoming more competent and you will begin feeling much more confident. Picking it up when it counts will go a long way in relaxing your swing. Do not worry about picking it off the rack clean. In competition, you can hit either side of the pin and still get it.

ADJUSTING FOR LANE CONDITIONS

The moves described so far are approximate because lane conditions may come into play and affect ball reaction as you adjust your angle to the spare. When this 3-6-9 system was developed, lane conditioner was applied in a more blended fashion. Now oil is applied in a more blocked pattern (figure 10.25), which makes the ball react differently as it crosses through the vastly different volumes of oil across the lane.

You may need to modify your adjustment according to how the ball is reacting to the lane conditions. If you make a proper move, adjust your shoulders, and make a good shot but the ball does not make it to the pin, you have to adjust the number of boards you move next time to allow for lane conditions.

For example, let's say you move six boards to the right to pick up the 4 pin, adjust your shoulders, and make a good shot but miss to the right. This shows you that you have to move more than six boards to the right to allow for how much the ball is sliding in the oil (figure 10.26).

In an advanced spare shooting system (see chapter 11), you can take the lane conditions out of play by using a separate ball that does not hook or take the hook out of your release and learn to shoot directly at spares, still using the cross-lane advantage. This is an excellent option when you are missing spares because it is challenging to calculate how much the ball is actually going to hook at the spares. It also is an excellent option to simplify spares when you bowl on a variety of conditions or when your strike line is out by the first arrow, where it can be difficult to make spare adjustments.

Becoming systematic while taking lane conditions into consideration when you calculate your adjustment will improve your spare shooting. It is a matter of staying mentally focused and following the system.

Be sure to consider lane conditions, especially when going for spares on the left (for a right-handed bowler) or on the right (for a left-handed bowler). You may have a lot of friction in your hook zone but come across a lot of oil in the center of the lane. You may have to adjust the number of boards you move your feet to allow for the lane conditions.

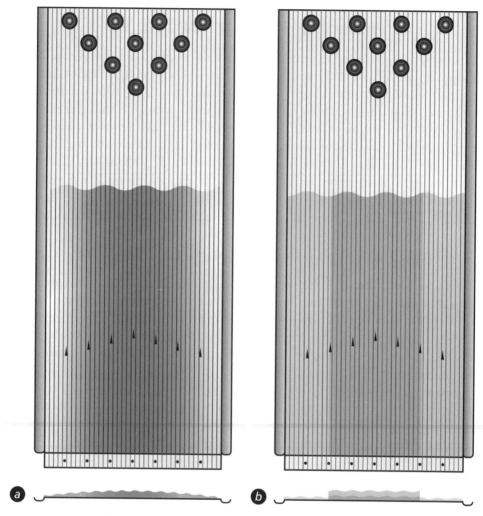

Figure 10.25 Oil patterns: *(a)* blended lane; *(b)* blocked lane.

Splits: Should You Go For It?

A spare is considered a split when there is a gap between the remaining pins. For some spares that are splits, you may consider it best to go for a good count rather than try to convert the spare. Anytime you have a split with the pins in the same row and more than a ball-width apart, strive to get as many pins as you can for the best pin count toward your score, especially when you leave a difficult split after a strike (see chapter 13). For these splits, it's best to go for pin count: 4-6, 4-6-7, 4-6-10, 4-6-7-10, 7-9, 7-10 & 8-10.

Though the pins are not in the same row, the conversion rates for the following splits are low but slightly higher than those previously mentioned. Try to pick up these splits at the risk of pin count: 4-10, 4-7-10, 6-7, 6-7-10, 2-4-(8)-10 (RH) and 3-(6)-7-9 (LH).

Though challenging, the following splits have higher conversion rates, and you will likely still knock down a pin, or pins, as you strive to make them. A split with the head pin standing is referred to as a washout. RH: 1-2-(4)-(8)-10, 2-(4)-10, 2-7-(8), 3-(9)-10, 4-5-(7), 4-7-(9), 5-7. LH: 1-3-(6)-7-(9), 3-(6)-7, 3-(9)-10, 2-7-(8) 5-6-(10), 5-10, 6-8-(10).

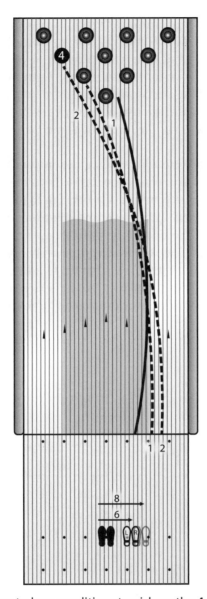

Figure 10.26 Adjusting to lane conditions to pick up the 4 pin.

SUMMARY

Spare shooting is a four-part process: identify the pins, calculate the adjustment, turn your shoulders, and make a good shot. Consider lane conditions to make modifications within your system. If you make a good shot but you still miss it, make the appropriate adjustment to your angle the next time. Being systematic, but flexible, is important.

Right-handers make the adjustments to pick up all spares on the left side of the headpin from the strike line. Use the strike target and move your feet incrementally to the right from the stance position of your strike shot.

Left-handers make the adjustments to pick up all the spares on the right side of the headpin from the strike line. Use the strike target and move your feet incrementally to the left from the stance position of your strike shot.

For the corner pin (10 pin for right-handers, 7 pin for left-handers), start on approximately board 35, using between the third and fourth arrows, face the pin, but walk straight. Make the rest of your moves for the spares on that side from this corner pin position, keeping the same target and moving your feet toward the center.

With a systematic spare shooting system, not only will you make more spares, but you will more easily troubleshoot misses. If you make a logical move but miss the spare, go back over your four-step system to identify what went wrong. If your shoulders were lined up properly and you executed well, adjust to create a bigger or smaller angle to convert the spare the next time.

When lane conditions create too much guesswork for spare adjustments, consider using a plastic ball for all spares. Chapter 11 addresses an advanced spare shooting system using a separate plastic ball for spares to simplify ball reaction so that spare shooting adjustments can become more routine again.

Chapter 11

Advanced Spare Shooting

Although the 3-6-9 board adjustment system has been around for a long time and is still taught, modifications in this system have become necessary because of how differently lanes are being oiled. In addition, people are bowling on so many different lane conditions that using just one formula makes picking up spares tricky.

When the 3-6-9 spare system was developed, the numbers worked almost flawlessly when oil was applied in a more blended pattern across the lane (i.e., lightly on the boards by the gutter and gradually and incrementally increasing in units toward the center of the lane).

However, on today's typical house shot (THS), the lanes are oiled differently from that blended shot years ago. The oil is much more built up in the center, with a more defined oil line between the oily and dry boards. There is a huge contrast between the units of oil in the middle and those that are outside toward the gutters. This creates a much less predictable reaction as the ball crosses through the wet and dry conditions of the lane. When the ball hits the high volume of oil (nicknamed wet), it just slides. When it hits the much drier boards, it hooks a lot.

In addition, people bowl in different bowling centers or on different lane conditions or in tournaments or other competitive events. If this is true for you, you may find that you cannot count on your ball hooking the way it does in week-to-week league play, and that your angle is critical for the proper reaction to your left-side spares (for right-handed bowlers) or right-side spares (for left-handed bowlers). If you are missing spares because of this and dealing with lane conditions becomes frustrating, consider taking lane reaction out of play. Rather than adjusting and continuing to use your performance ball, try using a plastic ball that doesn't hook to roll straight to the spares, so you can simply rely on angle.

Finally, when you are playing way outside on the lane, as in the first arrow, you are so far out that when you try to move more to get your spares, you are actually too close to the gutter to make some of the adjustments in the 3-6-9 system. This is another reason to learn to shoot more directly at your spares, independent of lane conditions, at least as an option.

CLOSING THE SHOULDERS

You will have to close your shoulders to shoot more directly at some spares. Closing your shoulders to make left-side spares (right-handed bowler) or right-side spares (left-handed bowler) is a very awkward feeling at first. This is because on all other shots, your shoulders are either parallel to the foul line or slightly open, as when you throw a hook ball or when you shoot at spares on the other side. It feels odd to close your shoulders because it is so different from what you are used to.

In fact, how it feels to close the shoulders is the biggest obstacle I see bowlers face, and it is typically why so many end up abandoning this system. It simply feels too weird at first, and so they do not stick to it to benefit from the advantages it provides.

Note: When you close your shoulders, also close up your hip and foot so that you are in alignment on the swing side of your body in the stance. This helps the spine to stay relaxed and makes it easier to stay in alignment throughout the approach.

What is also very different is seeing the ball go straight. This is the very reason your shoulders need to be closed to throw the ball cross-lane. Often, it takes only going directly toward a spare with a plastic ball in league play and missing it to quickly abandon the system. This is especially true when your teammates give you a hard time, telling you, "If you had hooked at it, you would have gotten it!" Rather, you just needed to execute better or adjust your angle. It takes practice to get comfortable executing at this direct angle.

There is a reason professional bowlers go more directly at spares, whether they flatten their wrists or use a spare ball. It is to take the lane conditions out of play. You may have to be a bit more accurate, but the advantages often outweigh the challenges to change. I encourage you to stay the course.

I know when I first learned to use this system, I always felt as though I wanted to pull the ball across my body when my shoulders were closed. It is simply a matter of getting used to turning your body, but still following through with your swing at a 90-degree angle in relation to your shoulders. Forget about any notion to stay parallel to the foul line.

Almost everyone who tries this for the first time feels as though she is facing the wall! But rest assured—you are not. It is just that the feeling of closed shoulders feels so drastically different from what you are used to on all other shots. The most closed you will ever have to be is when shooting the 7 pin (right-handed bowler) or the 10 pin (left-handed bowler) with a plastic ball.

Demonstrating Shoulder Angle

Have a partner stand behind you and extend her arms over your shoulders toward the pins (figure 11.1). This will show you where you are actually facing.

Figure 11.1 Demonstrating shoulder angle drill.

When you close your shoulders, also close your hips and feet in your stance so that everything stays aligned and relaxed. You do not want torque in your spine. In the stance, align your swing shoulder, hip, and foot so that your entire side is uniformly closed to face the spare. The biggest obstacle I see facing bowlers is getting comfortable with how foreign it feels at first to close the shoulders directly toward a spare but still follow through straight at 90 degrees.

I frequently have to stand behind my students and put my arms over their shoulders with my hands pointing to the pins to reflect the angle they are actually facing versus what they think they are facing. Almost every time, the bowler is not closed enough, although she feels as though she is. Once she sees where my arms and hands are pointing, she learns to close the shoulders more than she thought she needed to. It's all about lining up the swing so it can follow through straight and get the spare.

STRAIGHT FOLLOW-THROUGH

When you close the shoulders to face the spare, you may feel the urge to pull the ball to go with it. Although you obviously still want to keep a 90-degree angle between your shoulders and your swing plane, it just plain feels odd to be that closed when you first learn to do it. This is simply because you are never that closed for any other shot.

If you pull at first, just keep at it until you learn to face that way and still follow through straight with a 90-degree angle from your shoulders (figure 11.2). You do not have to be parallel to the foul line. This angle is different and more direct to the pin.

Figure 11.2 Shoulders closed, 90-degree follow-through.

MAINTAINING SHOULDER ANGLE

Many bowlers have learned to face the spare while in their stance and follow through straight at delivery. However, they end up missing the spare because their shoulders turn during the approach. Preset your shoulders in the stance and maintain this position.

The key is to set your shoulders in position and lock your core in place to face the spare throughout the entire approach. Even as the momentum of the swing passes your body, do not let the force turn your shoulders. If you do, your shoulders will open and your swing will no longer be lined up to get the spare. In that case if you do still get the spare, it would be because you pulled it, and that is typically a short-term solution.

I see many bowlers attempt this system only to abandon it before they give themselves enough time to get used to it. Typically, they are pushed over the edge and finally stop doing it because they invariably miss a spare trying to shoot straight at it and their teammates give them a hard time, saying they missed it because they threw it straight. I beg to differ. They missed it because something went wrong in the execution.

Having bowled on so many lane conditions and seeing the imbalance of oil in the center of the lane as compared to outside on the THS, I really believe that using a plastic ball is the way to go. In fact, it is how I shot my spares on tour. It took the lane out of play, and I just had to execute. That is why you see professionals throw straight at their spares. I believe that getting used to how it feels and not seeing your ball hook is a small price to pay for the success you will have making your spares.

In this system, using a plastic ball, there are six basic shots for single-pin spares (figure 11.3). Once you determine where to stand for both pins in the corners using a target near the middle of the lane, adjust your angle for the remaining pins by moving from these positions in three-board increments toward the middle of the lane, keeping the same target. It's a very simple but effective system.

This spare system is presented separately for right-handed and left-handed bowlers. Left-handed bowlers may skip ahead to their section.

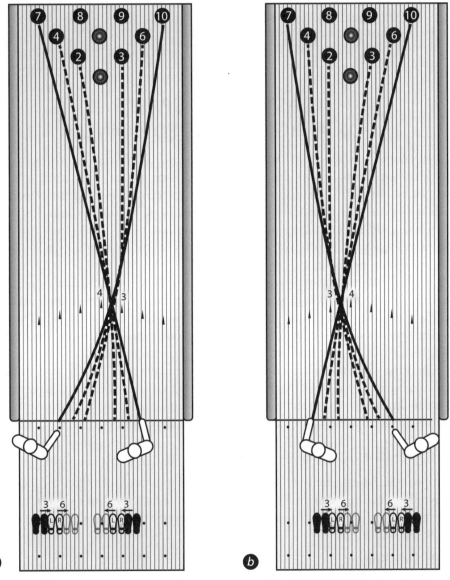

Figure 11.3 Six basic shots for single-pin spares: (a) right-handed bowler; (b) left-handed bowler.

Making Changes: Watching the Ball Go Straight

It can be a much different visual to watch the ball go straight when you are learning to shoot spares with a plastic ball. Some bowlers just want to see the ball hook, believing this creates more room to miss. This is understandable, but the flip side is that you have to take lane conditions into consideration, and that room doesn't seem to work when you do not effectively manage the oil on the lane.

Getting used to seeing the ball go straight is an adjustment in itself. But keep in mind that although you have to be a little bit more accurate, you get to take the lane conditions out of play. This takes so much of the guesswork out of the equation. You still have some room to play when you use good angles and make the proper adjustments. You just don't have to worry about the ball hooking or sliding past the spare.

PLASTIC BALL SPARES FOR A RIGHT-HANDED BOWLER

As in chapter 10, spares are broken down into left-side and right-side spares, with the emphasis in this chapter on the left-side spares. This is because the angles for the right-side spares are the same as those presented in chapter 10. The only difference is that you will be using a plastic ball to eliminate ball reaction when shooting these spares. The starting point for the 10 pin is the same (approximately board 35), and the adjustments for the remaining spares on the right side are the same.

What is different in this system is that you will not be moving from your strike line when you shoot left-side spares. Rather, you first will develop a separate angle toward the 7 pin, using your plastic ball, and then adjust for the remainder of the spares on the left by moving from this arbitrary angle. I will start with single-pin spares, followed by multiple-pin spare combinations.

Shooting straight at spares definitely has a different feel. This section explains what to expect as you make this transition to using a plastic ball toward these spares. This includes addressing technique as well as common obstacles that may undermine your commitment to this system. Left-handers can skip to the next section.

Single-Pin Spares

For pins on the left, you first have to establish a separate 7-pin shot, independent of your strike line. Once you have determined this angle, move from here for the remaining spares on the left side, maintaining the target that you used on your 7-pin shot.

Left-Side Spares

When you pick up spares with a separate plastic ball, you no longer move from your strike line for pins on the left side. Moving off your strike line when you are using a completely different ball makes no sense. You do not want to use your strike target to shoot spares on the left side of the lane because you are using an entirely different ball. So, just as you established an arbitrary angle for the corner-pin shot (the 10 pin) to shoot right-side spares, you need to do the same for the 7 pin to shoot left-side spares using this plastic ball system.

Establishing a 7-Pin Shot Use a target somewhere around the center of the lane—let's say, between the third and fourth arrows. Move over to the right and figure out an approximate place to stand that looks right to hit this target and get the 7 pin.

Make sure you turn, or close, your shoulders to face the 7 pin (figure 11.4). Remember that this plastic ball does not hook; you are throwing it directly at the pin. Closing your shoulders can seem a bit awkward, because you never close them like this for any other shot.

Where to stand for this side is less clear because the amount of drift toward the target in an attempt to keep the shoulders closed and facing the pin varies from bowler to bowler.

It may sound a bit contradictory to the notion of walking straight, but you do not walk straight when your shoulders are closed, aligned to the 7 pin. Because your arm swing is on the right side of your body, you need to walk toward your target to keep your swing on the intended target line toward the pins on the lane and still follow through at a 90-degree angle to your shoulders. Where I am consistent about drift is that you never walk right *toward* your arm swing.

Figure 11.4 Right-handed bowler with (a) shoulders closed to the 7 pin (b) walks toward the 7 pin.

> ## Making Changes:
> ## Shoulders Closed and Walking Toward the 7 Pin
>
> When you are facing the left-side spare with your shoulders closed, you have to walk toward the pin to keep your shoulders closed and be able to follow through at a 90-degree angle. The more to the right you start, the more you will have to drift. It comes down to how it looks visually and what you establish as your comfort zone to keep your shoulders closed and be able to hit your target. This might sound like a contradiction; however, the consistent thought is that you never want to walk right into your arm swing.

Walk straight when your shoulders are open; walk slightly toward target when your shoulders are closed.

Some bowlers drift more than others do and have to start more to the right. Some drift less and should start closer to the target. This has to be discovered through trial and error. Typically, bowlers start somewhere around the 15 board and walk slightly toward the center of the approach for the 7 pin. Again, the only time you walk toward your target is when your shoulders are closed, and in this case you are not walking into your swing plane.

Adjusting for the Remaining Left-Side Spares   Just as you adjusted for the spares on the right by moving from your 10-pin position, to pick up the remaining spares on the left, you must adjust your angle off your 7-pin shot. The other pins on the left side of the lane can be broken down into two columns based on their relationship to the 7 pin. For these spares, move your feet to the left from the 7-pin shot, keeping the 7-pin target.

There are two columns of pins to the right of the 7 pin: the 4 pin and the 2/8 pins. Keep the target that you had for the 7-pin shot, between the third and fourth arrows.

For the 4 pin, move your feet three boards to the left from where you stood for your 7-pin shot (figure 11.5).

For the 2 pin or 8 pin, move your feet six boards to the left (figure 11.6). (*Note:* There is not a nine-board move from this side, because you would end up back at the headpin, which is a strike shot.)

Remember, the adjustment for these pins is not made based on their relationship to the headpin. Instead, it is made based on their relationship to the 7 pin.

Right-Side Spares

Right-side spares are virtually the same in this system as they were in chapter 10. The only difference is that you are using your plastic ball to get them. The adjustments are the same as if you were using your strike ball, only you are throwing straighter at the pins, taking ball reaction out of play. This will be to your advantage.

Just remember that on this side, you do walk straight but face the spare with your shoulders. Since your shoulders are open for this side, you should end on the same board at the foul line that you started on in the stance.

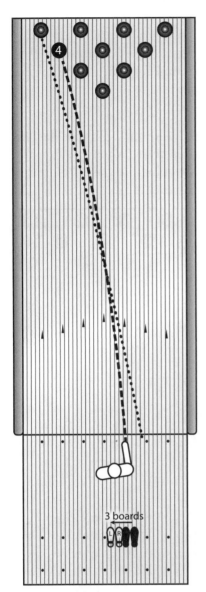

Figure 11.5   Converting the 4-pin spare, right-handed bowler.

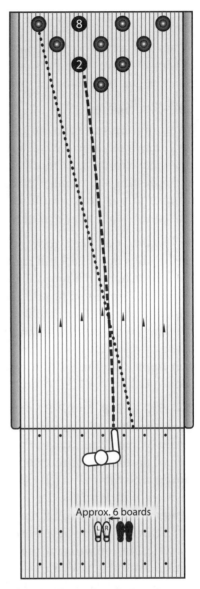

Figure 11.6   Converting the 2- or 8-pin spare, right-handed bowler.

To review the adjustments from chapter 10:

- For the 6 pin, move your feet three boards to the right from where you stood for your 10-pin shot.
- For the 3 pin or 9 pin, move your feet six boards to the right. (*Note:* There is not a nine-board move from this side, because you would end up back at the headpin, which is a strike shot.)

See figure 10.8 in chapter 10 or figure 11.3.

Multiple-Pin Spares

When you leave two-pin spares, adjust so that the ball goes between the pins. When you leave three pins or more, you have to consider which is the key pin (i.e., the one closest to you toward the front of the rack).

Left-Side Spares

To pick up the spares on the left, adjust your angle from your 7-pin shot, keeping the same 7-pin target between the third and fourth arrows. When you leave two pins, move to the left from your 7-pin position, keeping the same 7-pin target and adjusting the number of boards to a number that is between the number you moved for either pin separately.

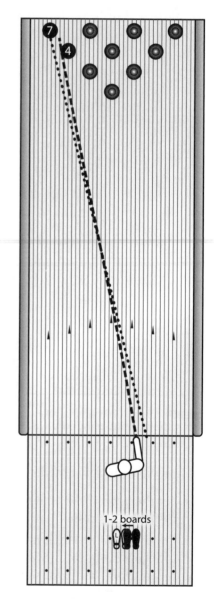

4-7 Spare Calculate your move so that the ball hits both the 4 pin and the 7 pin. For a right-handed bowler, the 7 pin is its own shot. Since you would move three boards to the left from the 7-pin shot for the 4 pin; you would move one and a half boards to the left from your 7-pin position to pick up the 4-7 pin combination (figure 11.7).

2-4-5, 2-4-5-8, and 2-8 Spares If you leave these combinations, your key pin would be the 2 pin. Again, the key pin is the pin closest to you. You normally would move six boards to the left from the 7-pin position to pick up the 2 pin, so try this adjustment for these combinations (figure 11.8). Obviously, you have to be a bit more accurate, but you will take the lane conditions out of play with this strategy. You may have to adjust a board either way.

2-4, 2-4-5-7, and 2-7 Split In all three of these combinations you are trying to hit the 2 pin and 4 pin, even in the case of the baby 2-7 split when the 4 pin isn't there. You would move three boards to the left for the 4 pin and six boards to the left for the 2 pin. Because you are trying to put the ball between the 2 pin and the 4 pin, you would move between three and six, or approximately four and a half, boards to the left from your 7-pin shot to pick this up (figure 11.9).

Figure 11.7 Converting the 4-7 spare, right-handed bowler.

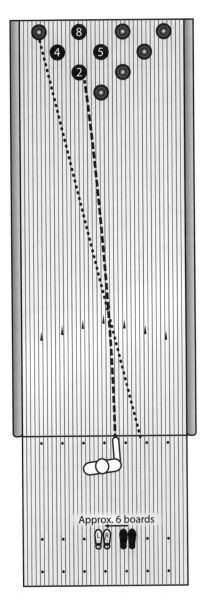

Figure 11.8 Converting the 2-4-5, 2-4-5-8, or 2-8 spare, right-handed bowler.

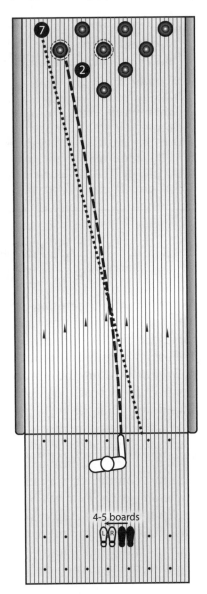

Figure 11.9 Converting the 2-4, 2-4-5-7, or 2-7 split, right-handed bowler.

Right-Side Spares: 3-6, 3-6-10, and 3-10 Split

All three combinations come down to trying to hit the 3 pin and 6 pin, even in the case of the baby 3-10 split when the 6 pin isn't there. Because you move three boards for the 6 pin and six boards for the 3 pin, move between, or four or five boards, to the right from your 10-pin position. See figure 10.14 in chapter 10.

Remember, the adjustment for these pins is not made based on their relationship to the headpin. Instead, it is made based on their relationship to the 10 pin.

The next section covers spares for left-handed bowlers. Right-handed bowlers may skip this section.

PLASTIC BALL SPARES FOR A LEFT-HANDED BOWLER

As in chapter 10, spares are broken down into right-side and left-side spares, with the emphasis in this chapter on the right-side spares. This is because the angles for the left-side spares are the same as those presented in chapter 10. The only difference is that you will be using a plastic ball to eliminate ball reaction when shooting these spares. The starting point for the 7 pin is the same (approximately board 35), and the adjustments for the remaining spares on the left side are the same.

What is different in this system is that you will not move from your strike line when shooting right-side spares. Rather, you first will develop a separate angle toward the 10 pin using your plastic ball, and then adjust for the remainder of the spares on the right by moving from this arbitrary angle. I will start with single-pin spares, followed by multiple-pin spare combinations.

Shooting straight at spares definitely has a different feel. This section explains what to expect as you make this transition to using a plastic ball toward these spares. This includes addressing technique as well as common obstacles that may undermine your commitment to this system.

Single-Pin Spares

For pins on the right, you first have to establish a separate 10-pin shot, independent of your strike line. Once you have determined this angle, move from here for the remaining spares on the right side, maintaining the target that you used on your 10-pin shot.

Right-Side Spares

When you pick up spares with a separate plastic ball, you no longer move from your strike line for pins on the right. Moving off your strike line when you are using a completely different ball makes no sense. You do not want to use your strike target to shoot spares on the right side of the lane because you are using an entirely different ball. So, just as you established an arbitrary angle for the corner-pin shot (7 pin) to shoot left-side spares, you need to do the same for the 10 pin to shoot right-side spares in this system.

Establishing a 10-Pin Shot Use a target somewhere around the center of the lane— let's say, between the third and fourth arrows. Move over to the left and figure out an approximate place to stand that looks right to hit this target and get the 10 pin.

Make sure you turn, or close, your shoulders to face the 10 pin (figure 11.10). Remember that this ball does not hook. You are throwing it directly at the pin. Closing your shoulders can seem a bit awkward, because you never close them like this for any other shot.

Where to stand for this side is less clear because the amount of drift toward the target in an attempt to keep the shoulders closed and facing the pin varies from bowler to bowler.

It may sound like a contradiction to the notion of walking straight, but you do not walk straight when your shoulders are closed toward the 10 pin. With your arm swing on the left side of your body, you need to walk toward your target to keep your swing on the intended target line toward the pins on the lane and still follow through at a 90-degree angle to your shoulders. Where I am consistent about drift is that you never walk left *toward* your arm swing. *Walk straight when your shoulders are open; walk slightly toward your target when your shoulders are closed.*

Figure 11.10 Left-handed bowler with *(a)* shoulders closed to the 10 pin *(b)* walks toward the 10 pin.

> ## Making Changes:
> ## Shoulders Closed and Walking Toward the 10 Pin
>
> When you are facing the right-side spare with your shoulders closed, you have to walk toward the pin to keep your shoulders closed and be able to follow through at a 90-degree angle. The more to the left you start, the more you will have to drift. It comes down to how it looks visually and what you establish as your comfort zone to keep your shoulders closed and be able to hit your target. This might sound like a contradiction. However, the consistent thought is that you never want to walk left into your arm swing.

Some bowlers drift more than others do and have to start more to the left. Some drift less and should start closer to the target. This has to be learned through trial and error. Typically, bowlers start somewhere around the 15 board and walk slightly toward the center of the approach for the 10 pin. Again, the only time you walk toward your target is when your shoulders are closed, and in this case you are not walking into your swing plane.

Adjusting for the Remaining Right-Side Spares Just as you adjusted for the spares on the left by moving from your 7-pin position, to pick up the remaining spares on the right, you must adjust your angle off your 10-pin shot. The other pins on the right side of the lane can be broken down into two columns based on their relationship to the 10 pin. For these spares, move your feet to the right from the 10-pin shot, keeping the 10-pin target.

There are two columns of pins to the left of the 10 pin: the 6 pin and the 3/9 pins. Keep the target that you had for the 10 pin, between the third and fourth arrows.

For the 6 pin, move your feet three boards to the right from where you stood for your 10-pin shot (figure 11.11).

For the 3 pin or 9 pin, move your feet six boards to the right (figure 11.12). (*Note:* There is not a nine-board move from this side, because you would end up back at the headpin, which is a strike shot.)

Remember, the adjustment for these pins is not made based on their relationship to the headpin. Instead, it is made based on their relationship to the 10 pin.

Left-Side Spares

Left-side spares are virtually the same in this system as they were in chapter 10. The only difference is that you use a plastic ball to get them. The adjustments are the same as if you were using your strike ball, but you are throwing straighter at the pins, taking ball reaction out of play. This will be to your advantage.

Just remember that on this side, you do walk straight but face the spare with your shoulders. Since your shoulders are open for this side, you should end on the same board at the foul line that you started on in the stance.

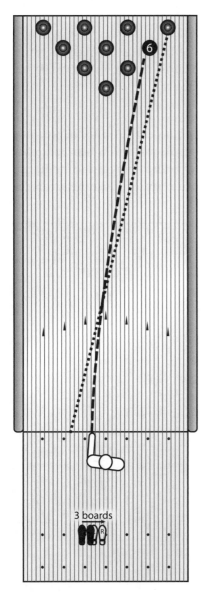

Figure 11.11 Converting the 6-pin spare, left-handed bowler.

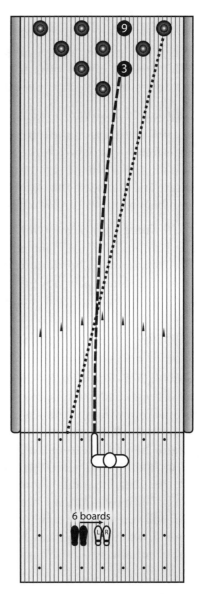

Figure 11.12 Converting the 3- or 9-pin spare, left-handed bowler.

To review the adjustments from chapter 10:

- For the 4 pin, move your feet three boards to the left from where you stood for your 7-pin shot.
- For the 2 pin or 8 pin, move your feet six boards to the left. (*Note:* There is not a nine-board move from this side, because you would end up back at the headpin, which is a strike shot.) See figure 10.17 in chapter 10.

Multiple-Pin Spares

When you leave two-pin spares, adjust so that the ball goes between the pins. When you leave three pins or more, you have to consider which is the key pin (i.e., the one closest to you toward the front of the rack).

Right-Side Spares

To pick up spares on the right, adjust your angle from your 10-pin shot, keeping the same 10-pin target between the third and fourth arrows. When you leave two pins, move to the right from your 10-pin position, keeping the same 10-pin target and adjusting the number of boards to a number that is in between the number you moved for either pin separately.

6-10 Spare   Calculate your move so that the ball hits both the 6 pin and the 10 pin. For a left-handed bowler, the 10 pin is its own shot. Since you move three boards to the right from the 10-pin shot for the 6 pin; you move one and a half boards to the right from your 10-pin position to pick up the 6-10 combination (figure 11.13).

3-5-6, 3-5-6-9, and 3-9 Spares   If you leave these combinations, your key pin would be the 3 pin. Again, the key pin is the pin closest to you. You normally would move six boards to the right from the 10-pin position to pick up the 3 pin, so try this adjustment for these combinations (figure 11.14). Obviously, you have to be a bit more accurate, but you will take the lane conditions out of play with this strategy. You may have to adjust a board either way.

3-6, 3-5-6-10, and 3-10 Split   In all three of these combinations you are trying to hit the 3 pin and 6 pin, even in the case of the baby 3-10 split when the 6 pin isn't there. You would move three boards for the 6 pin and six boards for the 3 pin. Because you are trying to put the ball between them, you would move between three and six, or approximately four and a half, boards to the right from your 10-pin shot to pick this up (figure 11.15).

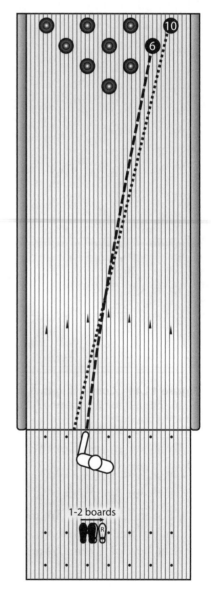

Figure 11.13   Converting the 6-10 spare, left-handed bowler.

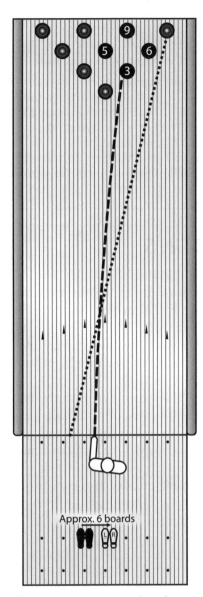

Figure 11.14 Converting the 3-5-6, 3-5-6-9, or 3-9 spare, left-handed bowler.

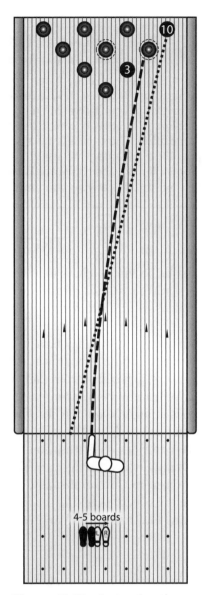

Figure 11.15 Converting the 3-6, 3-5-6-10, or 3-10 split, left-handed bowler.

Left-Side Spares: 2-4, 2-4-7, and 2-7 Split

All three combinations come down to trying to hit the 2 pin and 4 pin, even in the case of the baby 2-7 split, when the 4 pin isn't there. Because you move three boards for the 4 pin and six boards for the 3 pin, move between, or about four or five boards, to the left from your 7-pin position. See figure 10.23 in chapter 10.

Remember, the adjustment for these pins is not made based on their relationship to the headpin. Instead, the adjustment is made based on their relationship to the 7 pin.

Making Changes:
Choosing Your Option for a 3-Pin Combination

In the heat of play, when you leave a 3-pin spare combination, pick your strategy. You may choose to hook at it using your strike ball, adjusting to the left from your strike line (using your strike target). Or you may choose to go directly at it with your plastic ball, adjusting to the right from your 10-pin position. The choice is always yours, depending on how you feel.

The advantage to using a plastic ball is that you take the lane condition out of play. The challenge is that you have to be a bit more accurate. Go with your gut. It's always your call.

TROUBLESHOOTING

In this system, you have to be sure of your initial 10-pin and 7-pin angles. The rest is math to make the remaining adjustments from these angles. In your warm-up, make sure you attempt a 7-pin and 10-pin pickup. Fine-tune your angle for the best reaction. Although angles will not vary much, because you are throwing a plastic ball, you may have to tweak them slightly on some conditions. It may just be a couple of boards at most. Once you determine the best angles at your corners, just adjust from there for the rest of the spares.

When you close down your shoulders to face the spares (because the ball goes straight), you may feel the urge to pull the ball in that direction. Because you want to follow through straight at 90 degrees from your shoulders, you just have to work on getting comfortable angling your shoulders to face the spare, but still follow through straight.

Once you are comfortable seeing your ball go straight and begin to appreciate the benefit of taking the lane conditions out of play on your spares, you will learn to trust yourself, and you will make more spares!

SUMMARY

Whether you bowl in multiple leagues or on various types of conditions, you can simplify your spare shooting by taking the variable of lane conditions out of play. It is a good idea to use a plastic ball for spares if you are not good at flattening out your roll to keep your strike ball from hooking at spares, or if you can't go back to hooking your strike ball once you flatten out your roll for a spare. The whole idea is to be able to release the ball about the same as you do on your strike ball without the ball hooking because it is plastic.

Using a plastic ball, there are six basic shots for the single-pin spares. Once you have established both your 7-pin and your 10-pin shots, you will use these angles as your point of origin for the rest of your spares. You do this by starting from the appropriate corner shot and adjusting your feet toward the center, either three or six boards, depending on where the remaining single pin is in relationship to either the 7 pin or the 10 pin. Your target for either side is between the third and fourth arrows. Move in between these adjustments when you leave adjacent two-pin combinations.

When using a plastic ball, remember to take your stance; align your shoulders, hips, and feet toward the target; and maintain this shoulder angle throughout the approach. When the shoulders are closed, a right-handed bowler walks toward the spares on the left and a left-hander walks toward the spares on the right. When the shoulders are open, a right-hander walks straight when the spares are on the right and a left-hander walks straight when the spares are on the left.

Finally, that is not to say that plastic balls never hook, because they can. If the lanes are so dry that even your plastic ball is hooking, you need to adjust your release to flatten your roll and minimize the hook at spares. Extreme circumstances call for extreme measures!

Chapter 12

Mental Game

A successful bowler must physically execute the skills necessary for knocking down the pins and also control the mental side of bowling. Developing a strong mental game will help you become a good bowler, whereas a great mental game will help you become a great bowler. The better your physical game is, the more important your mental game becomes to your success. Developing your mental game is just as much work as developing your physical game, only it's invisible. However, the effects on your performance are not.

Your mental game involves remaining calm and relaxed under stressful conditions. You may be just bowling for fun and need to strike to shoot your highest score, or you may be competing in a league and need a strike to win for your team. You may simply need to figure out how to adjust on a difficult lane condition, or you may be in a tournament trying to qualify for the finals. You can learn to conquer any challenges in the face of pressure by learning how to stay calm and focused.

Controlling your emotions helps you stay on task and focus on what you can control, without worrying about what you can't control. You can control your own performance, but you cannot control the performance of another bowler or even the outcome of a game or tournament.

Be flexible and adapt to your environment. You will be bowling on different lanes, in different bowling centers, and on different lane conditions. You have to learn to adjust, and this includes expanding your comfort zones. This is a mental process.

There are many possible thoughts that can go through your mind at any time. Learning to discipline your thoughts and create more effective thoughts is the cornerstone of a sound mental game, and it will help you bowl better.

DEVELOPING A SHOT MAKING ROUTINE

Developing a shot making routine will enhance your ability to repeat your technique. It involves both a physical and mental regimen and is as important in bowling as it is in golf, another game of repetition.

A shot making routine is a physical ritual paired with a mental process that is used for every shot. Preparing the same way for each shot improves your ability to repeat your technique. Professional golfers go through a consistent routine before every shot because they have to make good shots, over and over. Consider these tips to develop a sound pre-shot making routine:

- As you approach the bowler's area on your turn, imagine a curtain drops behind you to separate you from everyone else. Channel your focus on the upcoming shot.
- Visualize the path of the ball to the pocket or spare.
- Use the same ritual every time you pick up the ball and set your stance.
- Clarify and simplify your thoughts. Commit completely to your strategy.

As part of your mental process, you should also have a postshot routine to analyze the outcome and react appropriately to it for the next shot. Here is a suggested postshot routine:

- Assess the outcome. Note ball reaction and any flaws in execution.
- Refocus if you left a spare to shoot.
- Strategize your next strike shot before you leave the bowler's area, and decide what adjustments, if any, you will make on the next shot to make it more successful. Do this before socializing between shots while the shot is fresh in your mind.

You may have determined that you simply did not focus properly on the last shot, so you resolve to do so on the next one. Or you may have determined that the ball hooked too much because you drifted, and so rather than adjust where you stand, you resolve to walk straighter next time. Or you may decide that you made a good shot, but need to make an adjustment because of the lane condition. This is the time to engineer the move you will make for the next frame and commit to it.

Note: Adjustments are always a series of educated guesses. That's all you ever have. So as long as your decision makes sense, commit to it without second-guessing it. This commitment and clarity will help you make a better, more relaxed shot. Because of your strong resolve, the quality of the swing may even determine the success of the next shot, even if the adjustment was not dead on!

Consider a golfer who is trying to decide between two clubs. His caddy can influence the mental frame of the golfer based on his reaction to the decision. If the golfer makes a decision on his own and the caddy questions it, the golfer may doubt his decision and not be as relaxed and trusting when he makes the shot as he would have if the caddy had expressed clear approval of the decision, even if he wasn't sure either! Committing to a questionable strategy with all your heart can lead to a better outcome than making a perfect decision but committing only halfway to it. The effect of that commitment on the quality of your physical shot can affect the outcome.

Don't be too concerned if sometimes you just don't feel like doing your shot making routine. I get it. You might be too upset from your last shot or distracted by the lucky shot your opponent got, or you might just feel lazy. This stuff takes a lot of energy to do every time! Again, working on the mental game is just as hard as working on the physical game; it just happens to be invisible. Some of the best bowlers I competed against on tour stuck relentlessly to their routines. This does not mean that it was easy to do. It means that they had trained themselves to do so, so that it had become automatic. Because of this, their mental games were very strong and their shot making was superb.

CONTROLLING EMOTIONS

When I first went out on tour, I took note of the demeanor of a veteran player, Jeanne Maiden (Naccarato), during qualifying. After each game, we had to move to the next pair of lanes, and I followed Jeanne. I was coming onto her pair as she came off to go to the next one. I was taken by how constant her demeanor was, whether she had just bowled a 150 or a 250. If I had just shot a 150, you knew it! I was visibly upset. Mentally, I would just bounce off my last outcome into my next performance. My focus was clearly interrupted or at least inconsistent. But Jeanne never seemed to change her disposition or outwardly react to her performance. She was able to maintain the same focus regardless of the situation. She appeared unaffected and always on task to perform from game to game. She understood how important it was to maintain a constant focus and had obviously honed her skill to do so. I was thoroughly impressed. Developing this focus will lead to success.

Have you ever gotten so mad at leaving a 10 pin that you blew picking it up? I understand that it can be very frustrating to leave the corner pin, especially on a good shot. However, if you get so upset that you are unable to focus well enough to pick it up, how upset are you now after you miss it? You allowed your reaction to disrupt your focus, which led to missing the spare. And you had made a good shot to begin with. You just needed to make your spare and change your strategy to strike the next time.

Learning to control your emotions is a process, and it's not easy! Just as I had finished writing about Jeanne, who impressed me so much, one of my students came into the pro shop. He had just watched a match I was in on YouTube. He was commenting on the focus I exuded. His timing was interesting to me. It dawned on me that he had happened to watch a video in which I was on top of my game. However, I immediately thought about the many times my focus was poor. It is humbling to think about the role focus, and the ability to refocus, plays in performance.

I have been to national amateur competitions and have competed professionally. It is amazing how much more common it is to see open frames come in clusters at the amateur level, whereas it is rare to see a professional follow an open frame with another open frame. This is because professionals recover more quickly from their mistakes than amateurs do, many of whom let a mistake linger in their heads. Professionals learn to manage and control their emotions to maintain focus. Furthermore, they learn how to refocus, regardless of the situation. Focus is essential to survive at the highest level, at which the mental game makes a big difference.

You can strike 10 times in a row at the beginning of a game or you can have an open in the previous frame. Theoretically, you should approach the next shot exactly as you did the previous one, regardless of the circumstance. Learning to maintain an even keel arms you with the ability to perform, regardless of the scenario. It's you, the ball, and the pins. Every time.

MANAGING YOUR THOUGHTS

I have a new passion of working out at the gym. I have been seeing a personal trainer for years and have learned that working out is all about functional training and balance. As the exercises have progressed into compound movements, they have continually challenged my balance. Although my body is trained to remain balanced, I am always taken by how much my focus matters to be able to keep my balance. Every time, it makes me think about how much influence good concentration and focus had on my career and the influence they have on the careers of others.

I have been trained to have good balance. But, when I lose my balance, it is almost always because my mind wandered and I lost focus. This is fascinating to me. When I refocus, I can accomplish the task at hand. I realize how important the relationship between the ability to maintain focus and performance truly is. It seems so obvious, but to experience it in another setting is amazing. This is such a simple and yet profound concept. The ability to focus and refocus makes all the difference.

CONTROLLING WHAT YOU CAN

You have to learn to be concerned only with what you can control and let go of the rest. The fact is that you can control only your own performance and your reaction to your surroundings.

How often have you let another player distract you only to admit that he stole your focus? Actually, what he did is not the problem. Your reaction to it is. You cannot control what another player does or doesn't do, but you can control your reaction to it. The other player did not steal your focus. Rather, you let what he did interfere with your ability to focus on what you can control.

How many times have you let a bad break take hold and steal your focus? The bad break wasn't the problem; your reaction to it was. The only thing you can do is make the best shot you can and adjust your strategy. That's all you have control over. You can shoot a great 279 game and get beat if your opponent shoots 280.

PERFORMANCE VERSUS OUTCOME

You can control your performance, but you cannot control the outcome. This is the reason for focusing on your performance, rather than on the outcome.

You can control making good shots, adjusting to the lanes, and making spares. These strategies are performance oriented. What you cannot control is the outcome. You may believe that you can focus on shooting 300, but in reality you can only make the best shots you can, every frame, and then look up at the end of the game to see the score. The goal of shooting 300 is outcome oriented; the goal of making the shots necessary to reach a 300 game is performance oriented. That is a goal you can work on and control.

My roommate on tour, Liz Johnson, was interviewed as she approached her sophomore year on tour after a spectacular rookie year. The reporter asked her how she would handle the sophomore slump that many seem to go through, especially after a strong rookie year. Her response was classic. Liz said, "I just have to focus on one tournament at a time. Actually, I can only focus on the next tournament." Thinking more, Liz continued, "Well, I really can only focus on the next block of games. No, I really just need to focus on each game." Finally, Liz nailed it: "I really just focus on making good shots and making my spares each frame; that's all I can control." Her response was so thoughtful and truly a reflection of a great champion's mental game. Liz has gone on to have a prolific championship career, winning several professional titles, including three U.S. Open Championships. She has represented the United States on Team USA and continues to bowl both nationally and internationally, among women and men. She is truly a great champion.

Trying to beat an opponent is another example of focusing on an outcome. You cannot control your opponent's performance. All you can really do is focus on the shots you make, create a strategy for adjusting to the conditions, and pick up your spares. When you look up, you hope that your score is better than your opponent's.

Actually, each bowler is playing her own game against the pins, and whoever ends up knocking down more pins is the winner. I have won with a 150 game, and I have lost with a 250 game.

IS IT YOU OR YOUR STRATEGY?

This can be a very tricky question! Let's start out by declaring that you cannot outperform a bad ball reaction! Sometimes a bowler who is not bowling or scoring well tries to perfect his form for better results when a poor reaction on the lanes is really the problem. If your lane play strategy is not good and your ball reaction is poor, meaning that you have little to no room for error, *you must improve your strategy to be able to make better shots*. When you have a little bit of room for error, you make better shots because you can relax your swing.

Tightening up your swing is a subconscious reaction. That's why it can be difficult to determine whether you or your reaction on the lanes (strategy) is the culprit. My personal story in chapter 5 of the Sam's Town Invitational demonstrates the effect ball reaction truly has on the swing. I bowled for a living, and yet at times I didn't realize that I had to change my strategy to loosen up, score, and in this case, win!

This is a lot to take in if you are the type of bowler who gets more upset about a bad shot than a bad break. You may tend to blame yourself and try to perfect your

Making Changes: What Type of Bowler Are You?

I like to pose this question to bowlers to evaluate their mental makeup: What makes you more upset: a bad break or making a bad shot? Players with the proper type of focus answer that making a bad shot is more upsetting because they take responsibility for the shot knowing it is all they can really control, not the outcome. I am a firm believer that breaks even out. We easily take notice when we get a bad break but forget about all the good ones. Your answer to the question will determine the type of bowler you are: performance oriented or outcome oriented.

execution when you really need to change your lane play strategy. By adjusting your equipment, line, or release, you can create forgiveness in less-than-perfect shots. This will relax your swing and help you make better shots again.

Recognizing when the problem is your strategy can be difficult in the heat of battle. When you don't realize that your reaction is causing you to make bad shots, your attempt to make more perfect ones only tightens you up more. Then, your poor results only frustrate you more, causing you to tighten up. I understand this all too well; I have been that player!

At the Sam's Town Invitational, I was very upset with myself for the way I was throwing the ball. I became equally upset with my ball rep, Doene, for thinking it was the ball and not me. While I just *knew* I had to throw it better, he insisted that I try another ball. Suddenly, my swing loosened up! Had I not given in to the change in strategy, I would have kept trying to throw the ball more perfectly. But what Doene could see was that I had no room for error to be able to relax and let it happen.

SPECIFIC VERSUS GENERAL CUES

Sometimes you need to focus on a specific skill to enhance your performance. If you are still working on something in your game that you cannot do without thinking about it, then focus on that specific cue. For example, if you are late pushing the ball, focus on pushing the ball out sooner. You have to spend more time working on it so that you do not have to think about it so much when you are bowling for score.

When your execution seems to be on, focus on more general cues such as relaxing or rolling the ball cleanly off your hand. These more general thoughts will help you maintain your performance.

Thoughts are going to occupy your mind one way or another. So, take action and harness your thoughts, whether you focus on something specific or more general, to keep your overall feel.

SELF-TALK: POSITIVE VERSUS NEGATIVE

Because we tend to become the reality we create in our minds, coach yourself in positives rather than in negatives. This can be especially difficult if you tend to get frustrated with yourself. However, instead of following the downward spiral

Making Changes: Dos Versus Don'ts

When you bowl, focus on what you do want to do rather than what you don't want to do. Always focus on positives, not negatives.

Your thoughts should reflect the things you can do, rather than what you do not want to do. In other words, coach yourself in dos, not don'ts. For example, rather than tell yourself not to pull the next shot, tell yourself to relax and just let it swing. Your brain will tend to hear and remember the verb in the thought. In the first example, the verb is *pull*. In the second, it is *relax and let it swing*. You are more likely to end up pulling the ball following the first thought and relaxing the swing following the second one.

I am very sensitive to this principle when I coach. I strive to ask bowlers to do what I want them to do rather than tell them what not to do. Trying to avoid doing something can be very counterproductive.

that negative thinking can create and perpetuate, lift yourself up with positive thoughts, especially when the going gets tough.

Talk to yourself the way you would encourage someone else. Yours will be the strongest voice you hear when you are bowling and competing; make sure your thoughts are encouraging rather than discouraging. Such thoughts will lead to actions that put you on the upward spiral that is so much more enjoyable and productive.

Be careful what you ask for, you just might get it! The mother of a young girl I coach asked me how she should respond when her daughter gets so down on herself when she bowls. This is a problem I know all too well. However, it really is a matter of just staying on task. If the girl has had enough lessons to know about her execution and lane play strategy, she is obviously getting down on herself because she is not performing well. This is when she needs to focus on what she needs to do, rather than on what she isn't doing well. In an ideal world, she should stop and try to figure out why her performance is lacking then focus on what she has learned. This goes back to the issue of controlling your emotions so you can settle down and address the issue at hand.

Sometimes you may not know what to do, which is truly frustrating. At other times, you just have to stop, refocus on what you know how to do, and work on your shot making routine.

Being able to troubleshoot is important. Is the problem your reaction, your execution, a lack of focus, a case of trying too hard, being tight, a lack of practice, or something else? Taking lessons can be of great assistance in this process. You need the knowledge about your game to know what to do. Furthermore, you need the clarity of mind (and emotion) to be able to recall the things you know when you need them.

REFOCUSING

Let's face it, sometimes you are going to mentally stray from the task at hand. Whether you are fatigued, distracted, experiencing a bad break, or allowing your emotions to get the best of you, your mental state may lag. The key is to be able to refocus and get your thoughts back on track.

A very specific experience comes back to me every time I try to convey this concept. I was on TV in the title match at the Sam's Town Invitational. I was very focused on my performance each frame and nothing else—so much so that I got up and reracked the pins on my lane as my opponent came off the approach from her last shot. She looked at me, puzzled, and said, "What are you doing?" I said, "I am reracking for the next shot because the pins are off." She replied, "But it's the 10th frame." Oh boy, that meant that she had another shot to make because she had just marked. I should have waited to rerack. Also now I knew it was the 10th frame, so I was now distracted and nervous, I began to lose my sharp focus.

At that point, all these thoughts came flooding forward that had not been on my mind during the prior frames—the title, the trophy, the money, the Major! All of this started to become my focus. I knew I was in trouble with these thoughts and had only a few moments to gather myself before it was my turn. I knew I had to strike.

Desperately trying to get my performance-oriented focus back, I began to think about how I approached all the other shots so many times, not just during this show, but all week long. I focused on my performance, on making a good shot. This was just one more frame.

Focusing on just the frame, I went through my shot making routine and focused on making a good shot. I got on the approach and executed. I knew I threw it well, but would it strike? Although it seemed to take over a year to get down the lane, it did! Because I was able to refocus my thoughts (which had clearly come out of focus), I won my Major title.

CONFIDENCE COMES FROM COMPETENCE

Confidence is not magic. Although some people seem to be more naturally confident than others, confidence generally comes from being competent. The more competent you are, the better your results will be, which will lead to more confidence in your ability.

Becoming confident is a matter of doing the work. It takes time and effort to become more competent at something. It also takes dedication and focus. If you are not very good at picking up the corner pin, guess what? You need to spend more time practicing it and work out what stops you from getting it so you can learn to pick it up again. Seeing yourself pick it up will breed more confidence that you will get it the next time you leave it.

When I see someone who is good at something, I think about how much he must have done it. If you want to become more confident about picking up the 10 pin, practice at it. Take a lesson if you need to. Learn to work on it productively and you will develop your skill and become confident once again.

BREATHING TO HANDLE PRESSURE

Diaphragmatic breathing can help you calm your heart rate, manage your anxiety, and relax your body. I gave lessons to a collegiate bowler who was bowling for the national championship on TV, and she said that the breathing we worked on was one of the things that helped her the most!

Here is how it works: Inhale slowly, through your nose, allowing your diaphragm to lower as you breathe in. (Your nose is designed to filter the air you breathe in.) This will expand your belly and leave more room in your chest cavity for your lungs to expand and fill every lobe with air. Take four seconds to complete this inhalation. Hold this breath for eight counts. Next, take four seconds to exhale through your mouth. Repeat until you feel your body become calm; inhale through your nose and exhale through your mouth until you feel ready to make the next shot. You can do this when you are in the bowler's area awaiting your turn or even just before your next shot when you feel your heart rate needs to calm down.

ADJUSTING YOUR MENTALITY FOR SCORING CONDITIONS

Given all of the lane patterns you could potentially be bowling on, you may need to adjust your expectations for the condition. If you are used to averaging 210 but you are on a much more difficult pattern, you need to modify your expectations so that you do not get too frustrated when you do not score as usual.

I had been bowling great my junior year in college and was scoring and winning a lot. I managed to win the Women's National Collegiate title that year, which gave me the chance to represent the United States in the World Cup. It was my first experience bowling internationally, and it was in Seoul, Korea.

I bowled the first block and averaged about 190. I was young, and I was fuming! I was used to the way I scored at college meets; it wasn't uncommon for me to average 220 in tournaments. I was embarrassed to travel all that way, to be representing my country and not be able to bowl the way I did at home. Mentally, I was done. And what a shame that was.

When I came back from break, I was still distraught, unable to forgive myself for my poor performance. Without even realizing it, I was in fifth! But I mentally took myself out of the competition, not realizing that I just had to adjust my mentality to the conditions. They were so much more challenging to score on, so unlike what I had bowled on at home, but I couldn't see straight and blamed myself. If only I had realized at the time that hitting the pocket and picking up spares would be enough to stay in contention. I realized it later but much too late. Tough lesson learned and shared here.

This can be a hard lesson to learn, but it is an important one. Tougher conditions require more patience. They also require an adjustment in your thinking about what scoring pace to expect. On tour, the conditions were typically more difficult in the major tournaments. In the morning blocks, it was often harder to strike than it was in later blocks when the lanes broke down and the conditions opened up. That's when the scores were higher, but you had to have a different mentality in the morning.

Such is the case when you bowl on sport and challenge patterns, when it can be difficult to hit the pocket, or on longer patterns, when you have a shallow angle into the pocket on fresh conditions. It is hard to carry from such an angle. Expect to leave a 5 pin, among others spares, and plan to pick it up. Until the lanes break down, you have to live with this reaction until the strikes come.

Bowlers who grind out each frame to keep getting marks are the ones who hang in there and maintain the scoring pace until the strikes come. Spares are absolutely the key. Although not striking very much can be frustrating, just accepting that spares are good until the lanes open up is the right focus to have.

Furthermore, when strikes are hard to come by, missing spares only compounds the problem because then you have to double just to make up for the open. Also, it is easy to start falling more behind by missing spares. Then you start feeling anxious about catching up, and all this can trigger a downward spiral in your thoughts with a decline in performance to follow.

Adjust your mentality to fit the pace of the scoring on the conditions you are on, and place extra focus on your spare shooting. Those who can grind when the going gets tough are the ones who are in position to move ahead of the pack when the strikes start coming!

SUMMARY

A great mental game depends on your ability to control your emotions and discipline your thoughts. You have to think better to bowl better. Let go of mistakes and learn to focus on your next shot.

In this digital age, in which everything is much faster and we have constant interactions at our fingertips, we can take so much more into our brains. To offset this overload, we must develop our ability to maintain proper focus. Work hard to develop a shot making routine to properly focus your energy and harness your thoughts.

Stay focused on your performance, not the outcome. Focus on what to do rather than on what not to do. Make sure you coach yourself in positives rather than negatives. Also, remember that the more you work on things, the more competent and confident you will become.

Managing your self-talk will make a big difference in your performance. Use breathing techniques to control your body and prepare yourself in pressure situations. Develop your shot making routine to maintain your focus and repeat your technique.

Finally, when you lose your stroke, question your strategy. As hard as this can be to do, you may be pleasantly surprised by what a change in lane play strategy does for your swing. I know!

Remember that overcoming a mental lapse can be more difficult than remaining mentally strong the whole time. The mental game is a lot of work! Consider this quote from Aleta Sill, bowling's first $1,000,000 woman: "Champions have a short memory."

Chapter 13

Open Bowling, League Play, and Tournament Play

Bowling for fun or practice is referred to as open bowling. The opportunity to open bowl depends on lane availability outside of league play. The cost of open play varies depending on the bowling center and lane availability. Specials may be offered at various times. Open bowling is available when leagues, parties, or special bookings are not occupying the lanes.

Many bowling centers offer organized leagues that you can join to compete regularly at a recreational or competitive level. League play is an opportunity for bowlers who enjoy the sport to get out, socialize, and have fun competing.

Most bowling centers offer a variety of league programs. Leagues vary in duration, time, team size, and skill level. Different types of leagues use different scoring systems to manage the team competition points to determine league standings from week to week. Weekly dues typically include bowling fees and may include additional money toward a prize fund that is dispersed at the end of the league season according to the final standings and any special awards given to individuals. If the league is a USBC-sanctioned league (United States Bowling Congress), you will pay dues to be a USBC member for the season, typically at the beginning of the league season (and receive the perks of membership).

You can join a league as a team, or you can ask to be placed on a team. Bowling centers run enough varied leagues to suit most bowlers. Inquire at your local bowling center about getting into a league. You may make new friends and enjoy being on the team. Eventually, you may form your own team with your friends, family members, coworkers, other couples, or fellow churchgoers. Your choice!

LEAGUE PLAY

If you are interested in league play, go to your local bowling center and find a league that fits you. There are women's leagues, men's leagues, youth leagues, mixed leagues, couples' leagues, seniors' leagues, church leagues, and more. There are recreational leagues and various ranges of competitive leagues, with varying lane conditions.

The staff at the bowling center will help you find a league that suits you. Bowling with others at a similar skill level will help you feel comfortable and have a good time as you develop your skills.

The lengths of league seasons vary. Generally, they range from 14 to 36 weeks. Leagues are offered at various times on different days of the week. Most are held weekly, but some are bimonthly (bowling every other week). Leagues are also popular on the weekends. Leagues can be made up of individuals or doubles teams, but are most commonly made up of teams of three, four, or five members.

The scoring system varies from league to league. The majority of leagues are handicapped leagues, but some are more competitive and based on your actual, or scratch, score. In a handicapped league, you receive a given number of pins per game to add to your score, based on the difference between your average score and a standard score set forth by that league. In a scratch league, no pins are added to handicap your level of play. Usually, there is a cap on the team average in this case. That is, the combined averages of the players on the team from the prior season cannot be above a certain number. This is how scratch leagues are kept competitive.

Handicaps are based on your average, which is tabulated and updated every week. To calculate your average, divide the number of games you bowl by your total score for those games. For example, if you bowl a 450 series (total score for three games), divide 450 by 3 to get an average score of 150 per game. In leagues, the league secretary keeps track of the total pinfall for all games bowled and divides the total pinfall by the total number of games that have been bowled to keep each bowler's average updated, week to week.

Leagues compete on a schedule. Each team is assigned to a different lane each week. Teams that share a pair of lanes compete against each other that week. Bowlers complete a game, alternating frames on each of the two lanes. Most leagues include three games. Competition points are kept according to the league rules, and the standings are updated each week.

A league secretary keeps track of the data for each bowler, each team, and the entire league. Each week, a standings sheet (figure 13.1) shows the current team standings, lane assignments of each team, and a listing of averages for each bowler in the league, organized by teams.

You may join a league as a team, or you can request to be put on a team in the league of your choice. Leagues do run all year round, but leagues are most abundant during the fall and winter. Late summer is a good time to inquire about fall and winter league openings. Late spring is a good time to inquire about shorter summer leagues.

Some bowlers have difficulty committing to an entire season, whether because they already know they will have some date conflicts or because they cannot make a portion of the season for some reason. Some teams develop rosters with more team members than they need so bowlers can rotate in and out of the lineup. Some leagues

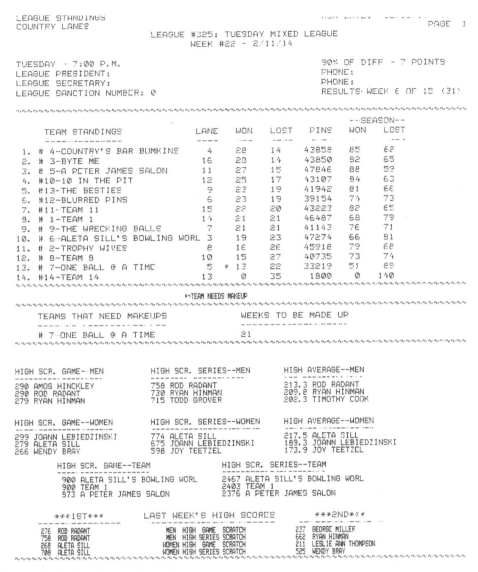

Figure 13.1 Sample standings sheet.

also allow substitutes. There are provisions in the rules to determine how to score for the absent bowler.

TOURNAMENT PLAY

You can boost your competitive experience by searching out tournaments to bowl in. The USBC hosts local city and state tournaments, as well as national tournaments. Additionally, other independent tournament associations offer organized local, state, and national competitions sanctioned by the USBC or other governing bodies at the international level. Go to your local USBC association for more information on what's out there for you.

There are many exciting opportunities for youth bowlers. In addition to youth leagues, there is an amazing sweep taking place across this country with high school

Making Changes: Getting a Coach

USBC Coaching is an organization committed to the development of quality coaching, to cultivate and create lifelong bowlers. USBC coaches are certified at Level I/II, Bronze, Silver, or Gold and provide coaching to bowlers of all skill levels. Coaching is the key to achieving the next level of play. With good coaching, any bowler can improve. Seek out a reputable coach so you can learn and improve and experience more enjoyment when you bowl.

bowling. I personally am passionate about high school bowling. Whereas I bowled with my grandpa when I was young, I did not bowl in youth leagues. If not for my high school starting a bowling team, I would not be where I am at today. The USBC has a goal to make high school bowling available in every state.

There are also various local traveling leagues and other tournament organizations that offer competitions for members and guests, in which bowlers can hone their competitive skills. Some of these also offer scholarship money for college. Some local bowling centers also host tournaments and have created their own college scholarship programs.

There is more exciting competition at the collegiate level, as well as many opportunities to accumulate scholarship money. In addition to local associations and bowling centers, many collegiate teams offer scholarships. You do not have to attend an NCAA college to be offered a scholarship.

Finally, like TEAM USA, there is also a Junior Team USA. Local Junior Gold qualifiers are held throughout the country to begin the selection process for Junior Team USA, culminating in the annual Junior Gold national tournament to select the final team each year.

For more information on both youth and adult opportunities, visit www.bowl.com.

KEEPING SCORE

Although the league secretary keeps track of the standings and averages, it's important for you to know how to keep score when you bowl. Just about all bowling centers have automatic scoring, but you need to understand how scores add up to realize the importance of your pin count in certain situations. With the advancement of automatic scoring, too many bowlers do not realize the significance that certain shots have on scoring, especially after a strike or spare.

Score is based on a possible two balls per frame. A complete game is 10 frames. The first score is recorded in the upper frame. Use a number to reflect the number of pins knocked down; use a symbol to reflect a strike or spare. A strike (usually indicated by an X) is knocking down all 10 pins in one shot. A spare (usually indicated by a slash) is knocking down all 10 pins in two shots. The score is then added from frame to frame and recorded on the bottom of the frame. Figure 13.2 shows a sample score sheet.

Each frame is figured separately and added to the next frame to keep the score. The values for strikes and spares depend on the pin count on subsequent shots. Once you know how to keep score, you can appreciate how much a strike or spare can be worth depending on how many pins are knocked down on the next shots.

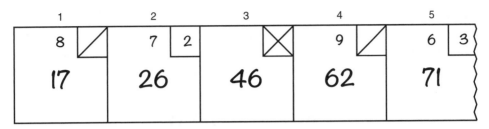

Figure 13.2 Sample score sheet.

To determine the score for the frame, add the number of pins knocked down for that frame. Strikes are worth 10, plus the total pinfall for the next two shots. Spares are worth 10, plus the total pinfall on the next shot. So, if in the first frame you have 8 and then knock down the remaining 2 pins to spare, that gives you at least 10 for that frame, plus the number of pins knocked down on the next shot. If you get 7 on your first shot of the next frame, you will add 7 to the spare in the previous frame to score a total of 17 in the first frame. If you get 2 on the next shot, you will receive a total of 9 for the second frame and add it to the score in the first frame, to have a score of 26 in the second frame. A strike on the next shot will be worth at least 10 in the third frame, depending on the total number of pins knocked down on the next two shots. If in the fourth frame you get 9 and spare, you will add a total of 10 more to the initial value of 10 for the strike, to get a total of 20 in the third frame. Added to the previous frame, that gives you a score of 46 in the third frame. The amount of the fourth frame depends on the pinfall of the next shot. If in the fifth frame you get 6 and pick up only 3 more, you will add 6 to the spare in the fourth frame, for a total of 16; then add it to the previous total in the third frame. That gives you 62 in the fourth, and for the fifth frame add the total of 9 pins to the fourth frame total, for a score of 71 in the fifth.

During open bowling at the bowling center, practice keeping score. Most bowling centers have paper score sheets at the control counter. These are either what they used before they installed automatic scoring or what they use when the technology fails. In either case, this old-fashioned method of tracking scores will enable you to compare your scoring to that of the automatic scorer. Compare your sheet to the automatic computer to detect any errors you may have made in your addition.

If your score is different from the automatic score, it may be the number of pins that you recorded for that frame. In that case, it was not your addition from frame to frame, but your recollection of how many pins you knocked down on that shot. It is between you and the automatic scorer to determine who is correct!

CALCULATING YOUR AVERAGE

Once you finish bowling, calculate your average score for the session by adding up your total game score (add the total scores for all the games you bowled), and then divide that total by the number of games you bowled. Sometimes, you can access this information on the automatic scoring computer.

If you came to open bowling to practice, you may have been busy working on your skills rather than trying to knock down pins. It is good to bowl to improve your skills without paying much attention to pinfall. Nevertheless, you still can do this average calculation just to learn how to determine your average. The scorer will work, regardless of your practice routine. If you are working on improving your skills and disregarding the pins, remember that this average calculation is just for practice. The average score you get may be significantly less than you are used to getting because you were not trying to knock down the pins.

LANE ETIQUETTE

During league play or open play, so many lanes are occupied at one time that rules of order are required to determine who goes up to bowl at any given time. Bowlers who are next to each other on consecutive lanes should not bowl at the same time. You must observe lane courtesy to ensure a flow to league or open play. Courtesy also allows all bowlers to focus on their shots. It is good bowling etiquette to look both ways before getting onto the approach so that you don't bowl at the same time as another bowler.

If two bowlers on consecutive lanes are ready to bowl at the same time, etiquette dictates that the player to the right goes first. You can assume this rule and let the bowler to your right go, or simply signal that the coast is clear. Usually a nod, a hand gesture, or even a comment will do. Once you extend lane courtesy to the player on your right, that player has the right to go or extend the courtesy back to you. The right to go is then yours. This courtesy allows everyone to bowl in turn with little distraction, and it keeps leagues running smoothly.

Refrain from talking to players once they have stepped onto the approach. Some players have a preshot routine that begins when they head toward the approach and pick up the ball. That is a good time to refrain from talking to them, because they are beginning to take their turn. Focus is a big part of bowling, as it is in all sports. As much as league bowling is a social occasion, each bowler needs to take uninterrupted time to focus on making a good shot.

During open bowling, when you practice your bowling skills, practice your bowling etiquette as well. Depending on how busy the center is, there may not be any bowlers directly to the right or left of you. If the center isn't very busy, bowlers a few lanes away may be distracting, so this may also be an appropriate time to extend courtesy. It is not essential but it can help both of you focus while practicing, even when not on neighboring lanes.

The common practice is to let the bowler to your right go first. If that bowler waves you on, you have been given the courtesy to go first.

FINAL FRAME

Bowling has one advantage over other sports: generations can bowl together. Whether you open-bowl for fun, decide to bowl in a league, or seek tournament play, bowling can be an individual, team, or even family sport. Bowling provides the opportunity to get out and enjoy a sport and socialize with little concern about skill level. Handicapped scoring levels out the playing field so bowlers of all ages, skill levels, and experience levels can bowl together comfortably and enjoy the game.

Bowling is a sport to enjoy with your family and friends, whether just for fun or in organized competition. For recreational and competitive bowlers, bowling is a great sport to play. Don't be surprised if you get hooked. You will soon discover that the more you know, the more there is to learn.

About the Author

Michelle Mullen, a United States Bowling Congress (USBC) Gold coach, has coached bowlers of all skill levels for almost three decades. She is co-owner of Your Bowling Coach (www.yourbowlingcoach.com) with renowned pro bowler Aleta Sill, and they operate Aleta Sill's Bowling World, a premier pro shop in metro Detroit.

Mullen has competed and won championships at every level, including high school and collegiate bowling and Professional Women's Bowling Association (PWBA) regional and national bowling. She holds four national titles (including a Major) and a record nine regional titles in the PWBA. She was also the 1990-1999 PWBA Regional Player of the Decade. In 1985 she represented the United States in the World Cup in Seoul, Korea, and is a former coach for the U.S. team.

Mullen is also an established international writer and author. She has been published in *Bowlers Journal International*, *Bowling Magazine*, *Bowling This Month*, *Asian Bowling Digest*, and various other publications. The first edition of *Bowling Fundamentals* was translated into Russian and Simplified Chinese. She is a member of the International Bowling Media Association.

Mullen enjoys working out, gardening, and cooking, but her greatest passion is to help homeless animals in need. She and Sill run an annual fundraising event, called "Bowl-4-Animal Rescue" (bowl4animalrescue.org), with 100 percent of the proceeds benefitting local animal charities. Mullen is from Chicago and lives in Livonia, Michigan, with her three dogs and four cats, who insist that "rescued is her favorite breed."

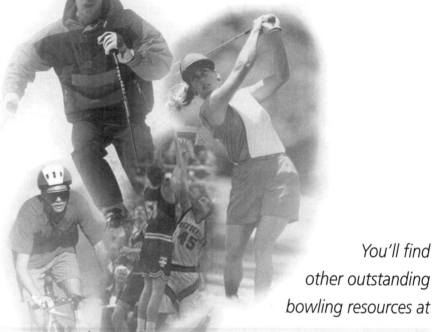